I0729712

COLOR
A Master Class

FLAMMARION

ENGLISH EDITION

Editorial Director
Kate Mascaro

Editor
Helen Adedotun

Translation from the French
Kate Robinson

Copyediting
Lindsay Porter

Design and Typesetting
Pierre-Yann Lallaizon, with Louise Gardebois
and Thibaud Sicard | Studio Recto Verso

Cover Design
Audrey Sednaoui

Proofreading
Nicole Foster

FRENCH EDITION

Editorial Director
Julie Rouart

Administration Manager
Delphine Montagne

Editor
Mélanie Puchault, assisted by Louise Pachurka

Picture Research
Claire Francillon

Production
Elodie Conjat

Color Separation
Hyphen, Bergamo, Italy

Printed in China by C&C Offset Printing

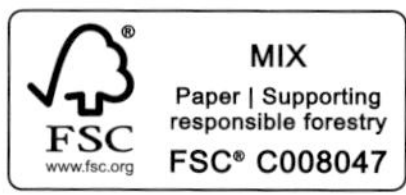

p. 10 Paul Signac, *Opus 217. Against the Enamel of a Background Rhythmic with Beats and Angles, Tones, and Tints, Portrait of M. Félix Fénéon in 1890* (detail).
p. 42 Rainbow flag.
p. 60 Sonia Delaunay, *Electric Prisms* (detail).
p. 188 Stained glass in Notre-Dame cathedral in Paris (detail).
p. 214 Piet Mondrian, *Composition with Large Red Plane, Yellow, Black, Gray, and Blue* (detail).

Camille Viéville

COLOR
A Master Class

Art History
Symbolism
Masterpieces
Materials

Flammarion

Contents

MATERIALS AND TECHNIQUES

APPENDIXES

Introduction

"THE ACTUAL BASIS OF COLOR IS INSTABILITY. ONCE YOU ACCEPT THAT . . . YOU BEGIN TO GET A WAY OF DEALING WITH IT." **BRIDGET RILEY**

The origin of the word "color," from the Latin *celare*, which means "to conceal or dissimulate," refers to color's hiding power. Color is as evasive as it is fascinating. Writing the history of color is a complicated undertaking, and it wasn't until the 1980s that historians began to address the question, led by French medievalist Michel Pastoureau, whose work has been widely recognized in academic circles and by the general public. Color is difficult to pin down because it intersects with many disciplines, including optics, chemistry, philosophy, religious and political studies, linguistics, literature, and the arts. Pastoureau reminds us of the profoundly social nature of this history: "It is the society that 'makes' the color, that gives it its definitions and meaning, that constructs its codes and values, that organizes its customs and determines its stakes. It is not the artist or the scholar; neither is it biological apparatus or the spectacle of nature." He also points out that the way colors are perceived is also a result of history.

This volume gives readers the keys to understanding how, in a given culture, painters, sculptors, printmakers, and videographers have used color. What colors were first used by prehistoric artists? How did the Greeks classify colors? Why are colors associated with music? What is Egyptian faience? What led to the invention of oil paint? What is International Klein Blue? How is gold leaf applied? These are just some of the questions that this informative, accessible book addresses through a selection of major and sometimes little-known works in the history of art.

Art History

"ONE CAN PAINT WITH TWO COLORS. . . . THREE, OR FOUR AT MOST, HAVE FOR CENTURIES BEEN ENOUGH FOR HUMANS TO RENDER SOMETHING IMPORTANT, ESSENTIAL, AND UNIQUE, THAT WHICH OTHERWISE WOULD HAVE BEEN IGNORED." **HENRI MICHAUX**

The history of color is incredibly rich. Each era, culture, language, and artistic movement has its own conception and perception of color. Like all fields of history, that of color involves diverse natural elements and has evolved according to material, scientific, social, economic, linguistic, philosophical, theological, literary, and, of course, artistic actualities. So the color we call "blue" today was neither identified nor viewed in the same way in ancient Egypt, ancient Greece, the medieval world, or by Pablo Picasso in 1901.

This chapter takes readers through thirty-two significant periods for color in the arts, from prehistory to the present day, in the West as well as in Japan and India. It provides tools for analyzing and understanding the historical roles that color has played and the ways in which artists have used it during different time periods and in various geographical regions. Each period features a reproduction of a work chosen to illustrate the analysis. Finally, this section retraces the evolution of social conventions related to color (primary and complementary colors, contrasts, etc.) and demonstrates the extent to which industrialization has influenced the standardization of color.

Symbolism

"I FOUND I COULD SAY THINGS WITH COLORS AND SHAPES THAT I COULDN'T SAY ANY OTHER WAY—THINGS I HAD NO WORDS FOR." **GEORGIA O'KEEFFE**

All color historians stress the fact that nothing is set in stone when it comes to the meaning of colors. These meanings are always changing and evolving, so that within the same society or the same historical period, each hue may take on contradictory, conflicting, or even opposing significations. This chapter provides a non-exhaustive exploration of the ever-shifting symbolism of colors.

Following the lead of Michel Pastoureau—a French medievalist and color specialist—we have focused on six main "basic" colors (black, white, red, yellow, green, and blue), as identified in European culture, as well as five "demi-" or "second rank" colors. The symbolic meaning of these eleven hues evolves as societies undergo ideological, economic, and political shifts. In addition to these colors, there exist innumerable shades with sometimes very poetic names but devoid of moral or spiritual significance. Gold and silver—unique tones derived from precious metals—are also addressed in this chapter. Finally, this section explores two ways of arranging different colors, each with its own particular meaning: stripes and the rainbow.

Masterpieces

"THE MOST POWERFUL ART IN LIFE IS TO TRANSFORM PAIN INTO A TALISMAN THAT HEALS. A BUTTERFLY IS REBORN IN A FESTIVAL OF COLORS!" **FRIDA KAHLO**

This chapter presents fifty-nine artworks selected for the artists' remarkable use of color. Each work has contributed to the history of art for many reasons, color being an essential aspect from both a technical and symbolic perspective. These works also demonstrate the close connection between color and art—both belong to a history of tastes and their social manifestations. The artistic production of a given period reflects the major political changes of the time. The austere colors advocated by the Reformation in sixteenth-century Europe, for instance, became characteristic of bourgeois portraits. In the centuries that followed, the bold use of color by the ruling classes evolved into the anarchist provocation of early-twentieth-century avant-garde painting. While painting has been the medium of choice for expressing color since the Renaissance, the selection in this chapter also includes sculptures, tapestries, and stained glass, as well as performances, installations, and videos from different cultures that use color to great effect.

Materials and Techniques

"TO MAKE ART AS BRILLIANT AS CAN BE, WE MUST DISCUSS THE GRINDING OF COLORS. . . . THERE ARE AS MANY BINDERS AND WAYS OF GRINDING AS THERE ARE COLORS." **CENNINO CENNINI**

This chapter focuses on the different materials and techniques that artists may use to create colors. For centuries, the tasks entailed in producing colors fell to artists; until the nineteenth century, they ground natural pigments and added binders themselves. Other techniques were involved that had an impact on the effects of color—such as applying a primer or undercoat to the support, or using varnish—and artists were also responsible for preparing these. These practices were passed down in studios from generation to generation. Each one called for a specific mastery of raw materials; some of the ingredients were highly toxic and required serious precautions to be taken. A color's chemistry would sometimes influence the symbolic meaning it acquired.

In the nineteenth century, the development of synthetic pigments produced new, often brighter shades. In the 1840s, the invention of the paint tube made it possible to buy ready-to-use colors. In the twentieth century, artists used unconventional, industrially produced materials to inject color into their work.

How to Use This Book

This book has four distinct chapters: Art History, Symbolism, Masterpieces, and Materials and Techniques. Each can be read separately or in connection with the others. Cross-references at the bottom of each page suggest further reading in other chapters. Sidebars present major historical evolutions, principal characteristics of artworks, or highlights in the career of an artist.

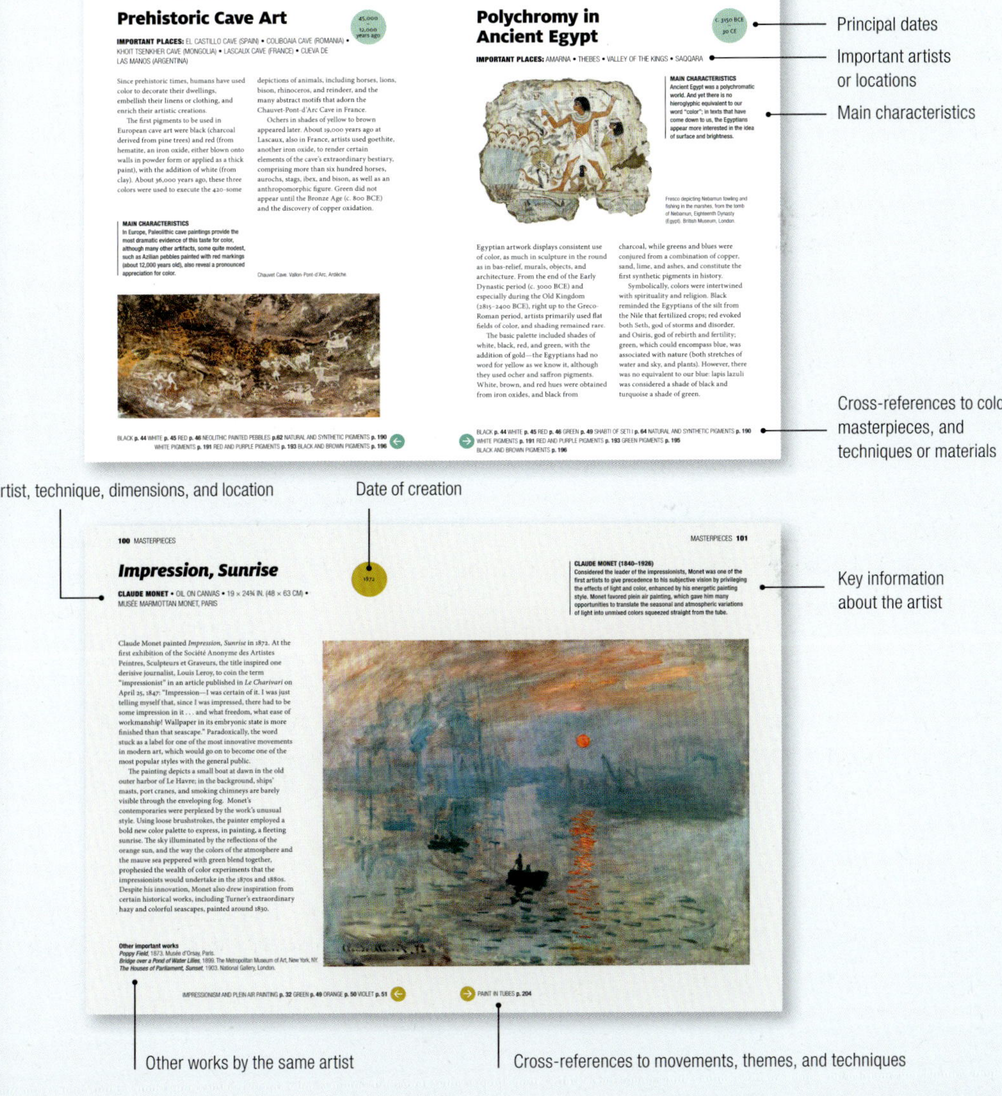

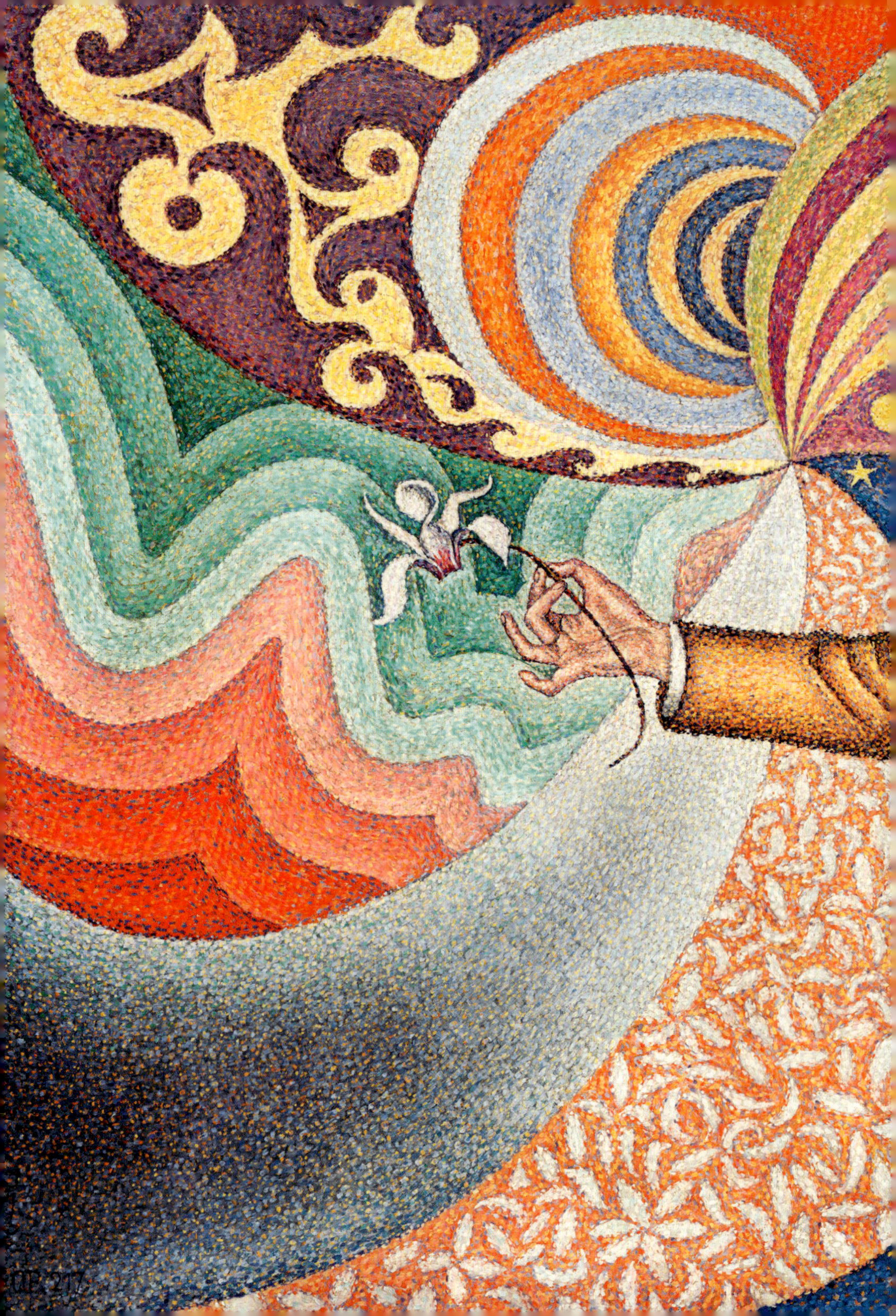

Art History

Prehistoric Cave Art

IMPORTANT PLACES: EL CASTILLO CAVE (SPAIN) • COLIBOAIA CAVE (ROMANIA) • KHOIT TSENKHER CAVE (MONGOLIA) • LASCAUX CAVE (FRANCE) • CUEVA DE LAS MANOS (ARGENTINA)

Since prehistoric times, humans have used color to decorate their dwellings, embellish their linens or clothing, and enrich their artistic creations.

The first pigments to be used in European cave art were black (charcoal derived from pine trees) and red (from hematite, an iron oxide, either blown onto walls in powder form or applied as a thick paint), with the addition of white (from clay). About 36,000 years ago, these three colors were used to execute the 420-some depictions of animals, including horses, lions, bison, rhinoceros, and reindeer, and the many abstract motifs that adorn the Chauvet-Pont-d'Arc Cave in France.

Ochers in shades of yellow to brown appeared later. About 19,000 years ago at Lascaux, also in France, artists used goethite, another iron oxide, to render certain elements of the cave's extraordinary bestiary, comprising more than six hundred horses, aurochs, stags, ibex, and bison, as well as an anthropomorphic figure. Green did not appear until the Bronze Age (c. 800 BCE) and the discovery of copper oxidation.

MAIN CHARACTERISTICS

In Europe, Paleolithic cave paintings provide the most dramatic evidence of this taste for color, although many other artifacts, some quite modest, such as Azilian pebbles painted with red markings (about 12,000 years old), also reveal a pronounced appreciation for color.

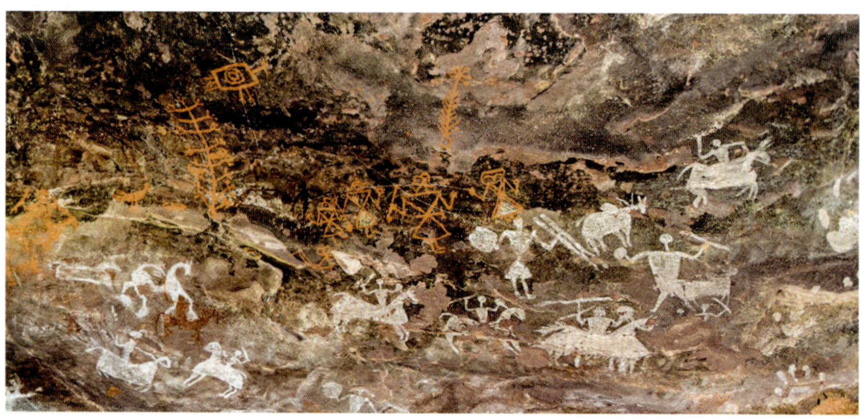

Chauvet Cave. Vallon-Pont-d'Arc, Ardèche.

Polychromy in Ancient Egypt

c. 3150 BCE – 30 CE

IMPORTANT PLACES: AMARNA • THEBES • VALLEY OF THE KINGS • SAQQARA

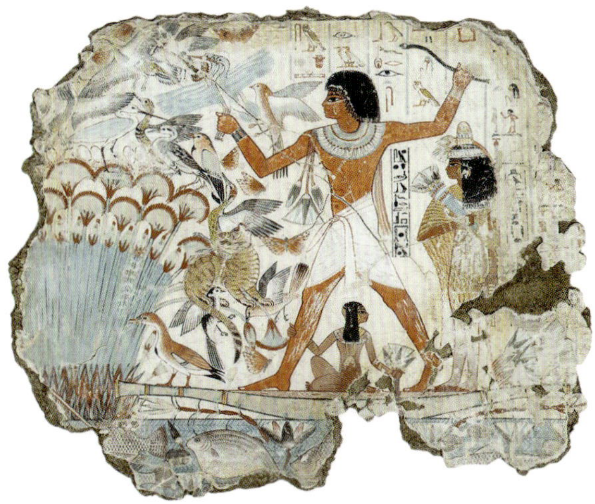

Fresco depicting Nebamun fowling and fishing in the marshes, from the tomb of Nebamun, Eighteenth Dynasty (Egypt). British Museum, London.

MAIN CHARACTERISTICS
Ancient Egypt was a polychromatic world. And yet there is no hieroglyphic equivalent to our word "color"; in texts that have come down to us, the Egyptians appear more interested in the idea of surface and brightness.

Egyptian artwork displays consistent use of color, as much in sculpture in the round as in bas-relief, murals, objects, and architecture. From the end of the Early Dynastic period (c. 3000 BCE) and especially during the Old Kingdom (2815–2400 BCE), right up to the Greco-Roman period, artists primarily used flat fields of color, and shading remained rare.

The basic palette included shades of white, black, red, and green, with the addition of gold—the Egyptians had no word for yellow as we know it, although they used ocher and saffron pigments. White, brown, and red hues were obtained from iron oxides, and black from charcoal, while greens and blues were conjured from a combination of copper, sand, lime, and ashes, and constitute the first synthetic pigments in history.

Symbolically, colors were intertwined with spirituality and religion. Black reminded the Egyptians of the silt from the Nile that fertilized crops; red evoked both Seth, god of storms and disorder, and Osiris, god of rebirth and fertility; green, which could encompass blue, was associated with nature (both stretches of water and sky, and plants). However, there was no equivalent to our blue: lapis lazuli was considered a shade of black and turquoise a shade of green.

Aristotle's Theory of Color

c. 800
–
31 BCE

IMPORTANT PLACES: ATHENS • OLYMPIA • EPHESUS

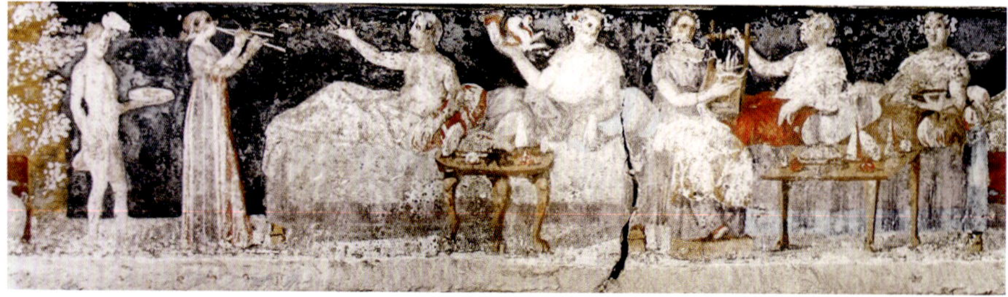

Mural depicting a banquet scene, from the tomb of Agios Athanasios, 325–300 BCE. Near Thessaloniki.

Throughout ancient Greece, theories of color and its associated meaning held many contradictions, so much so that modern readers may find them difficult to grasp. In his treatise *On Colors,* Aristotle (384–322 BCE) helped to clarify and structure the color system by organizing unmixed colors—red, violet, blue, and gray or yellow—on a scale from dark to light, or from black to white, for a total of seven hues, most likely modeled after the music scale.

Greek art made broad use of color: in painted murals, marble or wood statues, and mosaics, as well as ceramics, which were often dominated by black and red. Color was an integral part of the creative process and there was nothing incidental about it. In the private sphere, color provided clues to an individual's persona (the subject's sex or social status, for example); in religious contexts, it emphasized the piety of the patron who commissioned the divine statue or donated to the temple; in politics, it magnified power (palace decor). Rome maintained and enriched the tradition of polychromy, notably through the use of new pigments sourced from conquered lands.

MAIN CHARACTERISTICS

For the Greeks, the word "color" referred primarily to a colored surface. Aristotle's color system, which classifies pure colors from darkest to lightest, dominated European thinking until Isaac Newton's discoveries in the seventeenth century.

RED **p. 46** YELLOW **p. 47** BLUE **p. 48** GREEN **p. 49** VIOLET **p. 51** GRAY **p. 54**
NATURAL AND SYNTHETIC PIGMENTS **p. 190** POLYCHROME SCULPTURE IN THE WEST **p. 198**

India's Holi Festival

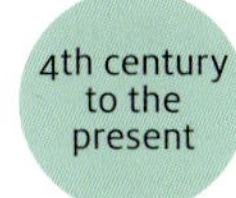

IMPORTANT CITIES: BARSANA • MATHURA • NANDGAON • VRINDAVAN

Each year in India, the Hindu festival of color, Holi (first cited in fourth-century texts), celebrates fertility and the arrival of spring. On the evening of the first day, a fire is lit to commemorate Vishnu's burning of the demoness Holika, and by the same occasion the triumph of good over evil. The next day, men and women of all ages and castes, dressed in white, throw pigments and tinted water at everyone they encounter.

Traditionally, dried and ground flowers of *Butea monosperma*, a sacred bush nicknamed "flame-of-the-forest," were mixed with water to form a yellow liquid; orangey curcuma and powdered red sandalwood were also used. The colors obtained symbolized faith (yellow); optimism (orange); and joy and love (red).

The palette has since expanded to include blue (vitality) and green (harmony). In northern India, the Holi festival is associated with the god Radha-Krishna, a dual divinity of eternal love. It is said that Krishna, fearing that Radha would reject him because of his dark complexion, asked the young woman to blow colored powder on his face—after which they fell in love.

KEY ARTWORK
In this eighteenth-century watercolor, Krishna and Radha, surrounded by *gopis*—the milkmaids with whom Krishna spent his adolescence—and young cowherds, use bamboo canes to blow powder and tinted water.

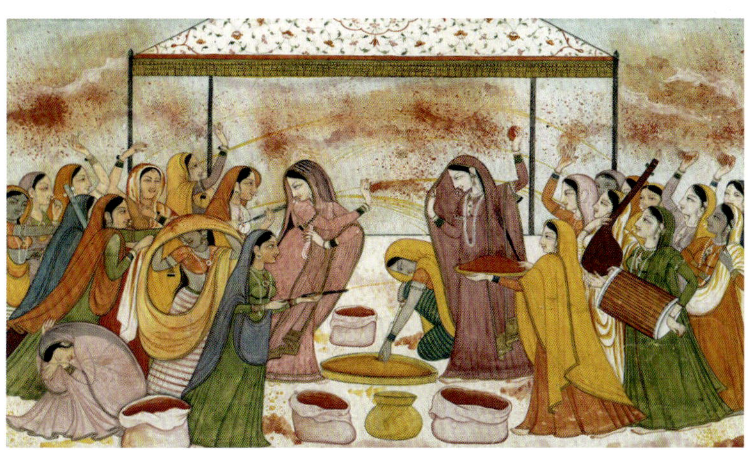

Unknown artist, *Krishna and Radha*, c. 1775–80. Watercolor. Victoria and Albert Museum, London.

RED **p. 46** YELLOW **p. 47** BLUE **p. 48** GREEN **p. 49** ORANGE **p. 50** NATURAL AND SYNTHETIC PIGMENTS **p. 190** YELLOW PIGMENTS **p. 192** RED AND PURPLE PIGMENTS **p. 193**

Colors and Heraldry

PRINCIPAL MANUSCRIPTS: THE GREAT EQUESTRIAN ARMORIAL OF THE GOLDEN FLEECE (FRANCE) • CONRAD GRÜNENBERG'S ARMORIAL (GERMANY) • DERING ROLL (ENGLAND) • THE GELRE ARMORIAL (BELGIUM)

12th century to the present

MAIN CHARACTERISTICS

The use of heraldic arms throughout Europe began in the twelfth century. This code, which grew out of knighthood, was used by families, institutions, and communities as a mark of identity. Knights were the first to paint a coat of arms on their shields, then on their tunic or their horse's caparison, to make themselves easy to identify during battles or tournaments.

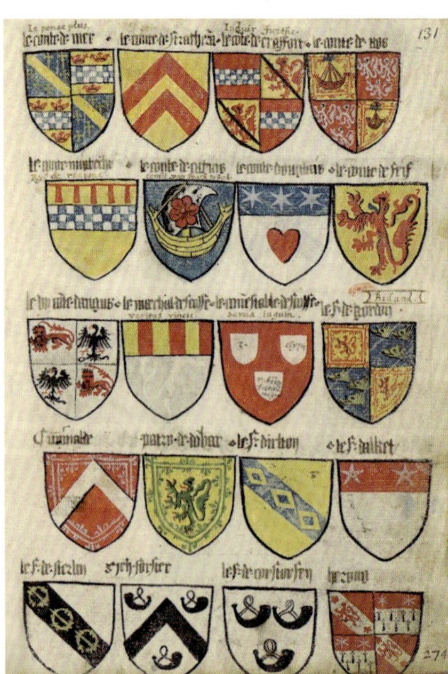

Colored armorial depicting the coats of arms of various princes and lords of France, Germany, Flanders, England, Spain, Italy, etc., fifteenth century. Bibliothèque Nationale de France, Paris.

Heraldry and its colors played a decisive role in medieval society. As historian Michel Pastoureau points out, the nobility was not the only group to adopt coats of arms: they were soon being used by high-ranking clergy, the bourgeoisie, craftsmen, and even peasants.

A coat of arms consists of figures and colors arranged according to a pre-established set of rules designed to be easily read. Figures included animal, plant, and geometric motifs. Colors, initially devoid of symbolism, were given names unique to heraldry: gold (yellow), silver (white), gules (red), sable (black), azure (blue), sinople (green), and purpure (violet). They were divided into two groups: gold and silver in the first, and the other five shades in the second. It was forbidden to combine two colors from the same group.

Gradually, these coats of arms came to represent family descent. As they spread, they began to be recorded by heralds in illuminated manuscripts known as heraldic manuals. These officers, who were tasked with announcing the heraldic feats and emblems of knights to the spectators at tournaments, began to specialize in codifying these crests in the fourteen and fifteenth centuries.

Divine Color

IMPORTANT ARTISTS: CIMABUE • GIOTTO • FRA ANGELICO

12th – 15th centuries

In the twelfth and thirteenth centuries, the Christian God became a divinity of light, a shield against darkness, and an uplifter of souls. Around 1130, Abbot Suger (1081–1151) oversaw the reconstruction of the Basilica of Saint-Denis (an abbey church at that time), located north of Paris, where he designed a sacred space bathed in color through the generous use of stained glass. Blue, henceforth associated with divine light, dominated his creation, although gold—a rival color inherited from Byzantine art—was still in use during this period.

In the early fourteenth century, the Florentine painter Giotto (c. 1266–1337), who developed the foundations of Renaissance painting by introducing more realism into his work, still used gold as a ground in his works, including his altarpiece *Saint Francis of Assisi Receiving the Stigmata* (c. 1300–1325).

A century later, in his work *On Painting* (1435–36), the theorist and writer Leon Battista Alberti (1404–1472)—a humanist who championed painting as a liberal art—deplored the excessive use of gold, which produced effects he considered too simplistic and insufficiently naturalistic.

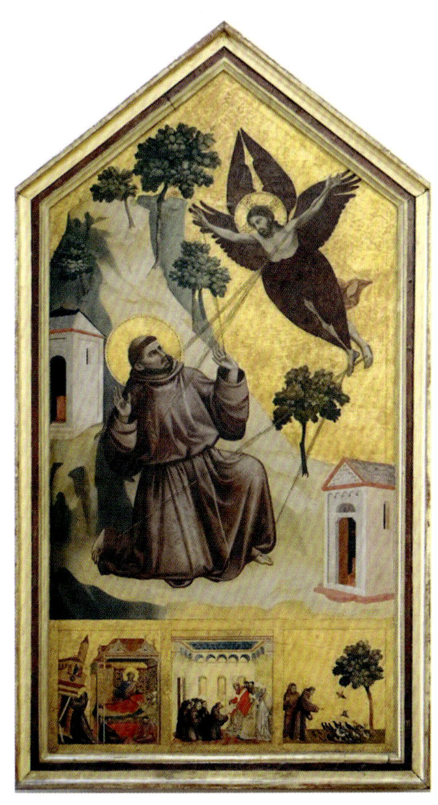

Giotto, *Saint Francis of Assisi Receiving the Stigmata*, c. 1300–1325. Tempera and gold on wood. Musée du Louvre, Paris.

KEY ARTWORK

In this work by Giotto, Saint Francis of Assisi, down on one knee, receives the stigmata from Christ, who is depicted as a seraphim. The background and the halos of the two figures are painted in gold— a brighter, more dazzling, and more blinding color than blue. The artist creates an illusion of depth by depicting a mountain rising behind Francis and incorporating architectural elements.

BLUE **p. 48** GOLD **p. 56** STAINED GLASS IN THE BASILICA OF SAINT-DENIS **p. 68** WORKING WITH GOLD **p. 199** STAINED GLASS **p. 207**

The Invention of Oil Paint

IMPORTANT ARTISTS: JAN VAN EYCK • ROGIER VAN DER WEYDEN • ANTONELLO DA MESSINA

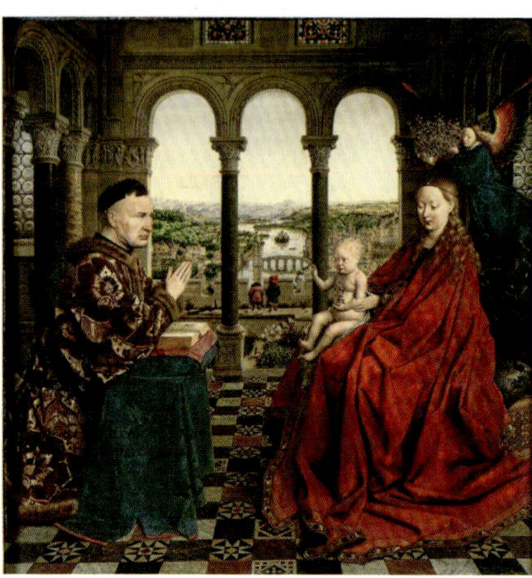

Jan Van Eyck, *Madonna of Chancellor Rolin,*
c. 1434–35. Oil on wood. Musée du Louvre, Paris.

Prior to the early decades of the fifteenth century, painters mainly worked in tempera (a mixture of pigments, water, and glue or egg yolk) and fresco (pigments applied to wet or dry lime plaster): two techniques with a very opaque finish. In the fifteenth century, an innovative way to paint with oil—which until that time had been used primarily as a varnish—was developed; by mixing pigments with cooked oil and a thinner (water and egg, and later turpentine oil, artists were able to obtain new color effects that were far more delicate, fluid, and translucent.

According to the legend popularized by Italian art historian Giorgio Vasari (1511–1574), Jan Van Eyck (c. 1390–1441) invented oil painting in the sixteenth century. In reality, the artist contributed to perfecting the technique.

In the sixteenth century, the oil painting revolution coincided with other artistic breakthroughs, such as illusionism, with the introduction of perspective; the development of chiaroscuro; and the use of canvas, which was lighter and easier to transport in rolls than wood panels, especially useful for large-format paintings.

KEY ARTIST

Jan Van Eyck contributed to the development of oil painting, applying color in a series of transparent films to create a glaze: light seems to enter the painting through the transparent layers of oil. Henceforth, great pains were taken to render textures, effects of shadow or reflections, and volumes naturalistically. The color palette expanded to include countless shades.

MADONNA OF CHANCELLOR ROLIN **p. 70** TEMPERA **p. 200** FRESCO **p. 201** OIL PAINT **p. 203**

The Color Renaissance

IMPORTANT ARTISTS: LORENZO LOTTO • TITIAN •
PAOLO VERONESE • TINTORETTO

15th
–
16th
centuries

The Renaissance was characterized by significant evolutions in philosophy and the arts. Unlike medieval thinking, humanist culture, steeped in ancient Greek and Roman knowledge, placed humanity at the center of the world. Writing against this backdrop in 1435–36, Florentine theorist and writer Leon Battista Alberti explains in his treatise for artists that a painting consists of three elements: composition, contour (line), and light (color). He describes black and white as regulating elements that allow painters to adjust values and chiaroscuro, and he pairs each of the four elements with a "pure" color: red for fire, blue for air, green for water, and gray (a mix of black and white,

notes Alberti) for earth. There is no mention of yellow, which was considered a derivative of green at that time.

Alberti recommended using a rich palette, breaking with medieval sobriety. This appreciation for color reached its height in the sixteenth century in Venice—the nerve center of luxury trade from all over the Mediterranean. Venetians, who encountered difficulties with fresco because of high humidity levels in their city, eagerly adopted a new technique: oil painting. Merchants specializing in the sale of pigments offered high-quality colors; in the rest of Italy, apothecaries supplied artists.

KEY ARTIST
Venetian painters like Titian (c. 1488–1576) and Paolo Veronese (1528–1588) excelled in the art of color—to the detriment of line and form, according to the art historian Giorgio Vasari.

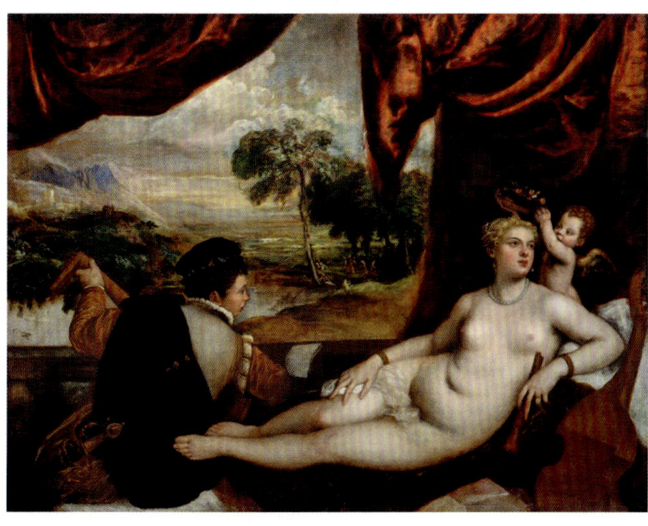

Titian, *Venus and the Lute Player*, c. 1565–70. Oil on canvas. The Metropolitan Museum of Art, New York, NY.

WHITE **p. 45** RED **p. 46** BLUE **p. 48** GREEN **p. 49** GRAY **p. 54** *LUCRETIA* **p. 76**
NATURAL AND SYNTHETIC PIGMENTS **p. 190** FRESCO **p. 201** OIL PAINT **p. 203**

Line and Form Versus Color

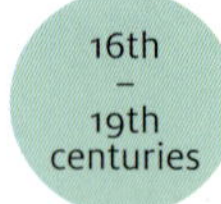

IMPORTANT ARTISTS: LEONARDO DA VINCI • MICHELANGELO • TITIAN • NICOLAS POUSSIN • PETER PAUL RUBENS

KEY ARTIST
Around 1508, in his *A Treatise on Painting*, the polymath Leonardo da Vinci (1452–1519) recommended that painters use a reduced and muted palette (with tones subdued by the addition of white or black) to compose paintings, notably through the use of shadow.

In the second edition of *The Lives of the Most Excellent Painters, Sculptors, and Architects* (1568), the art historian Giorgio Vasari mentions two traditions in sixteenth-century painting: one, originating in Tuscany, that privileged line and form, and which Michelangelo (1475–1564) would come to embody; and

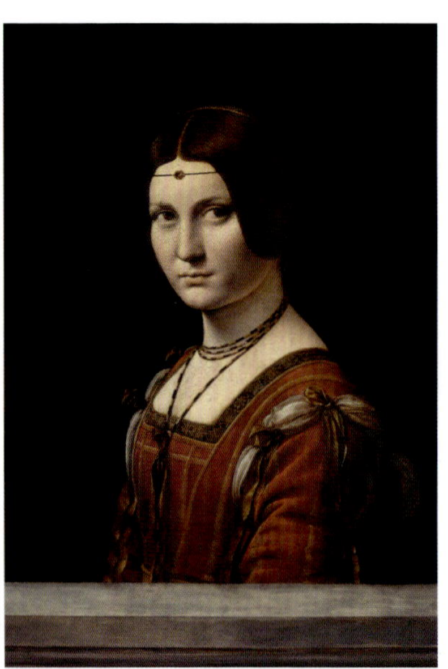

another, from Venice, that venerated color, led by Titian (c. 1488–1576).

While this quarrel between line and color was often exaggerated, it nevertheless spread to seventeenth-century France where, within the Royal Academy of Painting and Sculpture, acolytes of Nicolas Poussin (1594–1665), recognized for his majestic draftsmanship, disputed with followers of Peter Paul Rubens (1577–1640), who was famous for his skillful use of color. A fervent advocate of literary, even rhetorical painting, Charles Le Brun (1619–1690), the first court painter under King Louis XIV (1638–1715), maintained that line and form satisfied the spirit while color pleased only the eyes.

In the following century, the intense palette and loose brushstrokes of Antoine Watteau (1684–1721), admitted into the Academy in 1717, and Jean-Honoré Fragonard (1732–1806), admitted in 1765, seemed to spell victory for colorists. Yet artistic debate revived the argument and continued it into the late nineteenth century, pitting, for example, the fine, precise draftsmanship of Jean-Auguste-Dominique Ingres (1780–1867) against the sensuous use of color by Eugène Delacroix (1798–1863).

Leonardo da Vinci, *Portrait of a Lady from the Court of Milan,* also known as *La Belle Ferronnière*, c. 1490–97. Oil on wood. Musée du Louvre, Paris.

BLACK **p. 44** WHITE **p. 45** *PORTRAIT OF A LADY FROM THE COURT OF MILAN* **p. 74** *THE DEATH OF SARDANAPALUS* **p. 86**

Color and Gender

IMPORTANT ARTISTS: PIERO DELLA FRANCESCA • HYACINTHE RIGAUD •
JEAN-AUGUSTE-DOMINIQUE INGRES

Renaissance
to the
present

In the collective imagination, certain colors are associated with gender. Pink and blue are the most obvious examples; the first is supposedly feminine and the second masculine. However, for a long time there was no term to designate the color pink as we know it today. In the past, the word "carmine" or "crimson" was sometimes used, in reference to a bright pink reminiscent of the European complexion. The color was seen as a derivative of red, and in this regard was associated with virility. Blue, on the other hand, was associated with femininity, as in the color of the Virgin Mary's cloak (Piero Della Francesca, *Madonna del Parto*, c. 1455, Museum of Monterchi). These meanings inverted during the French Revolution. Men, who under the French ancien régime had long hair and wore high heels, stockings, and lace (Hyacinthe Rigaud, *Portrait of Louis XIV*, see pp. 82–83), cast aside their finery in favor of dark, dour clothing (Jean-Auguste-Dominique Ingres, *Portrait of Monsieur Bertin*, 1832, Louvre, Paris), and the color red took on feminine connotations.

The color gray, as French critic and essayist Roland Barthes explained in his lecture on color at the Collège de France in the late 1970s, is a neutral color and denotes gender neutrality. Shades of gray (grisaille) were used to decorate the exterior panels of altarpieces, and seemed at odds with the hidden richness of colors on the interior panels. Johann Wolfgang von Goethe considered gray to be a middle tint that contained the other colors combined, and so harmonized with every hue.

MAIN CHARACTERISTICS

Before the nineteenth century, pink and blue were not colors specifically assigned to girls and boys respectively, as evidenced in this portrait of a young boy by the British artist Thomas Gainsborough (1727–1788). But following advances in chemistry which made it easier to obtain pastel colors, they became increasingly associated with children, and the French haute bourgeoisie dressed girls in light pink and boys in sky blue. This division spread through the rest of society during the twentieth century.

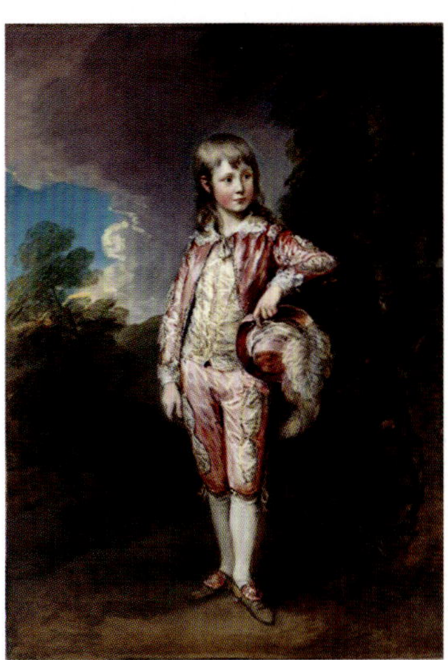

Thomas Gainsborough, *The Pink Boy*, 1782.
Oil on canvas. National Trust Waddesdon Manor, Buckinghamshire.

BLUE **p. 48** PINK **p. 53** GRAY **p. 54** *PORTRAIT OF LOUIS XIV* **p. 82**

The Color Reformation

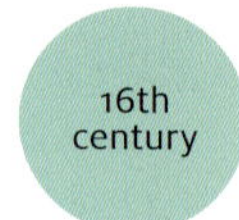

IMPORTANT ARTISTS: LUCAS CRANACH THE ELDER • HANS HOLBEIN THE YOUNGER

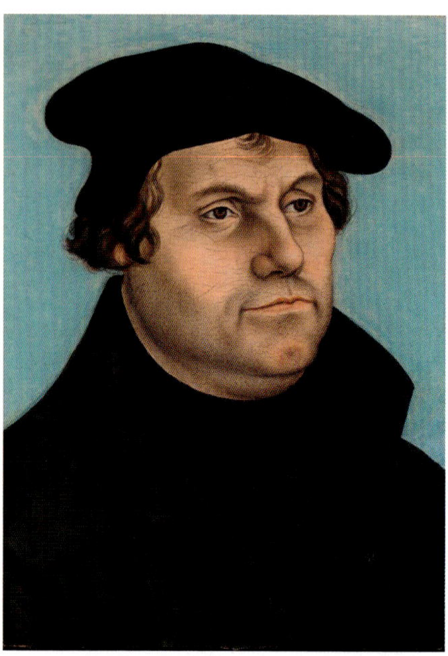

Lucas Cranach the Elder, *Martin Luther*, c. 1532. Oil on wood. The Metropolitan Museum of Art, New York, NY.

KEY ARTIST
The painter Lucas Cranach (1472–1553), working in service to the Reformation, carried out several portraits of his friend Martin Luther. These images, consistent with Protestant rigor, circulated widely as black-and-white prints, a format appreciated by advocates of the Reformed Church because they could be disseminated widely and were inexpensive to produce.

In 1517, the Protestant Reformation, spearheaded by Martin Luther (1483–1546), created a schism within the Christian religion, between Catholic Latin Europe and the now Protestant Northern Europe. Within this complex context, Protestant morality deplored—in both clothing and painting—the assertive use of color: a symbol of extravagant papistry and profligate aristocracy. In daily life, Luther and his followers, Ulrich Zwingli (1484–1531) in German-speaking Switzerland and southern Germany, and Jean Calvin (1509–1564) in the French-speaking world, advocated humility and austerity. Although he condemned Catholic idolatry, Luther understood the power of images, especially in the context of religious teaching, and encouraged their use in order to transmit his ideas. On the other hand, Zwingli was wary of such images and Calvin strictly forbade their use.

The values of the Reformation were expressed in clothing and in artistic representation through a use of black that broke with the crude appeal of color—now synonymous with deceit and dishonesty. The bourgeoisie dressed in black, a fact reflected in the portraits they commissioned.

Limited Color and the Rise of the Bourgeoisie

17th – 19th centuries

IMPORTANT ARTISTS: JACQUES-LOUIS DAVID • ADÉLAÏDE LABILLE-GUIARD • FRANS HALS • JEAN-AUGUSTE-DOMINIQUE INGRES • REMBRANDT

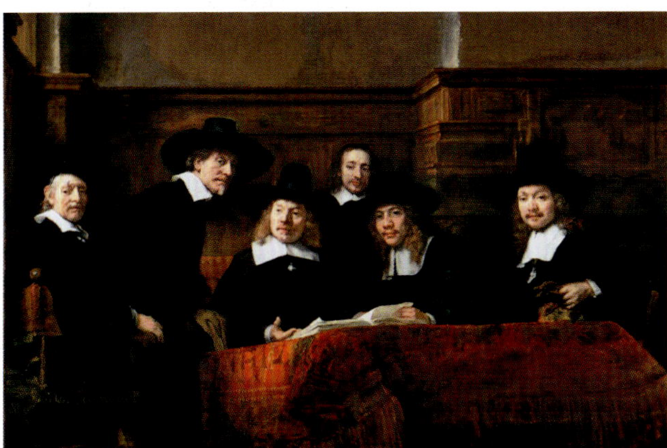

Rembrandt, *The Sampling Officials of the Amsterdam Drapers' Guild*, known as *The Syndics*, 1662. Oil on canvas. Rijksmuseum, Amsterdam.

In the sixteenth century, the Protestant Reformation found support in the emerging bourgeoisie. In response to an ostentatious Catholic monarchy that encouraged the conspicuous use of color in clothing and decor, a culture of austerity developed, dominated by the color black.

Certain bodies dictated the kind of clothing its members could wear: in France, for example, the Estates General of 1789 codified, among other things, the "uniform" of its congressmen. While representatives of the clergy were allowed to wear purple and members of the nobility could flaunt gold trim and white feathers, representatives of the Third Estate had to wear "frock coat, jacket, and breeches of black cloth, black stockings, with a short coat of silk or muslin, [and] a hat turned up on three sides,

without tassels or buttons." Leading up to the French Revolution, painters' palettes had already begun to grow muted, perhaps a portent of the crisis to come.

In the nineteenth century, a similar austerity prevailed in representations of the bourgeoisie, whose political and economic power continued to grow across Europe with the rise of the industrial revolution and capitalism.

A frugal use of color became synonymous with good taste, discretion, and temperance, considered virtues even by today's middle classes.

KEY APPLICATIONS
Severe portraits of merchant families dressed in black proliferated in seventeenth-century Dutch painting.

BLACK **p. 44** WHITE **p. 45** VIOLET **p. 51** GOLD **p. 56**

Chiaroscuro

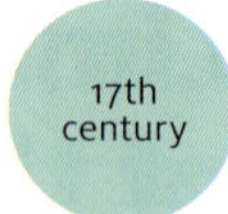

IMPORTANT ARTISTS: CARAVAGGIO • ARTEMISIA GENTILESCHI • VALENTIN DE BOULOGNE • JUSEPE DE RIBERA

KEY ARTIST
Early in his career, Caravaggio realized the dramatic power of chiaroscuro and its capacity to emphasize or to obliterate form. Using this technique, he captured decisive moments with a raw intensity, inspired by scenes from everyday life.

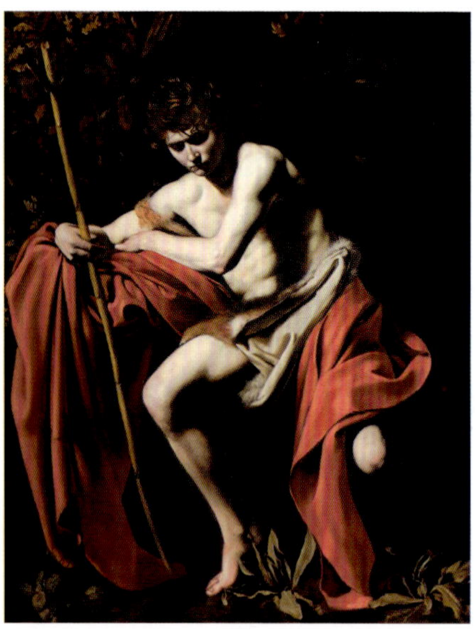

Caravaggio, *Saint John the Baptist in the Wilderness*, 1602–4. Oil on canvas. The Nelson-Atkins Museum of Art, Kansas City, MO.

At the turn of the seventeenth century, the Lombardi painter Caravaggio (c. 1571–1610) undertook a systematic effort to depict everyday and nocturnal scenes. He did not invent chiaroscuro, a technique involving contrasting areas of light and dark, but he was the leading master and employed the technique to dramatic, even violent, effect.

In Caravaggio's work, the source of light, rarely identified, seems to burst forth from the pigments themselves, from the pictorial matter. This is more than simply a technique, but represents the divine light that drives out the shadows of ignorance. To create a wealth of tones, from darkest to lightest, Caravaggio painted on red-brown, gray, or green ground layers. He avoided pure colors, restricted his palette, and used the glazing technique (applying successive layers of transparent color) to illuminate specific areas of the composition.

Although he had no students, Caravaggio influenced several generations of painters who discovered his work in Rome and Naples. Influenced by his dramatic effects and the choice of his subjects, artists like the Frenchman Valentin de Boulogne (1591–1632) and the Spaniard José de Ribera (1591–1662) adopted his naturalistic approach and his attention to chiaroscuro, and contributed to spreading his style throughout Europe.

BLACK **p. 44** RED **p. 46** GRAY **p. 54** *THE REPENTANT MAGDALEN* **p. 78** *WITCHES' SABBATH* **p. 84**

Contrasts

IMPORTANT THEORISTS: ARISTOTLE • ISAAC NEWTON • JOHANN WOLFGANG VON GOETHE • MICHEL-EUGÈNE CHEVREUL

17th – 19th centuries

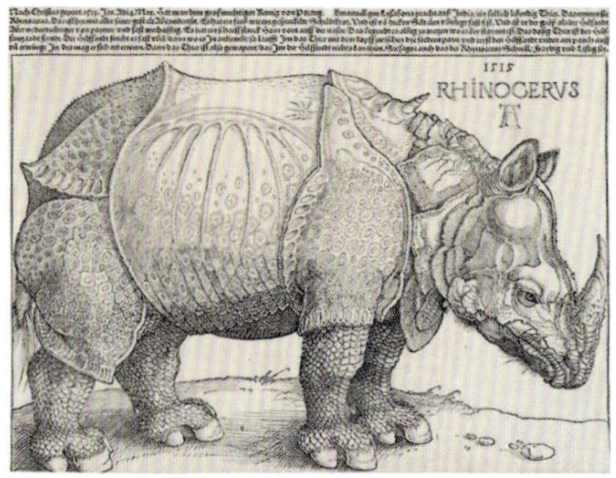

Albrecht Dürer, *The Rhinoceros*, 1515. Woodcut.
The Art Institute of Chicago, Chicago, IL.

MAIN CHARACTERISTICS

The current classification of colors into warm and cool hues is largely derived from research into visual perception carried out by Johann Wolfgang von Goethe in the early nineteenth century. Starting in the late fifteenth century, the early printing industry favored the use of black ink on white paper, establishing black and white as the standard for the strongest and most legible contrast in texts and prints.

The perception and classification of colors are essentially cultural and historical facts. In the West, several conventions prevail: the opposition of warm and cool hues, the contrast between black and white, the primary colors, and the complementary colors. The concept of warm and cool colors, as we know it today, developed in artistic circles during the eighteenth century. The German writer Johann Wolfgang von Goethe (1749–1832) revisits the idea in his *Theory of Color* (1810), writing that warm and active reds, oranges, and yellows stand out from their complements: cool and passive greens, blues, and violets.

While this opposition is relative—the historian Michel Pastoureau reminds us that in the Middle Ages, blue, for example, was considered a warm color—research into retinal ganglion cells has demonstrated a similar dualism in the evolution of the way mammals perceive colors.

The idea that black and white are not colors emerged from the work of Isaac Newton (1642–1727). Rejecting Aristotle's linear conception of colors (white, yellow or gray, red, violet, green, blue, black), he proposed a circular classification based on the colors of the rainbow (see p. 26). Black and white were excluded from his classification; placed at opposite ends of a scale ranging from lightest to darkest, they became, in the West, synonymous with contrast—a concept reinforced by the invention of printing.

Newton's Color Wheel

1704

IMPORTANT ARTISTS: J.M.W. TURNER • GEORGES SEURAT • PAUL SIGNAC •
PAUL SÉRUSIER • FRANTIŠEK KUPKA

Isaac Newton (1642–1727) revolutionized scientific thought, and many of his discoveries in the fields of mathematics and physics—his main areas of study—paved the way for modern science. In 1666, he began his research into optics, which would last several years, and made a key observation: white light refracted in a prism comprises a spectrum of colors. He distinguished six colors in the visible spectrum (violet, blue, green, yellow, orange, and red), setting aside black and white. But, as historian Michel Pastoureau points out, Newton conformed to the symbolic conventions of his day, which were based on systems with seven or twelve elements, and he added indigo (a second blue), making a total of seven fundamental colors, following the model of the music scale. The seven colors of the rainbow as we know them today were thus established.

In 1704, Newton published the results of his research in a book entitled *Opticks*. He formalized the division of colors in the spectrum according to wavelength in a color wheel (also known as Newton's Disc), breaking with Aristotle's linear representation of colors. In this way, he also introduced the notion of complementary colors, which are placed diametrically opposite each other on the wheel.

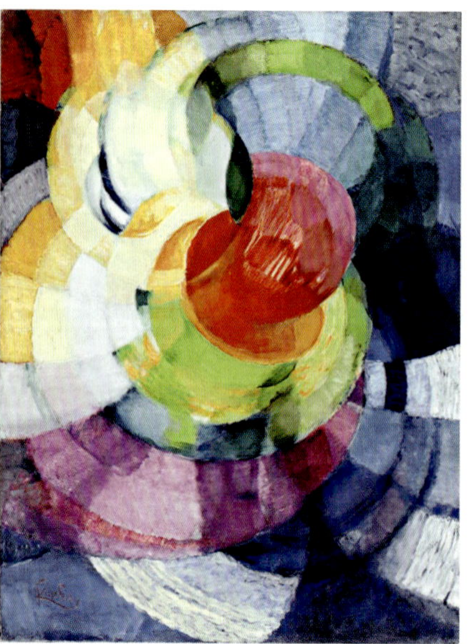

František Kupka, *Disks of Newton*, 1912. Oil on canvas. Philadelphia Museum of Art, Philadelphia, PA.

KEY APPLICATIONS

In the nineteenth century, color theorists proposed increasingly sophisticated versions of the color wheel, which aroused the interest of many painters, from J.M.W. Turner (1775–1851) to Georges Seurat (1859–1891).

Primary and Complementary Colors

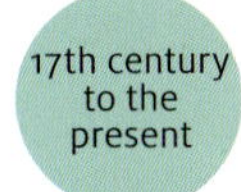

IMPORTANT THEORISTS: CLAUDE BOUTET • MOSES HARRIS • JOHANN WOLFGANG VON GOETHE • JOHANNES ITTEN

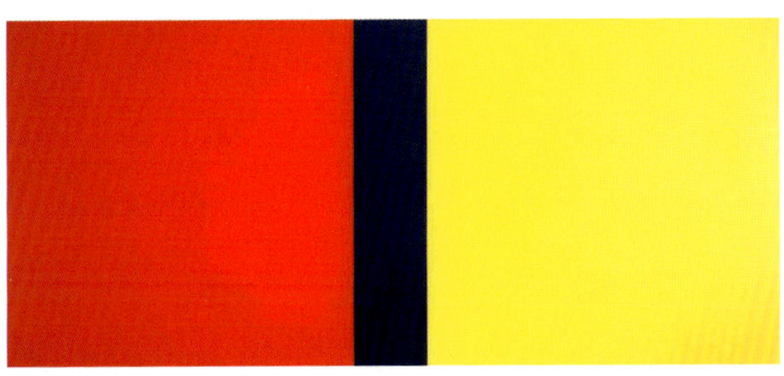

Barnett Newman, *Who's Afraid of Red, Yellow and Blue IV*, 1969–70. Acrylic on canvas. Nationalgalerie, Berlin.

The concept of three primary colors—yellow, red, and blue—that, according to popular belief, are capable of producing every other color, appeared in the late seventeenth century. In the early twentieth century, the Bauhaus, through members like the painter and theorist Johannes Itten (1888–1967), endowed primary colors with enduring connotations of purity and modernity. Several decades later, many artists relished challenging these strong connotations, producing ironically titled works such as Barnett Newman's series *Who's Afraid of Red, Yellow and Blue.*

The idea of facilitating the identification of complementary colors by classifying them on the color wheel is inherited from scientific research. In his work *The Natural System of Colours* (c. 1770), illustrated with a new color wheel, the naturalist Moses Harris (1730–1785) writes, "If a contrast is wanting to any colour or teint, look for the colour or teint in the system, and directly opposite to it you will find the contrast wanted." In the fiftieth paragraph of his *Theory of Colors* (1810), the German writer

Johann Wolfgang von Goethe considers how colors opposite each other on the wheel call out to each other in the eye of the viewer: "for the colours diametrically opposed to each other in this diagram are those which reciprocally evoke each other in the eye. Thus, yellow demands purple; orange, blue; red, green; and *vice versa.*" This approach was highly popular in the nineteenth century, particularly with painters like J. M. W. Turner (1775–1851) and Philipp Otto Runge (1777–1810). From the early 1850s, it was incorporated into many treatises, all of which mention that complementary colors are harmonious provided they are placed side by side and not mixed—for when they are, they turn into a drab gray hue.

KEY AUTHOR

The notion of three primary colors emerged in *Traité de la peinture en miniature* (Treatise on Miniature Painting), published in 1673 and attributed to Claude Boutet: "Properly speaking, there are only three primitive colors, which cannot be composed of other colors, but of which all others may be composed. These three colors are yellow, red, and blue."

RED **p. 46** YELLOW **p. 47** BLUE **p. 48** GREEN **p. 49** ORANGE **p. 50** VIOLET **p. 51** *COMPOSITION WITH LARGE RED PLANE, YELLOW, BLACK, GRAY, AND BLUE* **p. 126** *SEVERAL CIRCLES* **p. 130** *SIX COLORFUL INSIDE JOBS* **p. 172**

Art and Science

18th – 19th centuries

IMPORTANT ARTISTS: VINCENT VAN GOGH • GEORGES SEURAT • PAUL SIGNAC

Color became a subject of scientific research following Isaac Newton's experiments with prisms in the late seventeenth century. Several decades later, while acknowledging Newton's discoveries, Georges-Louis Leclerc, Comte de Buffon (1707–1788), turned his attention to the physiology of color and the importance of perception in his *Dissertation sur les couleurs accidentelles* (Dissertation on Accidental Colors) of 1743. In the nineteenth century, these two complementary approaches benefited from new research that generated unprecedented interest on the part of artists.

In 1839, the chemist Michel Eugène Chevreul (1786–1889), director of dyes at the national Gobelins textile factory in Paris, published *On the Law of Simultaneous Contrast of Colors*, which details how neighboring colors affect visual perception. The work, rarely read in its entirety, was popularized in the press, but also by another author, Charles Blanc (1813–1882): an engraver, art historian, and former director of the École des Beaux-Arts. In his *Grammar of Painting and Engraving* (1867), Blanc devotes a chapter to an accessible overview of color that found an audience with painters like Vincent Van Gogh (1853–1890), Georges Seurat (1859–1891), and Paul Signac (1863–1935): "To put a color upon canvas," writes Blanc quoting Chevreul, "is not merely to tint with this color everything that the pencil has touched; it is also to color with its complement the surrounding space."

KEY AUTHOR
Artists' enduring familiarity with Michel Eugène Chevreul, a major color theorist, owes much to the seventy-two-shade color wheel that he developed in the early 1860s for the Gobelins textile factory, and which is still used today.

Chevreul's color wheel.

THE RAINBOW **p. 59** *FIELD WITH IRISES NEAR ARLES* **p. 102** *THE CIRCUS* **p. 104**

Romantic Color

IMPORTANT ARTISTS: THÉODORE GÉRICAULT • CASPAR DAVID FRIEDRICH • EUGÈNE DELACROIX

1800
–
1850

In Europe, the Romantic movement redefined art, literature, and philosophy, and elevated emotion and imagination above reason. In France, a quarrel broke out between the old guard, who defended academic rules (a hierarchy of genres in painting and unity of place, time, and action in theater), and the moderns who broke those rules. This newfound freedom of the artist in relation to established institutions raised fears that the use of color soon came to symbolize.

In 1830, the play *Hernani*, by Victor Hugo (1802–1885), provoked a heated debate between supporters of classical theater and advocates of the Romantic "revolution." At the premiere on February 25 at the Théâtre-Français, the young Théophile Gautier (1811–1872)—a painter in training, future author, and supporter of Hugo—caused a sensation when he appeared with long hair, wearing what has been described as a red satin waistcoat. This provocative display symbolized Romantic liberation and provoked "the coarse laughter of the bourgeois." In *A History of Romanticism* (1872), Gautier writes, "I wanted a return to life, light, movement, audacity in thought and execution, to the fair times of the Renaissance and real antiquity, so that I rejected the faint colouring, the thin, dry drawing, and the compositions that looked like groups of lay figures, which the Empire had bequeathed to the Restoration."

Eugène Delacroix, *The Death of Sardanapalus*, 1827. Oil on canvas. Musée du Louvre, Paris.

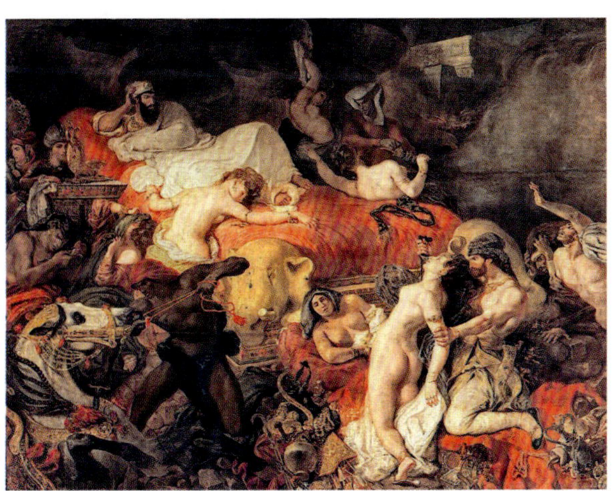

KEY ARTWORK

In 1827, Eugène Delacroix caused a scandal with *The Death of Sardanapalus*. Seated in his palace, surrounded by his possessions, slaves and mistresses, and horses and dogs, the Assyrian ruler chooses immolation over surrender. The primacy of color—the image is dominated by the red of the blood soon to be spilled—and the turbulent composition shocked defenders of academic beauty and neoclassical virtue.

RED **p. 46** *THE DEATH OF SARDANAPALUS* **p. 86**

In Praise of Shadows in Japan

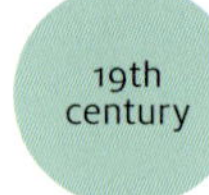

IMPORTANT ARTISTS: HOKUSAI • HIROSHIGE • UTAMARO • UTAGAWA KUNIYOSHI

In his essay *In Praise of Shadows* (1933), Japanese writer Junichiro Tanizaki (1886–1965) contrasted Japan's Western-driven modernization with a defense of traditional aesthetics rooted in a reverence for twilight, dusk, darkness, and *sabi* (an appreciation for timeworn patina): "This is true too of our household implements. We [the Japanese] prefer colors compounded of darkness. They [Westerners] prefer the colors of sunlight." Women of the middle and upper classes inhabited a domestic world whose architecture made use of chiaroscuro to create many shadowy nooks and alcoves. Tanizaki writes that their clothing "was in effect no more than a part of the darkness" and that they blackened their teeth. In Japanese culture, black and white are thought to contain all the other colors.

KEY ARTWORK

Color expressed as the relationship between light and shadow is singularly conveyed in a representation of the god of thunder and lightning by painter and printmaker Hokusai (1760–1849). A black cloud, partially rendered using the crachis technique, signifies the storm's violence and envelops the fiery god, who throws scarlet bolts of lightning: in Japanese, the word "red" (*aka*) also means "brightness."

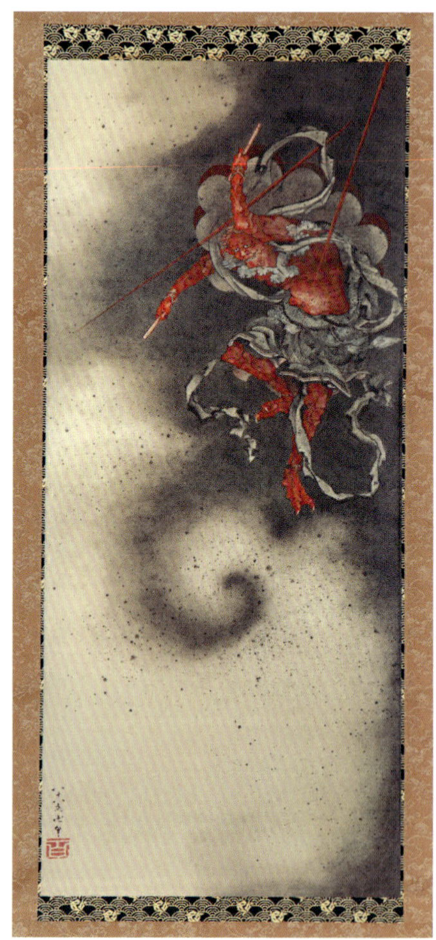

Hokusai, *Thunder God*, 1847. Ink and color on paper. National Museum of Asian Art, Washington, DC.

BLACK **p. 44** WHITE **p. 45** RED **p. 46** *THUNDER GOD* **p. 90** COLOR PRINTMAKING **p. 208**

The Magic of Electricity

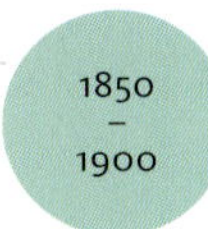

IMPORTANT ARTISTS: EDGAR DEGAS • HENRI DE TOULOUSE-LAUTREC •
LOUIS ANQUETIN

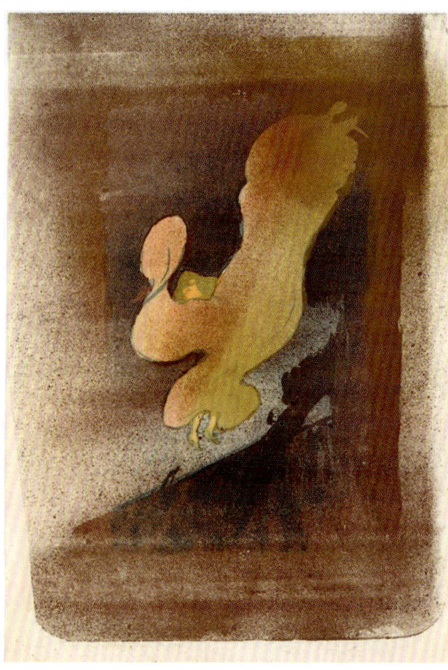

Henri de Toulouse-Lautrec, *Miss Loïe Fuller*, c. 1893. Color
lithograph with gold powder. Brooklyn Museum, New York, NY.

KEY ARTWORK
Loïe Fuller was a performer known for her
Serpentine Dance, which fascinated artists
with its dazzling energy. Draped in billowing
silk, she twirled around, surrounded by mirrors,
as color projectors lit her performance on all
sides: "For illumination," she writes in *Fifteen
Years of a Dancer's Life* (1913), "I intended to
have a lantern with colored glass. . . . I wanted
to dance the last one in total darkness with a
single ray of yellow light crossing the stage."
Toulouse-Lautrec's painting of her captures
this sense of light and color.

The invention of electric light and its
spread throughout public and private
spaces in the nineteenth century modified
the way colors were perceived. In the arts,
electricity encouraged representations of
nocturnal scenes now flooded with
uniform and often urban brightness, and
no longer bathed in a mysterious
chiaroscuro. As art historian Bruno
Foucart notes, "the intensity, whiteness,
density, and silence of electric lighting
astonished those who were used to the
quiver and crackle of flames, and the soft
blue of gas lighting. . . . Electric light is in
some way the tangible manifestation, the
colorful transcription of the forces that
ensure our mastery over the world"
("L'électricité et les artistes ou la baguette
et le balai," *Bulletin d'histoire de
l'électricité* ["Electricity and Artists, or the
Wand and the Broomstick," *History of
Electricity Bulletin*], 1991).

Paris as the city of pleasure became a
recurring theme in the work of artists
such as Edgar Degas (1834–1917), Henri de
Toulouse-Lautrec (1864–1901), and Louis
Anquetin (1861–1932), who turned their
attention to the electrified nightlife on the
Grands Boulevards, the supercharged
atmosphere of the cabarets, and the bawdy
brothels. The colors in their work are often
garish—bright pink, daffodil yellow, apple
green—in keeping with the harshness of
the selected motifs.

YELLOW **p. 47** GREEN **p. 49** PINK **p. 53** COLOR PRINTMAKING **p. 208** THE WORLD IN COLOR **p. 213**

Impressionism and Plein Air Painting

IMPORTANT ARTISTS: CAMILLE PISSARRO • ALFRED SISLEY • CLAUDE MONET • BERTHE MORISOT • AUGUSTE RENOIR

In the 1860s, the impressionist painters—including Camille Pissarro (1830–1903), Alfred Sisley (1839–1899), Claude Monet (1840–1926), Berthe Morisot (1841–1895), and Auguste Renoir (1841–1919)—developed a new approach to landscape painting. They abandoned traditional notions of structure and composition, choosing instead to convey their visual perceptions. Shimmering light, rustling foliage, and reflections on water are among the fleeting sensations that these artists sought to depict on canvas.

To this end, color was essential, as it could express changing atmospheric conditions and seasons. The introduction of unmixed color and the development of paint in tubes led to innovative, intuitive practices that were reaffirmed by scientific works on optics and color theory. In this way, chiaroscuro—popular with painters since the Renaissance—gave way to shadows rendered in color, with transitions between semi-darkness and light that combined the cool tones of the former and the warm tones of the latter using small brushstrokes. In the work of the impressionists, this method broke with the smooth finish of conventional, rule-bound academic art.

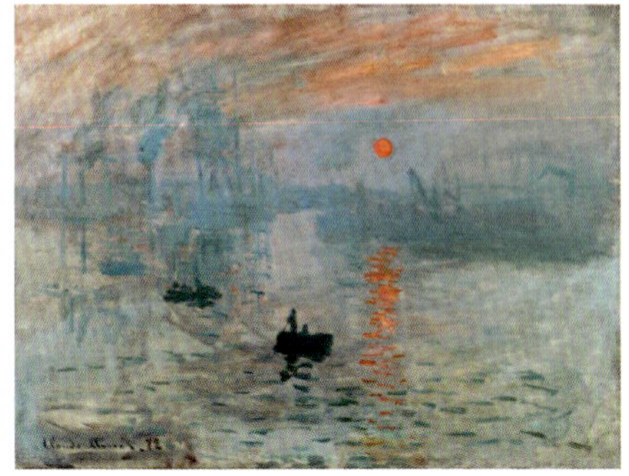

Claude Monet, *Impression, Sunrise*, 1872. Oil on canvas. Musée Marmottan Monet, Paris.

KEY ARTWORK

In 1872, Claude Monet painted *Impression, Sunrise*, which prompted a derisive journalist to coin the word "impressionist." The painting, which depicts daybreak over the Port du Havre, baffled Monet's contemporaries with its colors and loose brushstrokes: the orange sun reflected in the water and the hazy transition between the sky and the mauve sea glimmering with hints of green prepared the ground for many experiments with color.

Pointillism and Optical Mixtures

1880
–
1900

IMPORTANT ARTISTS: GEORGES SEURAT • PAUL SIGNAC • HENRI-EDMOND CROSS

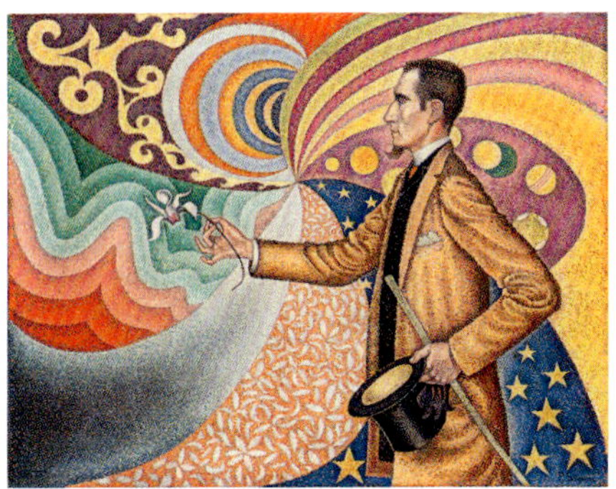

Paul Signac, *Opus 217. Against the Enamel of a Background Rhythmic with Beats and Angles, Tones, and Tints, Portrait of M. Félix Fénéon in 1890*, 1890. Oil on canvas. Museum of Modern Art, New York, NY.

KEY ARTIST

Paul Signac met his friend and mentor Georges Seurat in 1884. Both embraced a new way of using color in painting, which in Signac's hands became looser and less restrained over time. After Seurat died, Signac continued to spread their ideas with the publication in 1899 of a theoretical work titled *D'Eugène Delacroix au néo-impressionnisme* (From Eugène Delacroix to Neo-impressionism).

Georges Seurat and Paul Signac pioneered pointillism, also referred to as divisionism or neo-impressionism. These terms demonstrate the movement's debt to the impressionists, who in the 1860s adopted a new approach to color, using loose brushstrokes to depict effects of light and shadow. However, the pointillists took a scientific rather than intuitive approach to painting.

As an adolescent, Seurat became familiar with art historian Charles Blanc, whose works incorporated research by French chemist Michel Eugène Chevreul into color contrasts and their perception. He also read an article by Charles Henry, "Introduction à une esthétique scientifique" (Introduction to a Scientific Aesthetics) in *La Revue Contemporaine* (August 1885), and Ogden Rood's *Modern Chromatics* (1879). Seurat developed a method that consisted of painting small, tightly packed dots of unmixed color that interacted to create subtle vibrations of colored light in the eye of the viewer. He relied on a color wheel of his own invention, composed of twenty-two opposing colors. This method was used in highly constructed compositions structured by ascending lines, with hieratic figures inspired by Egyptian art, classical painting, and the mural painting of Pierre Puvis de Chavannes (1824–1898).

THE RAINBOW **p. 59** *THE CIRCUS* **p. 104**

Symbolist Colors

IMPORTANT ARTISTS: GUSTAVE MOREAU • PAUL GAUGUIN • PAUL SÉRUSIER

1875
–
1900

What is known as symbolism was a diverse movement that swept through European literature and art in the closing years of the nineteenth century. Symbolist painting united artists as diverse as Gustave Moreau (1826–1898), Félicien Rops (1833–1898), and Odilon Redon (1840–1916).

Among them, the painters of the Pont-Aven school and their successors, the Nabis, took the most liberty with color. Gabriel Albert Aurier (1865–1892), in his article "Symbolism in Painting: Paul Gauguin," published in *Mercure de France* (March 1891), was the first to define symbolism as an aesthetic, describing it thus: "1. *Ideist,* since its unique ideal is the expression of the idea; 2. *Symbolist,* since it expresses the idea by means of forms; 3. *Synthetic*, since it writes out those forms, these signs, according to a mode susceptible to general comprehension; 4. *Subjective*, since the object depicted is not considered as an object, but as a sign of an idea perceived by the subject; 5. And (as a consequence) *decorative*—inasmuch as decorative painting . . . is only a manifestation of an art that is at once subjective, synthetic, symbolist, and ideist."

Paul Gauguin (1848–1903), Charles Filiger (1863–1928), and Émile Bernard (1868–1941), followed by Paul Sérusier (1864–1927) and Maurice Denis (1870–1943), simplified form, using black contours, and applied flat fields of unmixed colors, often breaking with descriptive color, i.e. the "realistic" colors of objects.

KEY ARTWORK

In *Vision of the Sermon (Jacob Wrestling with the Angel)* from 1888, Paul Gauguin brings together in a single scene Breton women leaving Mass and the vision of Jacob's struggle with the angel that haunts their imaginations. The figures, cow, and tree are schematized, the space flattened, and the Breton grassland depicted in blood red.

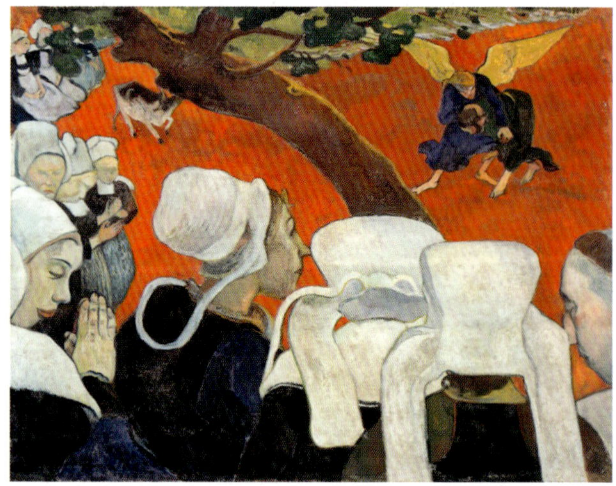

Paul Gauguin, *Vision of the Sermon (Jacob Wrestling with the Angel)*, 1888. Oil on canvas. National Galleries of Scotland, Edinburgh.

BLACK **p. 44** RED **p. 46**

Violent Use of Color

1900
–
1915

IMPORTANT ARTISTS: HENRI MATISSE • ANDRÉ DERAIN •
MAURICE DE VLAMINCK • ERNST LUDWIG KIRCHNER • EMIL NOLDE

In the early years of the twentieth century, painters on both sides of the Rhine experimented with color in an unprecedented and extreme way. Around 1905, the fauves in France—including Henri Matisse (1869–1954), André Derain (1880–1954), Maurice de Vlaminck (1876–1958), Albert Marquet (1875–1947), and Charles Camoin (1879–1965)—and members of Die Brücke (The Bridge) in Germany—including Ernst Ludwig Kirchner (1880–1938), Karl Schmidt-Rottluff (1884–1976), Emil Nolde (1867–1956), Max Pechstein (1881–1965), and Otto Mueller (1874–1930)—gave color new importance. Independent and unmoored to reality, color was at once expressive, a reflection of the artist's subjectivity; primitivist, a sign of authenticity; and rebellious, a sign of revolt against aesthetic, even social norms. Color emerged pure, from paint tubes, translated a large palette of emotions, and, at times, could be garish—orange and purple trees, faces tinted green or scarlet, yellow streets, or blue and pink hills. The primitivist color was often matched with simple, rapid lines influenced by the popular arts, wood engraving, and children's drawings.

This intense use of color was short-lived. The fauves quickly abandoned their experiments and in 1907–8 adopted a muted palette and more geometric forms. As for Die Brücke, its members disbanded in 1913.

Henri Matisse, *Woman with a Hat*, 1905. Oil on canvas.
San Francisco Museum of Modern Art, San Francisco, CA.

KEY ARTIST
Henri Matisse, who was passionate about pigments, explained, "Colors have a beauty of their own which must be preserved, as one strives to preserve tonal quality in music. It is a question of organization and construction which is sensitive to maintaining this beautiful freshness of color" (*Matisse On Art*, 1978).

RED **p. 46** YELLOW **p. 47** BLUE **p. 48** GREEN **p. 49** ORANGE **p. 50** VIOLET **p. 51** PINK **p. 53** PAINT IN TUBES **p. 204**

Monochromes

IMPORTANT ARTISTS: KAZIMIR MALEVICH • ALEXANDER RODCHENKO •
ROBERT RAUSCHENBERG • YVES KLEIN

1915
–
1970

Until the early twentieth century, the term "monochrome" referred to a painting executed in shades of a single color, an example being grisaille, based on shades of gray. Kazimir Malevich (1879–1935) was one of the first artists to experiment with a more radical monochrome technique. In works like *Suprematist Composition: White on White* (1918, MoMA, New York), the Russian painter attempted to achieve a transcendent form of art through pure, abstract forms, and in doing so expressed the first stirrings of a crisis in art—the death of painting. The same idea prevailed in the work of other painters like Alexander Rodchenko (1891–1956), in *Pure Red Color, Pure Yellow Color,* and *Pure Blue Color* (1921): all three are monochromes in the modern sense of the word.

Following World War II, this idea of the "supreme" painting (which led to the name "suprematism") gave way to other approaches to the monochrome. *White Paintings* (1951) by American painter Robert Rauschenberg (1925–2008) is a series of white canvases that appear free of all human intervention and receptive to the world around them. In line with a conceptual approach, these works could be refabricated again and again, sometimes by the artist's assistants, and notably when Rauschenberg reused them for other paintings. Since the late twentieth century, the monochrome has lost its power, becoming another pictorial genre, much like portraiture and still life.

Yves Klein, *Blue Monochrome*, 1961. Dry pigment in polyvinyl acetate on cotton over plywood. Museum of Modern Art, New York, NY.

KEY ARTIST
For his monochromes, Yves Klein (1928–1962) used an intense blue—he registered the formula at the National Industrial Property Institute in Paris under the name IKB (International Klein Blue)—and sometimes gold or pink: "The monochrome is the only physical way of painting—permitting us to attain the spiritual absolute" ("The Monochrome Adventure," 1955).

WHITE **p. 45** RED **p. 46** BLUE **p. 48** PINK **p. 53** GOLD **p. 56** *CONCETTO SPAZIALE. ATTESE (T. 104)* **p. 150**
BLUE MONOCHROME **p. 152** *PAINTING 324 × 362 CM, 1986 (POLYPTYCH I)* **p. 176**

Pure Color

IMPORTANT ARTISTS: MARK ROTHKO • HELEN FRANKENTHALER •
MORRIS LOUIS • KENNETH NOLAND

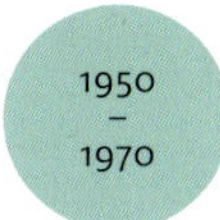

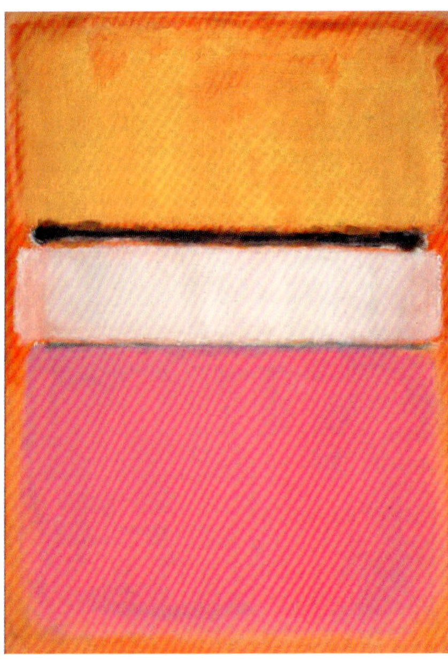

Mark Rothko, *White Center (Yellow, Pink and Lavender on Rose)*, 1950. Oil on canvas. Private collection.

KEY ARTIST
The works of Mark Rothko (1903–1970), composed of rectangles of color with blurry contours, were described by art critic Clement Greenberg as color field painting. However, Rothko always refused to accept this label.

If there was one pictorial movement that placed color at the heart of its aesthetic concerns, it was color field painting. The term was invented in 1955 by Clement Greenberg (1909–1994), best known as an advocate for abstract expressionism. Illusionism, motif, and controlled brushstrokes were banished in favor of fields of color, which revealed the two-dimensionality of the artwork—often very large in format—as a flat surface, and rejected the idea of painting as a window onto another world. Saturated pigments were chosen for their formal qualities, brightness, and vibration.

The painter Helen Frankenthaler (1928–2011) was among those artists paving this new path within abstract expressionism—a path that was less gestural and virile than the one being explored by Willem De Kooning (1904–1997) and Jackson Pollock (1912–1956). In the early 1950s, Frankenthaler developed the soak-stain technique. She applied pigments diluted in turpentine to raw canvas placed on the ground, unsupported by easel or frame: the highly volatile pigments literally soaked into the cloth. Morris Louis (1912–1962) and Kenneth Noland (1924–2010) visited her studio in the spring of 1953, and her innovative technique convinced them to pursue this approach to color and planarity.

RED **p. 46** YELLOW **p. 47** BLUE **p. 48** GREEN **p. 49** PINK **p. 53** *WHITE CENTER* **p. 144** *FLOOD* **p. 160**

Optical Illusions

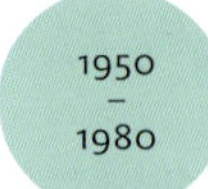

IMPORTANT ARTISTS: JESÚS RAFAEL SOTO • VICTOR VASARELY •
JULIO LE PARC • BRIDGET RILEY

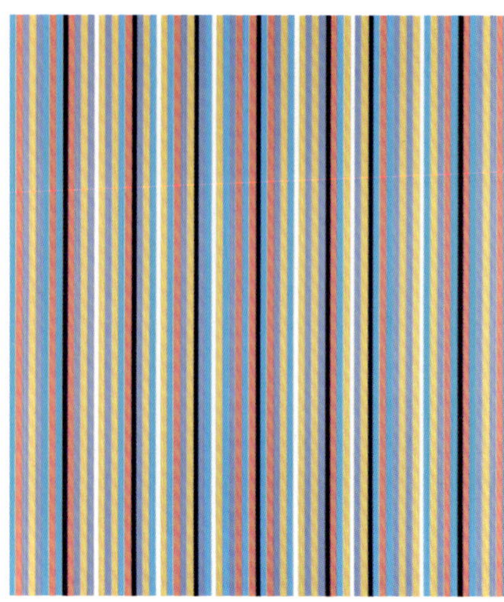

Bridget Riley, *Shade*, 1981. Oil on canvas.
Kunsthaus Zürich, Zurich.

KEY ARTIST
After working for many years in black and
white, the British artist Bridget Riley (born 1931)
embraced the instability of color and the relativity
of perception, and in 1967 she introduced unmixed
color into her painting.

Op and kinetic art—a protean, international movement that emerged in the 1950s—exploited the optical effects of visual perception. Its practitioners, who sometimes took differing approaches, deconstructed the traditional structure of pictorial composition and, in some cases, integrated the work into the surrounding space in a new way. *Great Panoramic Vibrant Wall* (1966) by Jesús Rafael Soto (1923–2005), for example, is composed of blue and black metal rods whose movement modifies the viewer's perception of a place. In so doing, these works engage the senses, often provoking a kinesthetic impression, and demystify the creative process: artists are no longer all-powerful creators, and viewers are made active participants. In this context, color takes on an important role, thanks to its vibrational qualities obtained through the use of abstract forms (undulating lines, circles, spirals, etc.) and a skillful command of contrasts. Some artists, such as Martha Boto (1925–2004), reinforced this quality by using light and electricity. This work with color, which relies on the eye's fallibility, intensifies visual energy, optical illusions, the persistence of vision, and sensations of vertigo or dizziness.

BLACK **p. 44** WHITE **p. 45** STRIPES **p. 58** THE RAINBOW **p. 59** *SHADE* **p. 174** INDUSTRIAL MATERIALS **p. 209**

Pop Colors

1960 – 1970

IMPORTANT ARTISTS: ARMAN • YVES KLEIN • ANDY WARHOL • CLAES OLDENBURG

In the late 1950s and 1960s, European and American artists used images and objects taken from popular culture (advertising, cinema, television, comics, etc.). The Coca-Cola bottle, Mickey Mouse, the pinup, and the hamburger became commonplace on canvases, screen-prints, and sculptures by Richard Hamilton (1922–2011), Andy Warhol (1928–1987), and Claes Oldenburg (1929–2022). This iconography of the ordinary burst onto the art scene in an explosion of color borrowed from industry and composed of pure colors that were uniform and standardized, as befit their original purpose—to arouse consumer desire.

In France, the New Realists—among them Arman (1928–2005), César (1921–1998), Raymond Hains (1926–2005), Yves Klein (1928–1962), Martial Raysse (born 1936), Niki de Saint Phalle (1930–2002), Daniel Spoerri (born 1930), Jean Tinguely (1925–1991), and Jacques Villeglé (1926–2022)—incorporated everyday objects into their work. As critic Pierre Restany (1930–2003) observed, "What we are rediscovering . . . is . . . our contemporary, industrial, mechanical, commercial nature: the landscapes of Arcadia are now driven back into the most mythical areas of our vision. The reality of our everyday context is the city or the factory"

(*Le Nouveau Réalisme à Paris et à New York*, 1961). This appropriation of a massively manufactured "reality" reached its apogee when Klein registered the formula for the intense blue (International Klein Blue) he used in his monochromes at the National Industrial Property Institute in Paris.

KEY ARTIST

In December 1961, Claes Oldenburg rented a small shop in New York where he sold objects that he had made and painted in bright colors. The objects mimicked the goods for sale in nearby stores. Barely larger than life, *Two Cheeseburgers* attests to the artist's questioning of the commodification of art.

Claes Oldenburg, *Two Cheeseburgers, with Everything (Dual Hamburgers)*, 1962. Burlap soaked in plaster, painted with enamel. Museum of Modern Art, New York, NY.

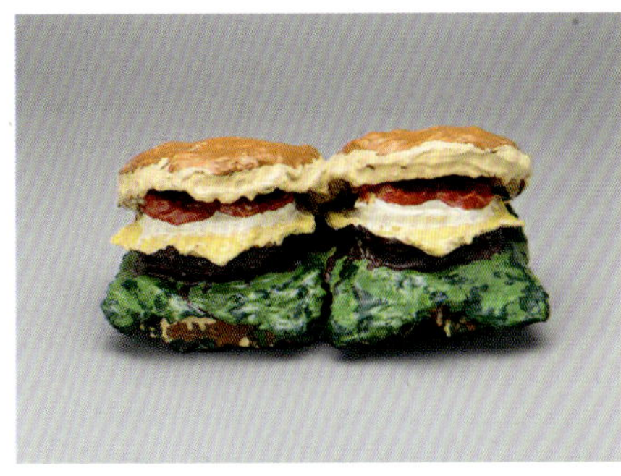

BLUE MONOCHROME **p. 152** SHOOTING PAINTING **p. 154** GOLD MARILYN MONROE **p. 156** INDUSTRIAL MATERIALS **p. 209**

The Artist's Studio and the Exhibition Space

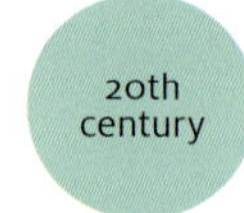

IMPORTANT ARTISTS: PIET MONDRIAN • GEORGIA O'KEEFFE

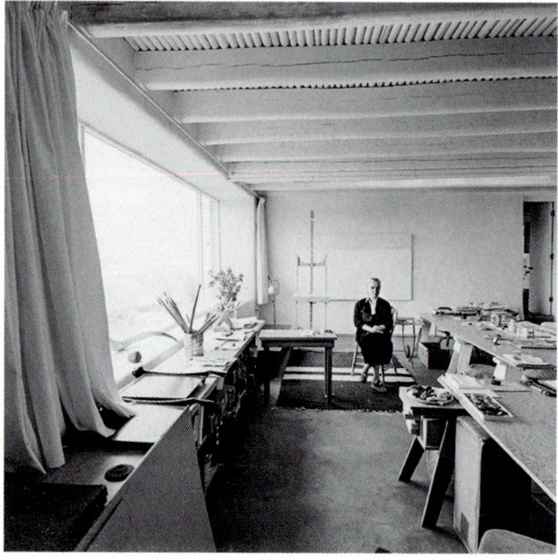

Georgia O'Keeffe in her studio in
Abiquiu, New Mexico.

MAIN CHARACTERISTICS
For some artists, the white wall offers
a potentially unlimited background
for works, while for others it draws
attention to the very flatness of the
material support.

Which color is most conducive to creating and showcasing artwork? Until the early twentieth century, the walls of studios as represented by painters were often dark, littered with paintings or plaster models and warmed up by a wall hanging or two. Similarly, galleries and salons were stuffed with artwork hanging from picture rails in shades of garnet, brown, or bottle green. Breaking with this tradition, modern artists like Piet Mondrian (1872–1944) and Georgia O'Keeffe (1887–1986) created an uncluttered workspace. Studio walls brightened to pale gray, cream, or white, and soon art galleries and museums, where color had formerly dominated, followed suit.

Upon reading the work of German-Baltic chemist Wilhelm Ostwald (1853–1932), members of avant-garde groups such as the Bauhaus and De Stijl regarded white as a neutral color. Gilded, finely worked frames were now passé, and unadorned walls framed abstractions with a limpid surround that accentuated their colors. Very fashionable since the 1960s and 1970s, the immaculate exhibition space has become the norm, losing its radical edge. As art critic Brian O'Doherty notes, "The development of the pristine, placeless white cube is one of modernism's triumphs—a development commercial, esthetic, and technological" (*Inside the White Cube: The Ideology of the Gallery Space*, 1976).

WHITE **p. 45** RED **p. 46** GREEN **p. 49** BROWN **p. 52** GRAY **p. 54**

Standardizing Color

PRINCIPAL MODELS: RGB • CMYK • PANTONE

Using four-color process printing, which became widespread in the twentieth century, it is possible to obtain a large range of colors through subtractive mixing (weakening certain wavelengths in the spectrum) of four primary colors (CMYK): cyan (blue-green), magenta (violet-red), yellow, and "key" (black). Computers use the RGB (red, green, blue) color model based on additive color mixing, either by overlapping lights of different colors or by placing dots of color next to each other in a mosaic form.

In 1866, an American company created the Pantone color chart for the cosmetics industry. At the time, it included a dozen colors. The company was bought by an employee, who developed it in the 1960s, making the Pantone Matching System a world-recognized reference for the publishing industry, then the plastic, textile, and paint industries. Contrary to four-color process printing, the Pantone system—in which each color has a particular number—involves creating a precise blend of inks prior to printing.

Today, it is common for brands in interior design and the cosmetics, textile, and automotive industries to develop their own color charts with the help of color experts.

MAIN CHARACTERISTICS

For centuries, color wheels have been used in an attempt to define and classify colors. The industrial revolution in the nineteenth century, then the emergence of mass consumer society in the following century, generated a need for standardized color. Many color systems and color charts were developed as a result, including RGB and Pantone.

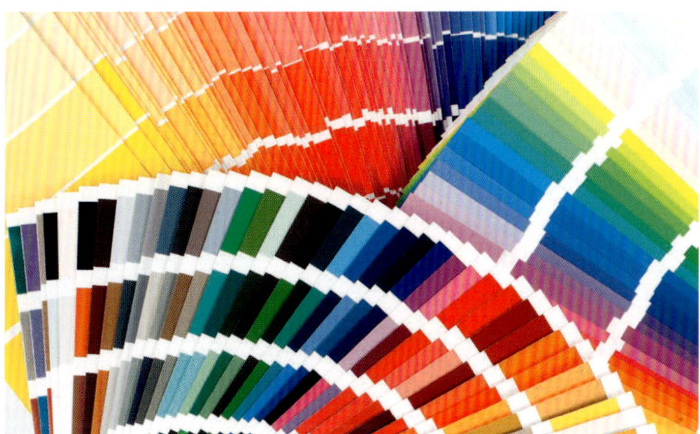

Acrylic paint color swatches and fan decks.

Symbolism

Black

MAIN SHADES: COAL • EBONY • KOHL • OBSIDIAN • ONYX • SABLE

MAIN CHARACTERISTICS

The Greek philosopher Aristotle counted seven colors, from black to white, but the physicist Isaac Newton removed black and white from the spectrum, giving these colors a separate status in the Western imagination.

Black was one of the first pigments, along with red and white, used to decorate cave walls in prehistoric times. It was obtained from charcoal, then later from iron oxides like magnetite. The word "black" appeared sometime before the twelfth century. Derived from the Middle English *blak*, it originally referred to the color of the night sky or the eye's pupil. In the Bible, black is associated with sin, turmoil, and darkness, in contrast with divine light. Black's macabre connotations reach as far back as classical antiquity, when the color was associated with Hades. This connection with death made it, in the Western world, the color of grief and of returning to the earth.

Black grew in popularity in the sixteenth century with the rise of the Protestant Reformation, which encouraged austerity and temperance in appearance and behavior. As the color spread through the bourgeoisie, it become synonymous with aesthetic restraint. But over the centuries the meaning of black changed dramatically: always a potent symbol, it represented, at different times, the sobriety of the Protestant Church or the bourgeoisie, the melancholy of the Romantic poets, or the rebellion of street movements, such as bikers or punks in the 1970s.

Since the nineteenth century, black has been cast as masculine, serious, and spiritual, as opposed to color, considered feminine and frivolous.

White

MAIN SHADES: ALABASTER • CHALK • CREAM • ECRU • IVORY • MILK • SNOW • VANILLA

White, along with black and red, was one of the first pigments to be mastered by humans. It is found in the form of clay (particularly kaolin) on the walls of the painted caves at Chauvet (about 36,000 years old) and Lascaux (about 19,000 years old), both in France.

The Greek philosopher Aristotle ordered colors on a scale from dark to light—from black to white, with red, violet, green, blue, and gray or yellow in between. The word "white" emerged in the twelfth century, derived from the Old English *hwīt*, meaning "bright or shining." Etymologically speaking, it expresses the idea of light or clarity, which foreshadowed the discoveries of the physicist Isaac Newton, for whom white was both the sum of all colors (in the prism) and the absence of color.

The idea of the "white" man (who is not white at all) in the Western imagination, and its racist implications, is based on the color's favorable values and stands in contrast to the "black" man (who is no more black than the white man is white), and all the negative connotations that darkness implies. On the rare occasion that white is used pejoratively, it is to express a lack or absence.

MAIN CHARACTERISTICS
White is probably the color with the most universally shared symbolic meaning: purity and virginity, innocence, cleanliness, even wisdom. In Asia, where death signifies a return to light, it is also the color of grief.

PREHISTORIC CAVE ART **p. 12** MONOCHROMES **p. 36** THE ARTIST'S STUDIO AND THE EXHIBITION SPACE **p. 40** *COMPOSITION WITH TRIANGLES, RECTANGLES, AND HALF-RINGS* **p. 124** WHITE PIGMENTS **p. 191** VISUAL COLOR AND MATERIAL COLOR **p. 211**

Red

MAIN SHADES: BORDEAUX • BRICK • CARMINE • CHERRY • CRIMSON • GRENADINE • GULES • SCARLET • TERRA-COTTA • VERMILION

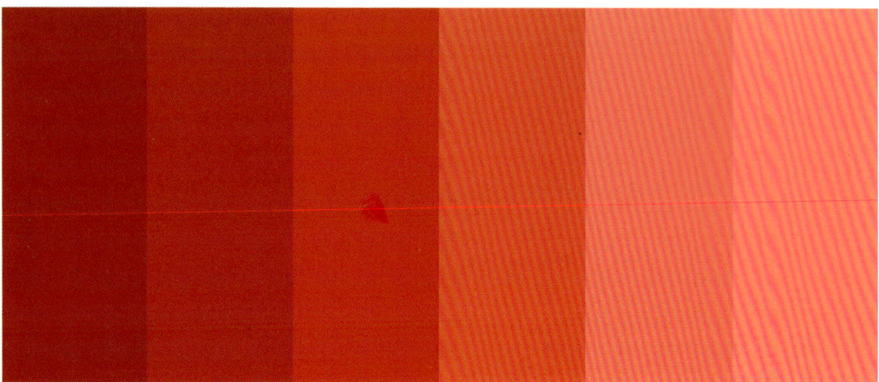

Associated with blood, life, and death, red encapsulates the ambiguities and power of color. The word "red" evolved from the Middle English *red*, *rede*, or *reed* in the twelfth century. Red pigments were among the first to be mastered, giving rise to stable, intense dyes and paints. Red was considered the ultimate color by the ancients, and its association with fire and blood earned it a central role in daily life—so much so that the Roman words for colored (*coloratus*) and red (*ruber*) were synonyms. By that time, it expressed religious and military power. In the Middle Ages, red symbolized the blood of Christ and, by extension, became the color of martyrs, and later of popes and cardinals. It often represented dignity and charity, but it could also depict temptation, or even hell. In the sixteenth century, the Protestant Reformation decried red as a symbol of papal excess, much like other bright colors including yellow, green, and violet.

Red had long been the color of power and of monarchs, but during the French Revolution, it took on a new and enduring meaning, becoming the symbol of popular revolt. Throughout the nineteenth century, this association intensified until red became the color of labor parties and then of the Soviet Union.

In the West, red clothing is often associated with female promiscuity or transgression, while in China, it is the color of luck and joy.

MAIN CHARACTERISTICS

On the electromagnetic spectrum, red has a wavelength of between 622 and 780 nanometers. Its complementary color is green.

PREHISTORIC CAVE ART **p. 12** PRIMARY AND COMPLEMENTARY COLORS **p. 27** *MADONNA OF CHANCELLOR ROLIN* **p. 70** *PORTRAIT OF LOUIS XIV* **p. 82** *THE DEATH OF SARDANAPALUS* **p. 86** *BELLBOY* **p. 128** *THE STUDIO* **p. 164** *FEMME* **p. 184** RED AND PURPLE PIGMENTS **p.193**

Yellow

MAIN SHADES: GAMBOGE • GOLDENROD • MARIGOLD • MUSTARD • NAPLES YELLOW • OCHER • SAFFRON • SUNFLOWER • WHEAT

MAIN CHARACTERISTICS
On the electromagnetic spectrum, yellow has a wavelength of between 577 and 597 nanometers. Its complementary color is violet.

Along with red, black, and white, yellow was one of the first pigments to be mastered by prehistoric humans. Yellow was popular during the Roman empire, when it symbolized joy and marriage. The Old English word *geolu* was related to the Latin word *helvus* and signified "the color of ripe lemons and sunflowers."

In medieval culture, gold gradually acquired yellow's positive connotations (light, energy, joy), leaving yellow with only the more macabre implications (fatigue, illness, betrayal). In Christian culture, the color became one of the attributes of the traitor Judas, who, from the twelfth century onward, was often depicted in a yellow robe. By extension, yellow was attributed to the Jewish people, and the Fourth Council of the Lateran (1215) obligated them to wear a yellow roundel or star as an identifying mark. The Nazis adopted this antisemitic practice in 1941.

In the sixteenth century, the Reformation was hardly more inclined to yellow. Along with red, green, and violet, Protestants considered the color to be immoral and prohibited its use in clothing. While yellow comes in and out of favor in the West, it is considered lucky in China.

The convention of three primary colors—yellow, blue, and red—based on the work of the physicist Isaac Newton, elevated yellow, particularly within European avant-garde art movements.

Blue

MAIN SHADES: AZURE • COBALT • CYAN • INDIGO • KLEIN BLUE • NAVY • PEACOCK • PRUSSIAN BLUE • ROYAL BLUE • SKY BLUE • TURQUOISE • ULTRAMARINE

The word "blue" is derived from Old High German via the Medieval Latin word *blavus*. Until the late twelfth century, its meaning remained vague and the word was used to refer to pale, bruised skin. The ancient Greeks had no word for blue, which they considered a shade of black. The Romans associated the color with childhood, but also with barbarism: Celtic warriors painted themselves blue to frighten their enemies. Today, blue symbolizes peace and harmony.

As blue acquired its current meaning, it became associated in Christian theology with divine light and has been incredibly popular ever since. It supplanted gold on the cloak of the Virgin Mary, and, by extension, became the emblem of monarchs, believed to have been appointed by divine right. Woad was the only plant in Europe that could produce blue dye, and French producers in Amiens and Toulouse made a fortune until the introduction of the indigo plant, discovered in the Americas and cultivated at lower cost with slave labor. The Reformation, which decried the colorful exuberance of the Catholic Church, felt differently about blue—unlike red, for example—and tolerated it alongside austere black.

In the nineteenth century, a tailor in San Francisco by the name of Levi Strauss (1829–1902) commercialized clothing made of rough cotton canvas dyed with indigo: blue jeans were born, first as work and then leisure wear, and later became a symbol of teenage rebellion in the 1960s. Blue has consistently ranked as the most popular color in the West since the first opinion polls were conducted 130 years ago.

MAIN CHARACTERISTICS
On the electromagnetic spectrum, blue has a wavelength of between 455 and 492 nanometers. Its complementary color is orange.

Green

MAIN SHADES: ALMOND • APPLE GREEN • AVOCADO • BOTTLE GREEN • CELADON • EAU DE NIL • EMERALD • KELLY • MOSS • PISTACHIO • SPRING GREEN • VERDIGRIS

Green pigment appeared in the Bronze Age, as humans mastered the use of copper, from which the pigment is derived. The word "green" is related to the Old English word *grōwan*, meaning to grow. The Latin word *viridis* also has connotations of growth and greenery.

The color's symbolic meaning has always been fraught with ambiguity. A dangerous, unstable pigment when produced from copper-based verdigris— releasing toxic substances when in contact with perspiration—it represents change, destiny, games of chance, and rebirth. It is also associated with poison, and with that most corrosive of emotions: envy.

Associated early on with the plant kingdom as an indication of unripe fruit or grain (thirteenth century), medieval thinking came to associate green with the short life cycles on earth. It was during the Renaissance, and especially the Romantic era, that the color came to represent nature. Because of this it is also associated with Islam, as the notion of paradise is closely linked to the garden.

Today, this connection with nature has led to the term "green" in reference to a concern for environmentalism, and has been taken up by a political movement, but it is often overused in communication and marketing, with the term "greenwashing" applying to companies whose ecological practices are superficial at best.

Green is now the second most popular color in the West, after blue, which remains unchallenged since the nineteenth century.

MAIN CHARACTERISTICS
On the electromagnetic spectrum, green has a wavelength of between 492 and 577 nanometers. Its complementary color is red.

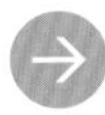

Orange

MAIN SHADES: AMBER • APRICOT • CARROT • GINGER • MANDARIN • PEACH • PUMPKIN • TANGERINE

It wasn't until the sixteenth century that the word orange was used to describe a color. Before that, it referred to the fruit, which had made its way west from China, and English speakers used the portmanteau *giolureade* or yellow-red for the color. Orange is a difficult hue to master. Until the Renaissance, mixing colors was considered impure and therefore forbidden—yellow and red were never mixed to create orange. It was only in the late eighteenth century that a more stable and non-toxic pigment, chrome orange, was created, before the release of the vivid but more noxious cadmium orange midway through the following century.

Orange has ambiguous connotations in Christian thinking. The color is associated with the revelation of divine love but also—due to its closeness to yellow— duplicity. Historian Michel Pastoureau notes how the color gradually acquired the virtues of gold—vitality, warmth, joy—as gold, deemed too flashy, fell from grace. Today, orange vies with yellow as a symbol of joy and warmth.

MAIN CHARACTERISTICS
On the electromagnetic spectrum, orange has a wavelength of between 597 and 622 nanometers. Its complementary color is blue.

IMPRESSION, SUNRISE **p. 100** *WHITE CENTER* **p. 144** *SIX COLORFUL INSIDE JOBS* **p. 172**
WALL DRAWING #610 **p. 180** *THE GATES* **p. 182** YELLOW PIGMENTS **p. 192**

Violet

MAIN SHADES: EGGPLANT • HELIOTROPE • LAVENDER • LILAC • MAUVE • PLUM • PURPLE

The word "violet" comes from the name of the eponymous flower, derived from the Latin word *viola*. From ancient Greece to the early Middle Ages, purple—a shade of violet—was an opulent color due to its highly priced pigments. Produced under the name Tyrian purple by the Phoenicians, who specialized in their manufacture, these pigments were the result of a long and complex, malodorous process involving the secretions of one of two Mediterranean shellfish, *Murex brandaris* and *Thais haemastoma*.

In Rome, purple was reserved for high-ranking officials (generals with the title *imperator*, senators, and emperors) and came to symbolize strength and power. The expertise needed to make Tyrian purple was lost when Constantinople fell to the Turks in 1204. Thereafter, carmine from cochineal mixed with indigo was often used to make this color.

In Christian symbolism, violet is considered a shade of black and was worn as a sign of half-mourning (a less severe period of mourning) or of penitence; since the fifteenth century it has colored clerical vestments during Lent. Today, it symbolizes melancholy and sadness, as well as the supernatural. It is the second least favored color in the West, after brown.

MAIN CHARACTERISTICS
On the electromagnetic spectrum, violet has a wavelength of between 390 and 455 nanometers. Its complementary color is yellow.

IMPRESSION, SUNRISE **p. 100** *FIELD WITH IRISES NEAR ARLES* **p. 102** *HOMAGE TO THE SQUARE: JOY* **p. 158** *PURPLE ATMOSPHERE* **p. 166** *MY PARENTS* **p. 170** *SIX COLORFUL INSIDE JOBS* **p. 172**

Brown

MAIN SHADES: BEIGE • BISTER • CAFÉ AU LAIT • CHESTNUT • CHOCOLATE • DUN •
UMBER • WALNUT

The use of brown pigments is ancient. Ocher was mined as far back as the Paleolithic period, and, when calcinated at temperatures greater than 480°F (250°C), it produces many shades, from the lightest yellows to the darkest browns. Brown—a color that occurs often in nature (bark, soil, animal fur, etc.)—was used by prehistoric humans to paint their extraordinary bestiary on cave walls.

In English, the word "brown" is derived from the Old English *brūn*, related to the Greek word *phrynē,* meaning toad. The Medieval Latin *brunus* emerged in the eleventh century to describe the color between black and reddish-brown. More specific words for the color brown emerged in Europe relatively late, between the twelfth and fourteenth centuries. The French word for brown, *marron*, takes its name from nature: it originally meant "big chestnut" (from the Italian *marrone*).

In the Christian era, brown was affiliated with other dark colors like black and gray, heavy with negative connotations, before being rehabilitated in the sixteenth century by followers of the Protestant Reformation, who equated severity with spiritual purity. Symbolically associated with humility, brown is also the color of many monastic habits.

MAIN CHARACTERISTICS
Brown is the least preferred color in the West.

Pink

MAIN SHADES: BLUSH • CANDY • CARNATION • CORAL • FUCHSIA • MAGENTA • ROSE • SALMON • SHOCKING PINK

Prior to the seventeenth century, the English word "pink" was used as a verb meaning to perforate. It was first used as a noun to describe a color in the seventeenth century and as an adjective in the eighteenth. The historian Michel Pastoureau notes that the word was ill-defined for centuries, and that "carnation" ("flesh-colored," in reference to Caucasian skin) was favored until the eighteenth century to describe the shade as we know it today.

Pink became very fashionable, especially in the French royal court under the influence of Louis XV (1710–1774), who named a tone of porcelain from the Sèvres porcelain factory—described in the registers as "very fresh and very pleasant"—*rose Pompadour* (Pompadour pink) in honor of his mistress, Madame de Pompadour (1721–1764).

MAIN CHARACTERISTICS
Once considered a masculine color because of its relationship to red, which was synonymous with power, pink became associated with femininity in the nineteenth century. It represents both naivety and eroticism, innocence and sensuality, sweetness and indulgence, romantic love, and little girls and women.

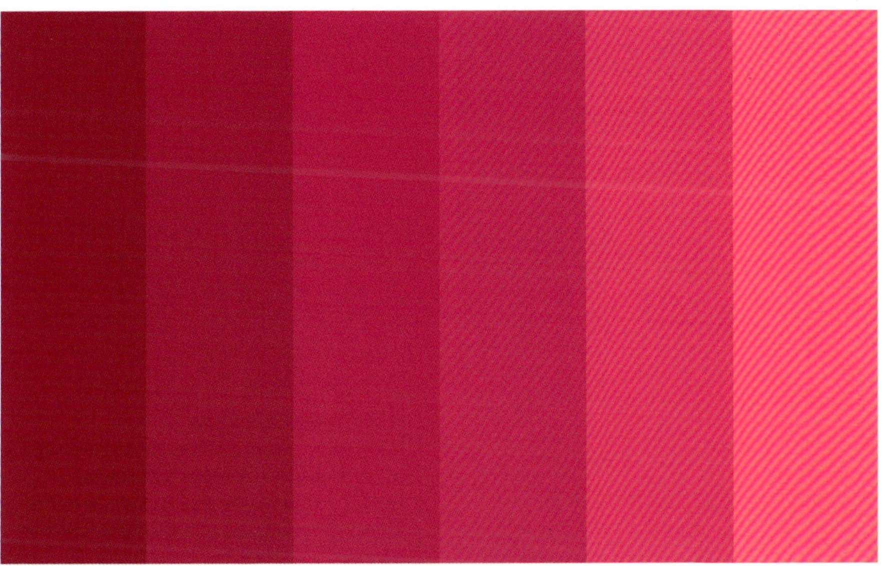

COLOR AND GENDER **p. 21** *SYMPHONY IN FLESH COLOUR AND PINK: PORTRAIT OF MRS. FRANCES LEYLAND* **p. 96** *SELF-PORTRAIT AS A TEHUANA* **p. 136** *WHITE CENTER* **p. 144** *THE STUDIO* **p. 164**

Gray

MAIN SHADES: CHARCOAL • DOVE • GRAPHITE • LEAD • MOUSE • PEARL • SLATE • SMOKE • STONE

The word "gray" comes from the Old English *græg*, which means having little or no color or luminosity. In the fourteenth century, gray began to be used as a verb associated with aging. However, in the late Middle Ages, as historian Michel Pastoureau points out, the color was perceived as the opposite of black and synonymous with hope. In the sixteenth century, the Protestant Reformation decried Rome's ostentatious displays and obsession with color and so valued gray for its discretion and austerity, along with other subdued hues, such as black and brown, and white. Gray's symbolic connection with age can also carry connotations of wisdom or intelligence.

The painter Paul Cézanne (1839–1906) summarized the color's ambiguous nature and the difficulties it raises in painting: "I was in Talloires. A temperate little town if ever there was one. Gray, gray, and more gray! . . . Surely it is still nature. But not as I see it. Do you understand? Gray upon gray. One is not a painter until one has painted a gray. Delacroix said the enemy of painting is gray. No: one is not a painter until one has painted a gray" (quoted in Joachim Gasquet, *Cézanne*, 1921).

MAIN CHARACTERISTICS
In the words of poet and theorist Johann Wolfgang von Goethe, gray is a middle tint obtained through the subtractive mixing of all colors: this achromatic quality makes it a suitable match for any hue.

THE COLOR REFORMATION **p. 22** *SUNBEAMS OR SUNLIGHT. DUST MOTES DANCING IN SUNBEAMS* **p. 108** *BLACK ABSTRACTION* **p. 132**

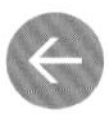

The Language of Color

The palette of six "basic" colors (white, black, red, yellow, green, blue) and five "demi-" or "second rank" colors (brown, orange, pink, violet, gray), as identified in European culture and noted by historian Michel Pastoureau, can be enriched with many shades. A shade, according to the dictionary, refers to the amount of black mixed into a particular color; a tint, how much white. But as Pastoureau reminds us, shades, unlike colors, are devoid of symbolism.

As languages developed, color nomenclature grew considerably between the tenth and thirteenth centuries, when most of the words for "basic" colors and "demi-colors" stabilized. In modern English, the names of well-known, stable shades like apricot, almond, azure, eggshell, lavender, olive, salmon, or turquoise are often borrowed by metonymy from nature—from minerals, plants, and animals—much like "demi-colors." They may also be composed of the name of a color and a qualifying adjective (for example, light blue) or a second color name (for example blue-green).

Shades are subject to the whims of fashion. Eighteenth-century France was rife with imaginative names for color: *ventre de biche* (doe's belly: a light reddish-brown); *puce* (flea: a brownish violet); *caca-dauphin* (dauphin's poop, in reference to the cloth diapers worn by the heir apparent, Dauphin Louis-Joseph de France, born in 1781), or *boue de Paris* (Paris mud: a reddish gray). In the nineteenth century, Werner's *Nomenclature of Color* (1814) included swatches with descriptive names such as "arterial blood red," "leek green," "liver brown," or "skimmed-milk white."

MAIN CHARACTERISTICS
Today, paint and textile brands develop their own color charts in which each shade is given a specific, intentionally affected name like mouse's back, mole's breath, obsidian green, or ashes of roses.

Gold

MAIN SHADES: MATTE GOLD • PALE GOLD • ROSE GOLD • YELLOW GOLD

Gold has been used by artists since antiquity for its dazzling hue and natural tendency to reflect light, as well as for its preciousness. It is found on Egyptian sarcophagi, on Greek statuary, and in Roman mosaics. It was also used to great effect in Byzantine icons and medieval Western illuminated manuscripts in the form of gold leaf applied to a moistened support or as a powder mixed with a binder. It represented the divine light that illuminated the world of believers and stood in contrast to the black of obscurity.

As the Catholic Church began to embrace color in the twelfth century, influenced especially by Abbot Suger, who was given the task of renovating the Basilica of Saint-Denis—a former abbey church just north of Paris—blue gradually supplanted gold. During the Renaissance, the search for more pictorial realism led artists to abandon gold grounds.

The Tuscan humanist Leon Battista Alberti, in his work *On Painting* (1435–36), deplored the excessive use of gold. He advocated for the elevation of painting to an art, rather than the work of craftsmen, and in that regard considered gold gaudy and insufficiently naturalistic. Less than a century later, the Protestant Reformation, in its rejection of papist splendor, decried the luxury represented by gold. In the twentieth century, gold made a noteworthy return to painting; during his Golden Phase, Gustav Klimt (1862–1918), the son of a goldsmith, created a series of paintings inspired by the Byzantine mosaics of Ravenna in northern Italy.

MAIN CHARACTERISTICS
Symbolically, gold is associated with warmth and joy, two connotations it shares with orange.

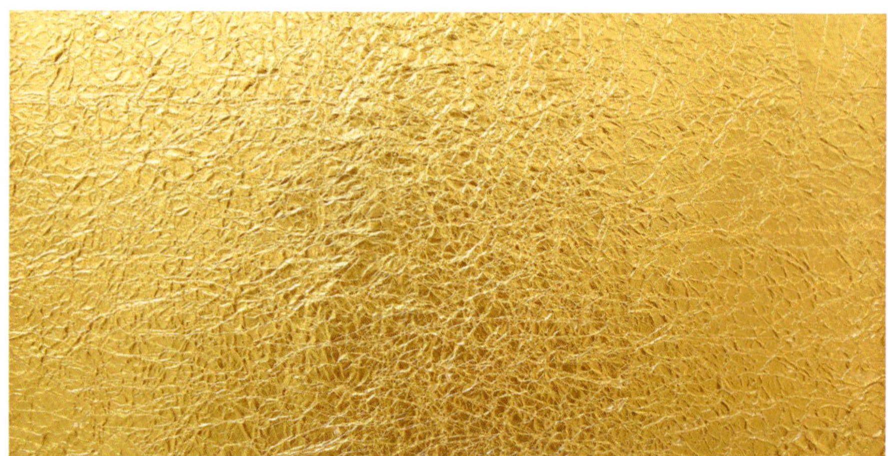

Silver

MAIN SHADES: ALUMINUM • CHROME • GUNMETAL • PLATINUM • STEEL

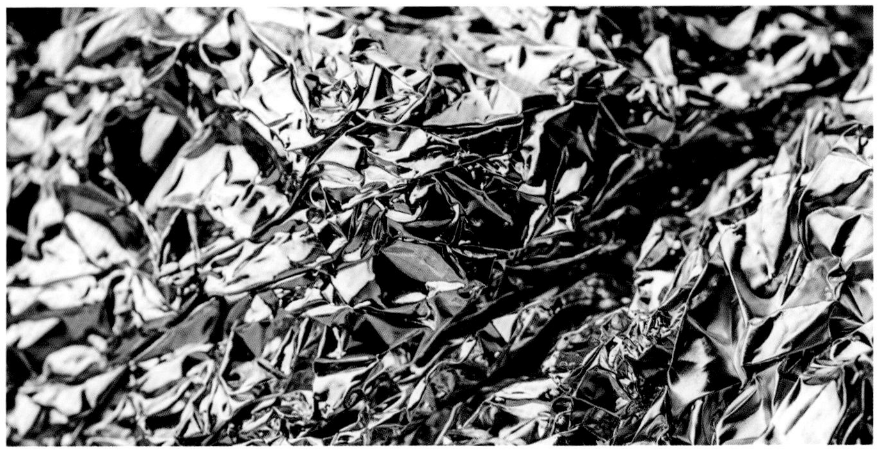

Silver refers to both a metal and a shiny shade of gray. As a pigment, it has been used less often in the history of art than its fellow precious metal, gold. Since antiquity, silver has figured more commonly as a raw material for certain objects such as statuettes, jewelry, and decorative accents on furniture. For example, ornate gilded silver frames, less expensive than pure gold, were used in the making of icons. Silver is also a component of a colorant that produces ocher-colored effects—silver stain—which was so valuable to glassmakers from the eighth century onward: an oxide of silver applied to glass and fired resulted in glass that was permanently stained yellow. In heraldry, silver is classified as a metal and is represented by a solid white ground, without hatching.

However, silver was used by medieval illuminators in leaf or powder form to create backgrounds and highlights in manuscripts. Like gold, although to a lesser extent, it enriched the work. With the development of oil paint, which spread through Europe from the fifteenth century, silver itself began to be represented on the canvas. The details made possible by the new technique gave artists the occasion to prove their virtuosity: depicting metallic objects demanded remarkable skill in rendering the light reflected on their surfaces. For centuries, this was silver's ticket onto the canvas.

MAIN CHARACTERISTICS

It wasn't until the twentieth century that silver was more widely used by painters, from *Painting [Silver over Black, White, Yellow and Red]* (1948) by Jackson Pollock (1912–1956) to *Electric Chair* (1964) by Andy Warhol (1928–1987). The Franco-Norwegian artist Anna-Eva Bergman (1909–1987) used silver leaf to depict a cold light in her sweeping abstract landscapes.

PORTRAIT OF ADELE BLOCH-BAUER / **p. 114**

Stripes

The history of striped clothing is a varied one. In Roman times, it was reserved for the lower classes, and the pejorative connotations associated with stripes intensified during the Middle Ages. Alternating colors implied disorder, discord, and impurity, and just as there was a taboo about mixing colors during the Middle Ages, it was forbidden to wear stripes, considered too demeaning, during the same period. Stripes were reserved for social outcasts such as prostitutes, jugglers, clowns, and hangmen, ensuring that the ostracized remained easy to identify.

However, stripes were looked upon more favorably during the Renaissance, when they acquired connotations of freedom and celebration, favorable counterparts to their medieval significations. A new code was established within a society that remained highly stratified: vertical stripes were for aristocrats and horizontal stripes for their servants. The stripe's political import reached its apogee in the late eighteenth century. The flag of the nascent United States of America had alternating bands of red and white to represent each of the original thirteen colonies declaring independence from Great Britain in 1776; the white stripes cutting through the red—a color that historically symbolized Britain—represented liberty and emancipation from British rule. In 1789, it was used in France for the tricolor cockade, also an emblem of liberty. The same idea prevailed in the early twentieth century when Gabrielle Chanel (1883–1971) borrowed the sailor's striped shirt, representing the freedom of the sea. However, the negative connotations of stripes persisted, associated as they were in the Middle Ages with ostracism: stripes were used on prisoners' clothing, and then during World War II on the uniforms worn by deportees sent to Nazi concentration camps.

MAIN CHARACTERISTICS

The original meaning of "stripe"—a line or band in cloth—dates to the fifteenth century, and is likely derived from the Middle English word meaning welt, long scar, or blow. The figurative meaning of "stripes" to refer to merit emerged in the late nineteenth century.

The Rainbow

MAIN CHARACTERISTICS
In Christian theology, the rainbow is the bridge between the earthly and divine worlds, but it can also herald the Last Judgement. More broadly, it symbolizes hope, impermanence, and harmony. Since 1978, its association with pacifism has made it the chosen emblem of LGBTQI+ communities.

The rainbow is an arc-shaped optic phenomenon produced in the sky in the presence of sun and rain that results from the dispersion of white sunlight in water droplets suspended in the atmosphere.

The colors in the visible spectrum blend, uninterrupted, into one another from violet (about 390 nanometers) to red (about 780 nanometers).

Depictions of the rainbow are subject to cultural conventions, and the number of colors contained in it has varied throughout history. In *Meteorology*, the Greek philosopher Aristotle counts three (red, green, and violet), a number repeated for centuries by scholars from Avicenna (980–1037 BCE) to Albert the Great (c. 1193–1280). As for the Roman poets Virgil (70–19 BCE) and Ovid (43 BCE–17 CE), they saw a thousand colors in the rainbow. The number three reappears in the Middle Ages, sometimes rivaled by four, in keeping with the thinking of the time, which conceived of four seasons, four bodily humors, and four stages of life. But the colors were not fixed and might include blue, purple, red, or green. Isaac Newton established the seven colors recognized in the rainbow today: red, orange, yellow, green, blue, indigo, and violet. However, this is yet another standard—as its depiction using colored bands attests—which seeks to define a natural phenomenon whose poetic power continues to fascinate humankind.

INDIA'S HOLI FESTIVAL **p. 15** NEWTON'S COLOR WHEEL **p. 26** STANDARDIZING COLOR **p. 41** *GROUP X, ALTARPIECE NO. 1* **p. 122** *UNTITLED (TO DON JUDD, COLORIST) 1–5* **p.178** HUE, SATURATION, AND BRIGHTNESS **p. 210**

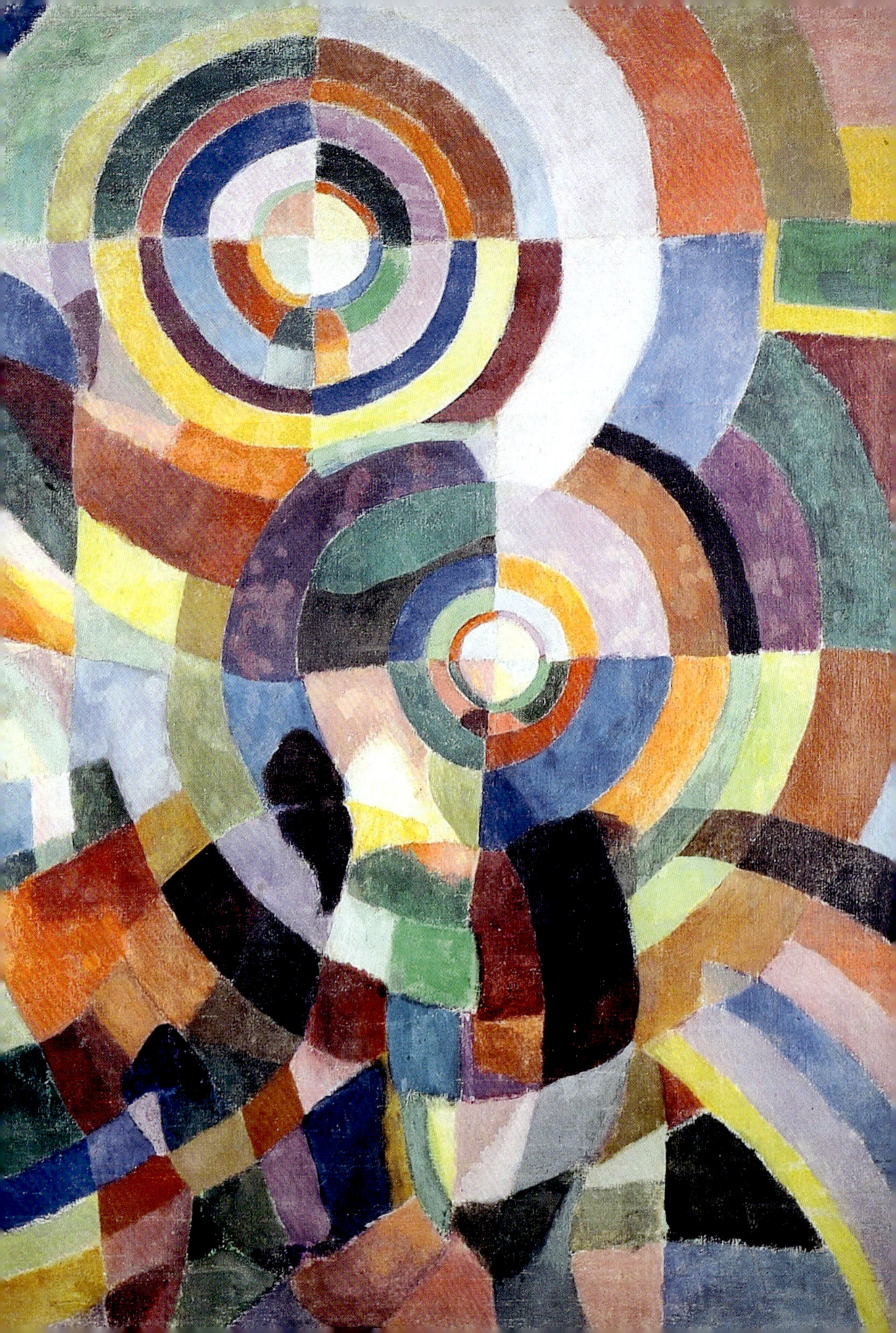

Masterpieces

Neolithic Painted Pebbles

SCHIST • DIFFERENT DIMENSIONS •
MUSÉE D'ARCHÉOLOGIE NATIONALE, SAINT-GERMAIN-EN-LAYE

In the late Neolithic period, artistic representation grew less figurative and more abstract, as demonstrated by painted or engraved Azilian pebbles. These decorated calcareous pebbles were found in the Mas-d'Azil cave in Ariège, France. Carefully selected for their often flat, oblong shape, they were decorated with motifs, primarily dots and lines that sometimes intersect to form a grid, as well as circles, ovals, curved lines, crosses, and frets— motifs traced in red ocher with a single movement of the finger, with no back-and-forth motion. The pigments used were sourced from an iron oxide deposit located upstream from the nearest river. Some of the pebbles are entirely painted on one side. They are estimated to be ten thousand to twelve thousand years old.

Iron oxides have been used since the Paleolithic period to create ocher hues. According to archeologist Édouard Piette, the pigments used at Mas-d'Azil were mixed with a binder—"a resin or fat"—that made it possible to apply the color in a thick, water-resistant layer. The symbolism of this portable art has sparked many interpretations since the pebbles were discovered in the late nineteenth century. Theories include systems for counting or record keeping (such as the lunar calendar), games, early writing, and schematized images of living things, both human and animal, yet the scientific community has not reached a consensus on any of these. The mystery of the Azilian pebbles remains unsolved.

PREHISTORIC CAVE ART **p.12** RED **p. 46** YELLOW **p.47** BROWN **p.52**

Other important works
Lubang Jeriji Saléh cave paintings,
c. 40,000 BP. Borneo.
Apollo 11 cave paintings, c. 30,000 BP. Namibia.
Lascaux cave paintings, c. 12,000 BP.
Montignac-Lascaux.

Three-quarters of the painted or engraved pebbles identified to date come from Mas-d'Azil, while the others were discovered at archaeological sites elsewhere in France (Troubat, Hautes-Pyrénées) and in Italy, Spain, and Switzerland (Monruz, Canton of Neuchâtel).

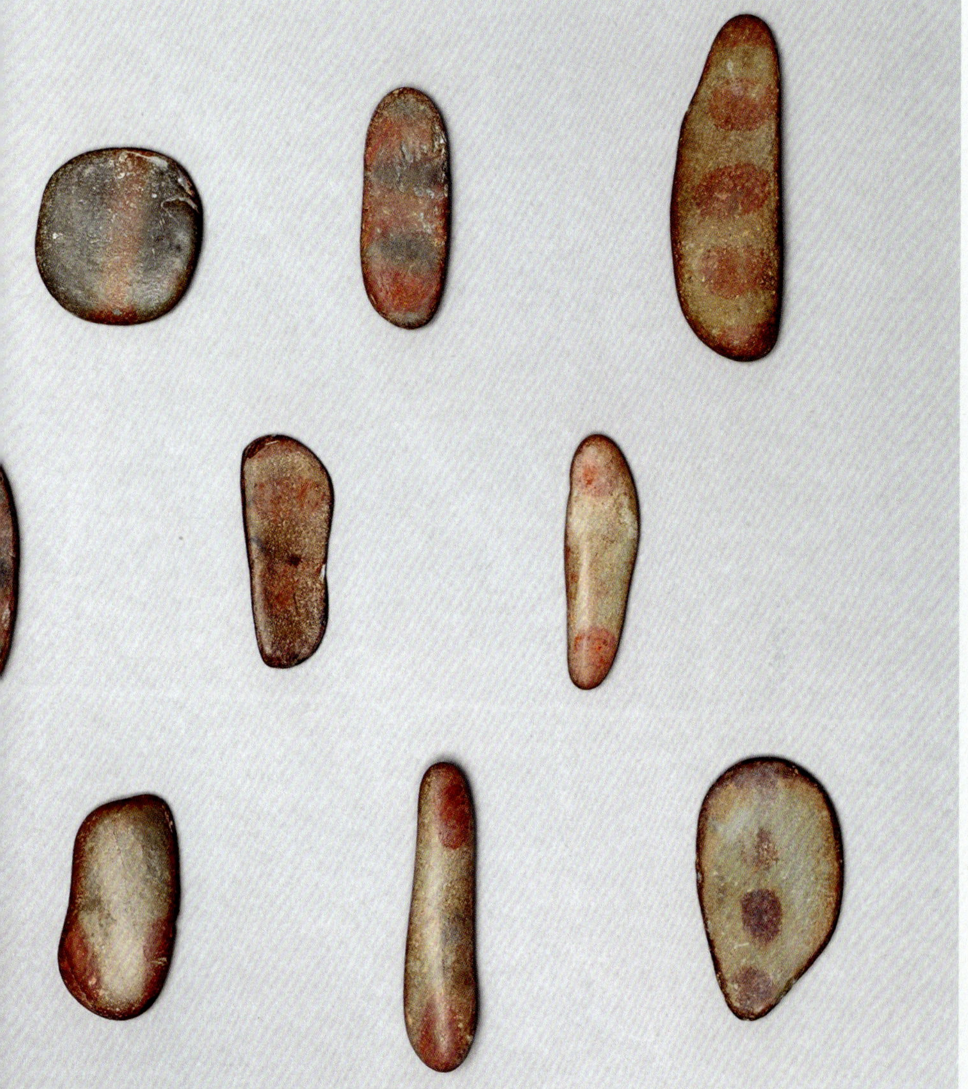

YELLOW PIGMENTS **p. 192** RED AND PURPLE PIGMENTS **p.193**

Shabti of Seti I

NINETEENTH DYNASTY • EGYPTIAN FAIENCE • H: 12 IN. (30.5 CM) •
THE METROPOLITAN MUSEUM OF ART, NEW YORK, NY

1294
–
1279
BCE

Other important works
Hippopotamus figurine, Middle Kingdom. Musée du Louvre, Paris.
Overseer Shabti of Taywheret, Twenty-First Dynasty. Musée du Louvre, Paris.
Scarab, New Kingdom—Twenty-First Dynasty. Manufacture et Musée Nationaux, Sèvres.

Egyptian faience, used to make a variety of small objects like beads, statuettes, and amulets, was a material favored by ancient Egyptian craftsmen. This faience, composed of a friable core of quartz grains, quartz sand, or flint containing silica, was characterized by a vitrified alkaline glaze made of silica, alkali (the ashes of plants or natron), lime, and metal oxides. During firing in a low-temperature, reduction atmosphere, the alkali reacts with the lime, copper oxide and melting silica to form a glaze on the object that ranges from green to bright blue. The Egyptians used several methods to create this glaze: cementation (raw materials buried in a paste or powder and fired); efflorescence or self-glazing (silica paste and a flux combined with pigments); and direct application (liquid paste applied to the dry or fired object).

Egyptian faience, developed during the Middle Kingdom, was used in particular to make *shabti* and *ushabti*: funerary statuettes that accompanied deceased members of the upper classes into the afterlife. These small figurines represent mummified figures and are decorated with inscriptions from the Book of the Dead. Ranging from green to blue, the colors of Egyptian faience were referred to with the hieroglyphic phoneme *ouadj* ("papyrus stalk"), which meant "greenery" or "rebirth." Associated with Osiris, the god of fertility as well as eternal rebirth, it was the most important color in the Egyptian imagination.

This funerary servant for Pharaoh Seti I, who reigned from 1294 to 1279 BCE, is a rare example of a large shabti in Egyptian faience that has survived nearly intact. The beautiful intense blue glaze is testament to the craftsman's skill.

POLYCHROMY IN ANCIENT EGYPT **p. 13** BLUE **p. 48**

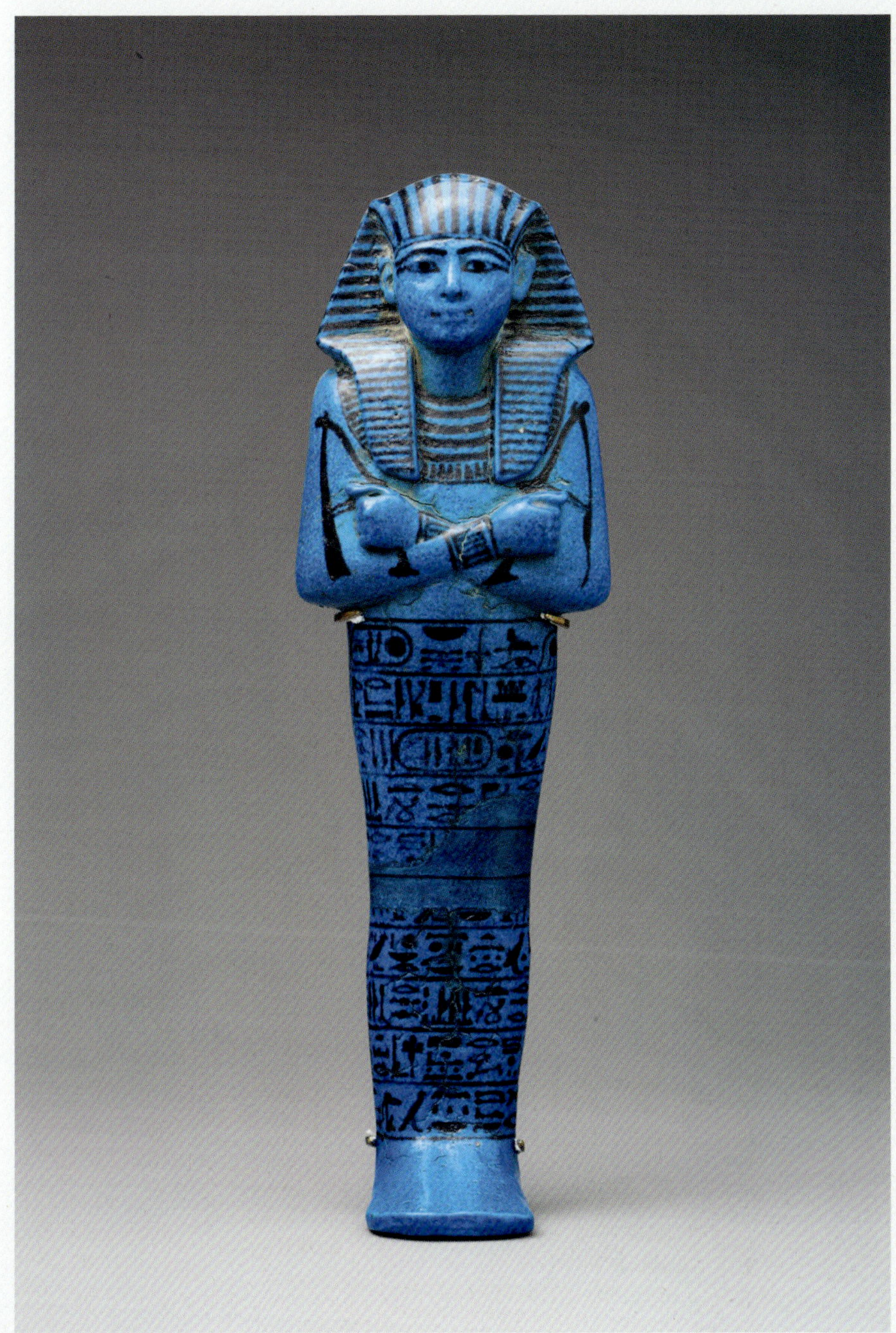

BLUE PIGMENTS **p. 194** GREEN PIGMENTS **p.195**

Triclinium of the Villa of Livia

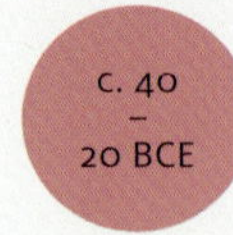

FRESCO • 19 FT. 4 IN. × 36 FT. 1 IN. (5.9 × 11 M) •
MUSEO NAZIONALE ROMANO, ROME

In 1863, a remarkable decorative ensemble featuring an illusionist rendering of nature was discovered in Prima Porta, in the country home of Livia Drusilla (c. 55–29 BCE), the wife of the emperor Augustus (63–14 BCE).

In a semi-underground room with little natural light—the triclinium was intended to provide relief during summer heatwaves—a fresco depicts a lush country garden. Laurel, pomegranate and date trees, strawberry, willow, reeds, boxwood, cypress, pine, quince and cherry trees, as well as roses, poppies, chrysanthemums, chamomile, acanthus, and ivy are meticulously rendered. A multitude of naturalistic details, like flying or pecking birds, and leaves rustling in the breeze, give the ensemble a peaceful atmosphere. The only two architectural elements depicted are a low retaining wall and a straw fence that structure the space. The soft, harmonious palette is dominated by shades of green—the vegetation in the foreground grows lighter in the background—and by the bright blue of the sky. Both colors are enhanced with touches of red, yellow, orange, brown, and white used for the fruit, flowers, and birds.

This ornamental cycle is remarkable for its intelligent design: the rich composition seems to enlarge the space, suggesting a lush landscape to those within, and the imagery reinforces the coolness of the semi-underground room. One detail, however, reminds viewers that they are still inside: the small bird cage perched on the outer wall.

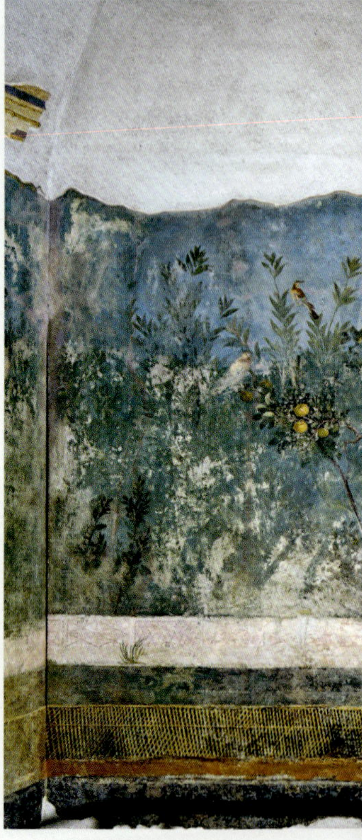

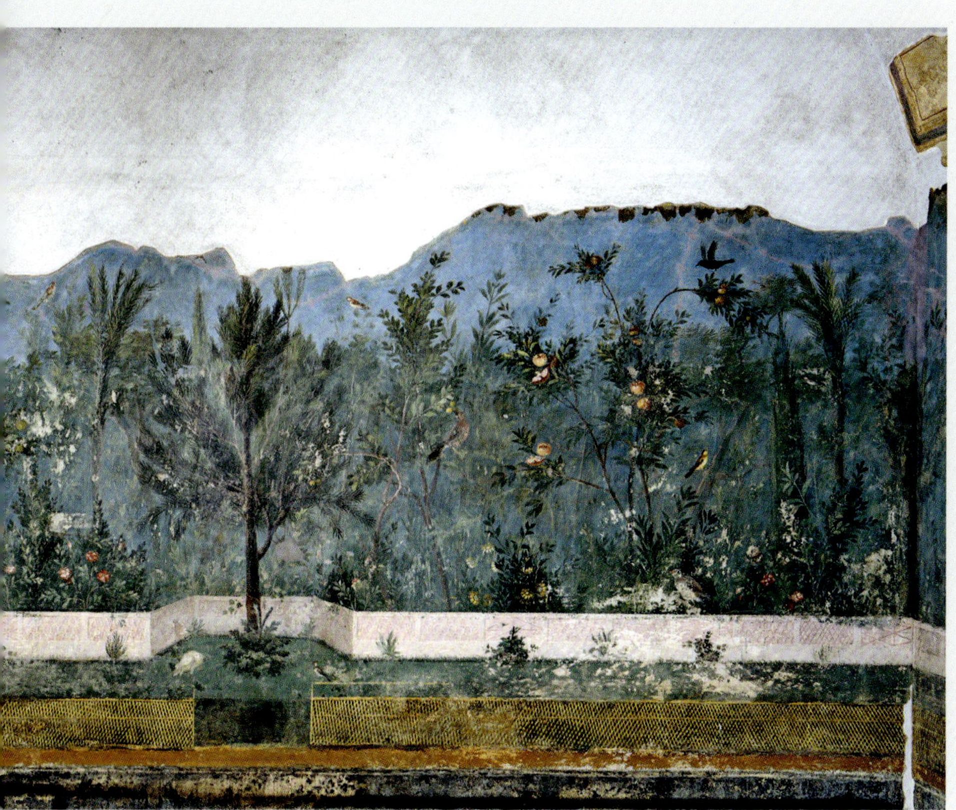

The Roman author Suetonius (c. 70–c. 140 CE) writes in *The Lives of the Twelve Caesars* that the Romans viewed dying laurels as an ill omen for the ruling power. However, lush vegetation such as this seems to have reassured Livia's husband, the emperor Augustus, that his reign will endure.

Other important works
Frescoes from the Villa of the Mysteries, c. 70 BCE. Pompeii.
Frescoes from the House of Julia Felix, c. 70 BCE. Pompeii.
Frescoes from the House of Augustus, c. 36 BCE. Rome.

FRESCO **p. 201**

Stained Glass in the Basilica of Saint-Denis

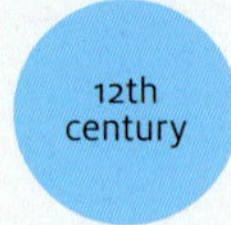

GLASS, LEAD • BASILICA, SAINT-DENIS

Other important works
Stained glass in Laon Cathedral, 12th century. Laon.
Stained glass in Cologne Cathedral, 13th–14th centuries. Cologne.
Stained glass in King's College Chapel, 16th century. Cambridge.

Breaking with the simple, dimly lit Romanesque style, the brightness that floods the basilica evokes the revelation of divine light, giving the lofty building the appearance of heavenly Jerusalem—a city bathed in light—and laying the foundations for the Gothic style.

Around 1130, Abbot Suger—advisor to Kings Louis VI (known as "the Fat") and Louis VII ("the Young")—was tasked with enlarging the Basilica of Saint-Denis, a former abbey church just north of Paris. Guided by a theological conception of light, he decided to give stained glass new importance. Drawing on the writings of the theologian Dionysius the Areopagite (fifth to sixth century), who described God as light, Suger created a high, bright radiating chapel with a ribbed vault supported by a multitude of slender columns and immense stained-glass walls.

Today, only five of the original stained-glass panels remain; the others were restored or designed in the thirteenth and eighteenth centuries. The upper portions of the stained-glass panels, destroyed during the French Revolution in 1789, were redesigned in the nineteenth century by the architect Eugène Viollet-le-Duc (1814–1879). The motifs are taken from the Old and New Testaments, and include innovative imagery like the Tree of Jesse, a representation of Christ's ancestors.

Suger adopted tinted glass, a precious material in the Middle Ages, for its ability to color light. To make the stained glass, which appears to have cost more than the stone reconstruction, Suger called on the best craftsmen, then recruited a master glassmaker to constantly monitor their progress. Blue, the dominant color, was achieved with cobalt; purple with manganese oxides; yellow with iron oxides; and green and red with copper oxides. In his writings, Suger compared the pervading blue to sapphire, a precious stone said to be incrusted in the wall of Heavenly Jerusalem, the holy city where, according to The Book of Revelation, the sons and daughters of God will live out eternity.

DIVINE COLOR **p. 17** RED **p. 46** YELLOW **p. 47** BLUE **p. 48** GREEN **p. 49**

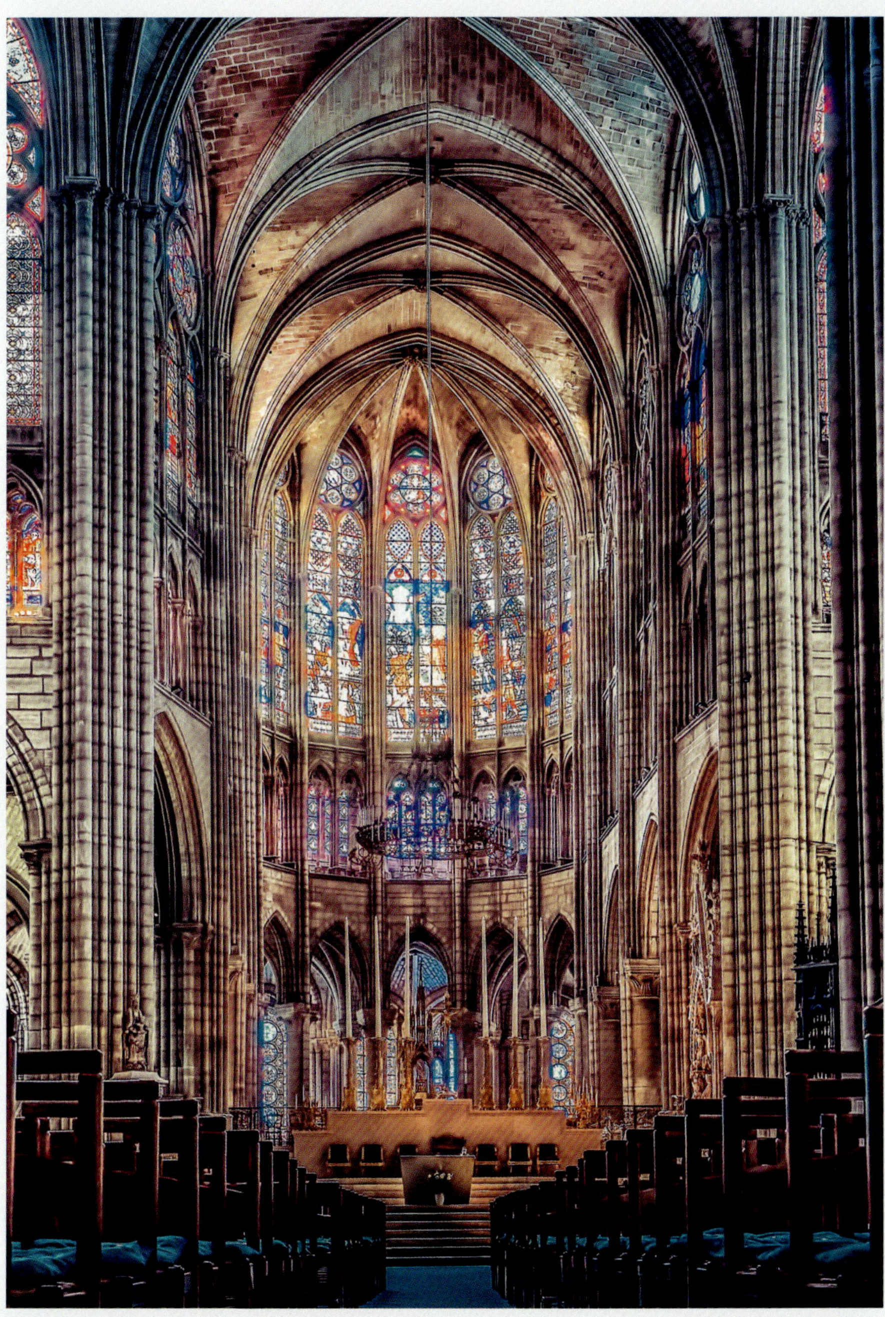

YELLOW PIGMENTS **p. 192** RED AND PURPLE PIGMENTS **p. 193** BLUE PIGMENTS **p. 194**
GREEN PIGMENTS **p. 195** STAINED GLASS **p. 207**

Madonna of Chancellor Rolin

JAN VAN EYCK • OIL ON WOOD • 26 × 24½ IN. (66 × 62 CM) •
MUSÉE DU LOUVRE, PARIS

C. 1434 – 1435

The two small figures outside the loggia may be an allusion to Philip the Good, Duke of Burgundy, and Charles VII, King of France, whom the chancellor Rolin helped to reconcile during the Treaty of Arras, putting an end to the civil war between Armagnacs and Burgundians in 1435. The two cities stretching out before them—the city of men on the left and the city of God on the right—as well as the rest of the landscape are rendered using aerial perspective in shades of brown, green, and blue.

Nicolas Rolin (c. 1376–1462), chancellor to the Duke of Burgundy, commissioned Jan Van Eyck to make a painting for his personal chapel in Autun. Using the iconography of the sacred conversation, a motif developed during the Renaissance, Rolin is depicted praying, facing the Madonna and Child. Jesus, holding a globe with a cross, blesses the chancellor. An angel places a crown on the Madonna's head. A triple archway evoking the Trinity frames a view from the loggia's opulent decor onto a river and an imaginary city. Behind the chancellor are visible bourgeois homes and a monastery—the city of men; behind the Madonna and Child stand a cathedral and churches—the city of God. The two banks, a tangible expression of the earthly and celestial worlds, are connected by a bridge in the center of the painting from

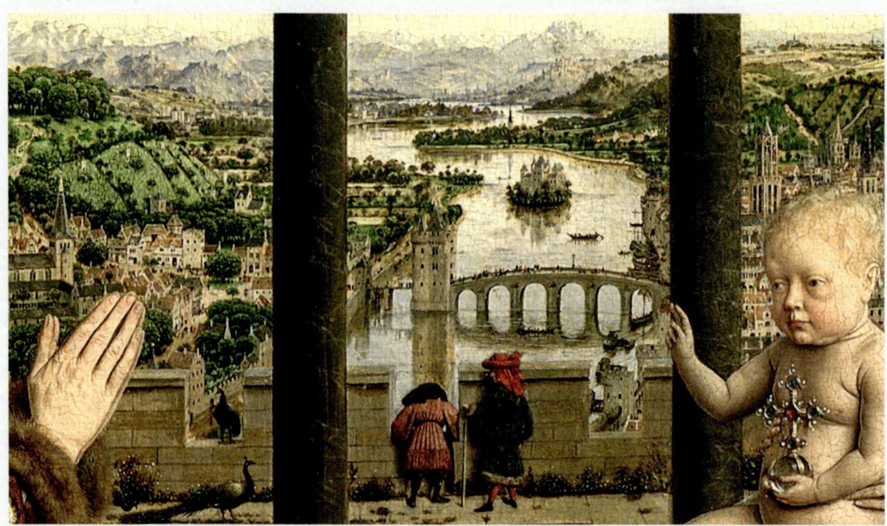

DIVINE COLOR **p. 17** THE INVENTION OF OIL PAINT **p. 18**
WHITE **p. 45** RED **p. 46** BLUE **p. 48** GOLD **p. 56**

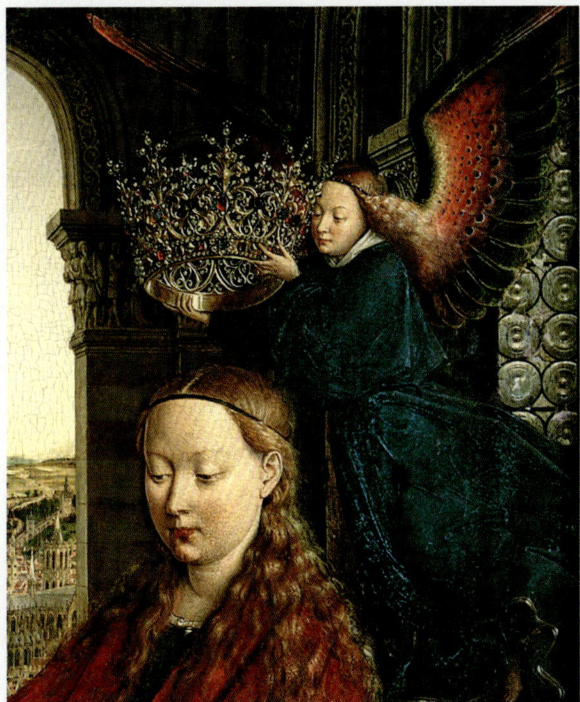

The crown that the angel places on the head of the Madonna reveals Van Eyck's extraordinary talent for rendering a multitude of details in his paintings. The gleam of the gemstones mounted in the finely crafted gold crown echoes the embroidery on the robe. The angel's gesture is an allusion to the Coronation of the Virgin, Queen of Heaven.

which a cross rises. A clever network of symbols structures the composition: the enclosed garden in the background represents Mary's virginity; the magpies symbolize death; the peacock represents Christ or vanity; the rabbits crushed by the column symbolize the struggle against lust, etc.

Van Eyck's mastery of oil painting, an innovation in fifteenth-century art, enabled him to skillfully render a multitude of realistic details in a complex painting that combines portraiture, religious art, and landscape. His attention to color is remarkable. The painter chose half-tones for the entire painting, except for gold, blue, red, and white, which he reserved for fabrics and attributes, as well as the stained glass. These colors were the most favored by the Christian religion: blue and gold were used to represent the light of God, red for dignity and charity, and white for purity.

JAN VAN EYCK (C. 1390–1441)

The Flemish painter Jan Van Eyck was one of the first artists to perfect the oil-painting technique. By applying successive thin layers of translucent paint over a more opaque layer (glazing), he played with the paint's transparency to create a glow—the work would appear illuminated from the inside—and achieve colors of unprecedented richness.

➡ OIL PAINT **p.203**

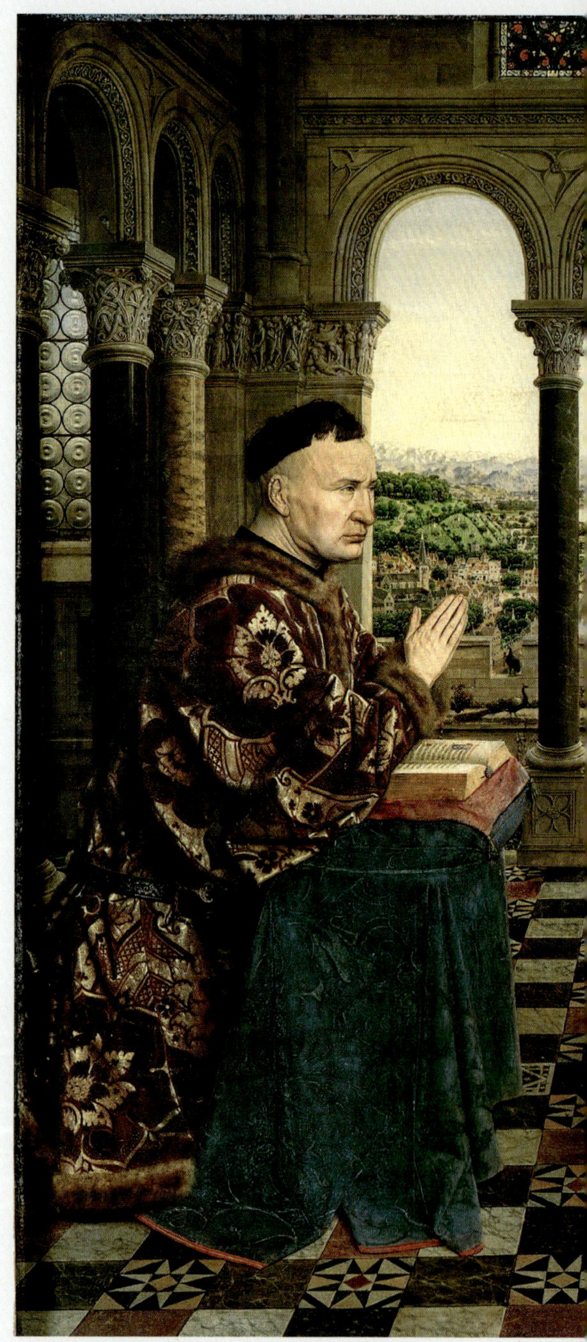

Other important works
The Ghent Altarpiece: Adoration of the Mystic Lamb, 1432.
Saint Bavo's Cathedral, Ghent.
Portrait of a Man (Self-Portrait),
1433. National Gallery, London.
The Arnolfini Portrait, 1434.
National Gallery, London.

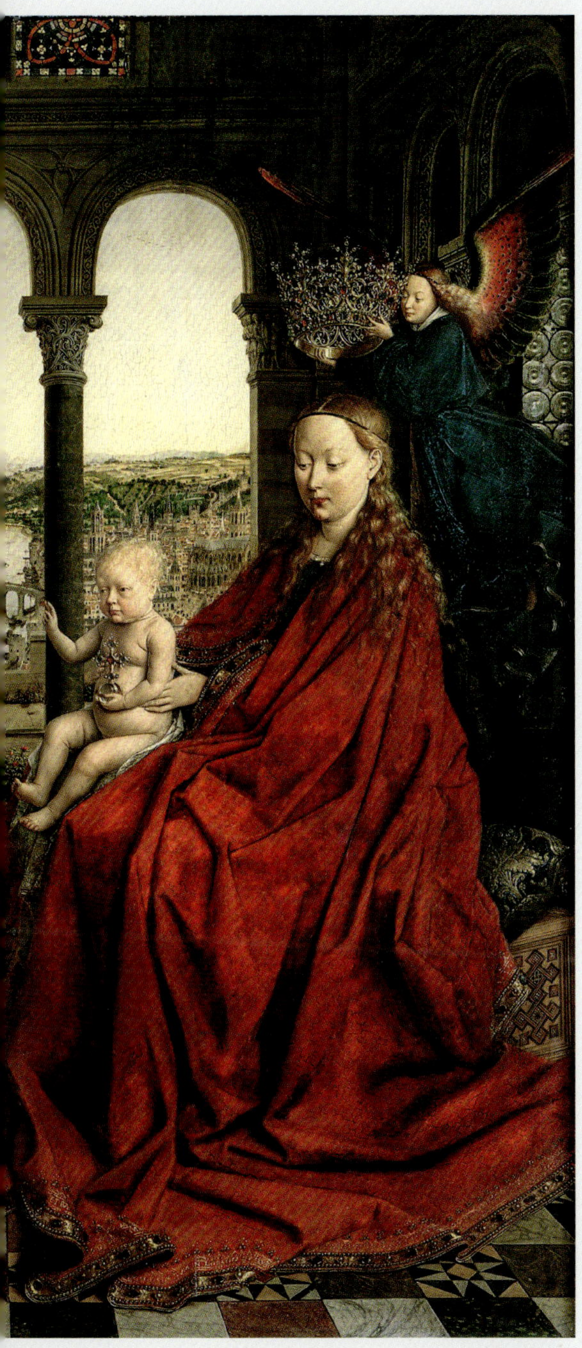

Portrait of a Lady from the Court of Milan, also known as La Belle Ferronnière

LEONARDO DA VINCI • OIL ON WOOD • 25¾ × 17¾ IN. (63 × 45 CM) • MUSÉE DU LOUVRE, PARIS

c. 1490 – 1497

LEONARDO DA VINCI (1452–1519)
Leonardo was the Renaissance genius par excellence, so much so that he has become a legend in the Western imagination. A polymath, who included painting and art theory among his many skills, he sought in his writings to develop a science of the visible. He explored the question of color by abandoning the bright, fanciful colors of Quattrocento painters in favor of brooding, muted tones to express the infinite shades of shadow.

The model for this portrait of a beautiful aristocrat is believed to have been Lucrezia Crivelli (c. 1464–1534), the mistress of Ludovic Sforza, the Duke of Milan (1451–1508); Béatrice d'Este (1475–1497), the Duke's wife; or Isabella of Aragon (1470–1498).

Leonardo da Vinci, then in service to the Duke of Milan, drew on the tradition of Lombardi portraiture, in which the model stands out from a dark, neutral ground. Influenced by Flemish painting, however, he modernized the style: seen from a more naturalistic three-quarter pose, the model almost appears in motion; the young woman's eyes look slightly behind her, and the artist chose to paint a bust to accentuate her sense of presence. In this painting, which foreshadowed the *Mona Lisa* (1503–19, Musée du Louvre, Paris), Leonardo sought to translate the emotions of his model and to reproduce her physical appearance while maintaining a certain air of mystery.

The palette is dominated by muted tones softened by the addition of white or black. Only the Spanish-style dress, in keeping with the fashion in the Milanese court, is painted in a stronger red symbolizing wealth, and is associated with other elegant embellishments (details in her clothing and jewelry). Several years later, in *A Treatise on Painting* (c. 1508), Leonardo would recommend this reduced palette for composition, in particular through the use of sfumato: a slow and meticulous glazing technique that softens the transition from areas of shadow to areas of light.

Other important works
The Last Supper, 1498.
Santa Maria delle Grazie, Milan.
Mona Lisa, 1503–19.
Musée du Louvre, Paris.
The Virgin and Child with Saint Anne, 1503–19.
Musée du Louvre, Paris.

THE INVENTION OF OIL PAINT **p. 18** LINE AND FORM VERSUS COLOR **p. 20**

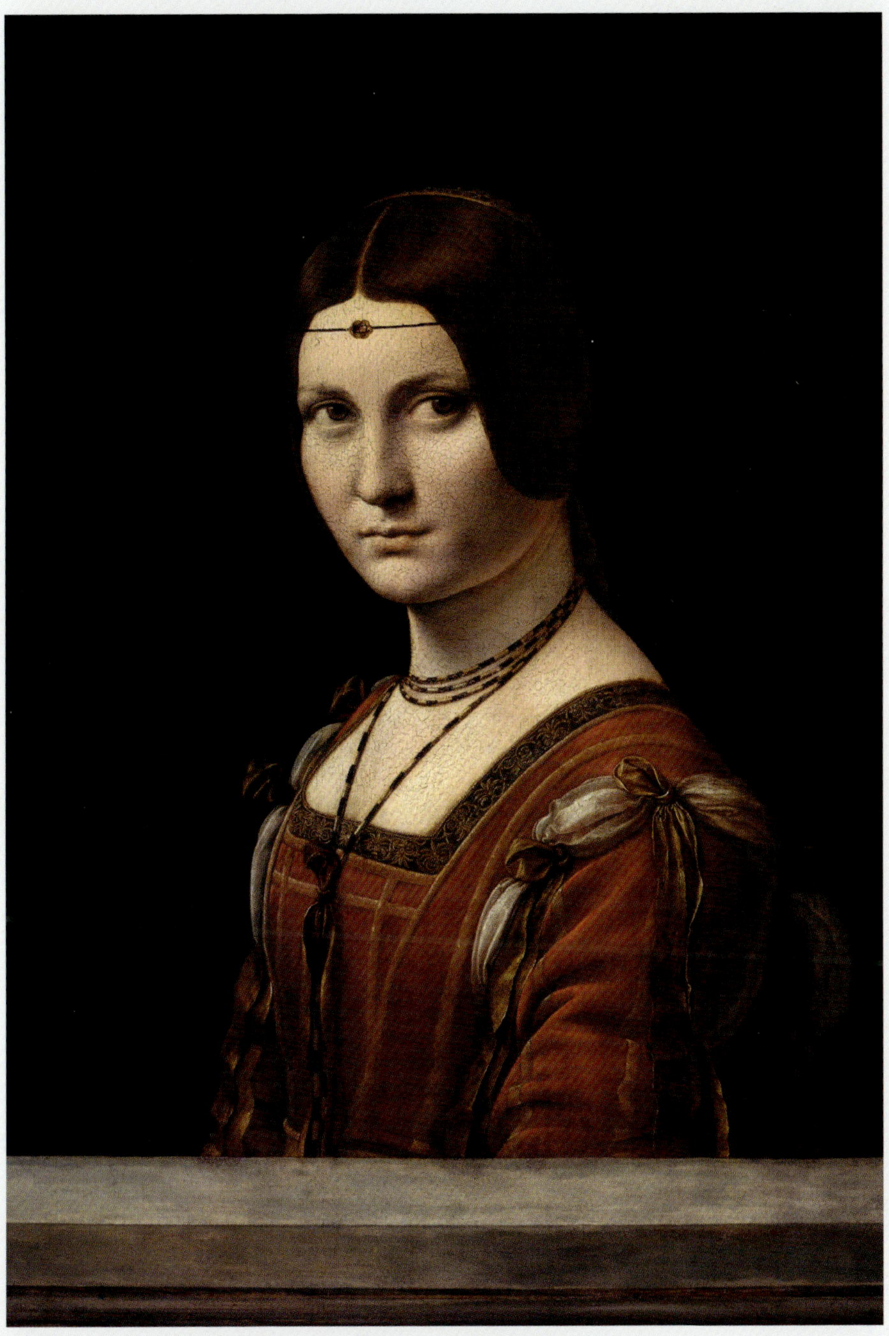

BLACK **p. 44** WHITE **p. 45** RED **p. 46**

Lucretia

PAOLO VERONESE • OIL ON CANVAS • 3 FT. 7 IN. × 3 FT. (109 × 91 CM) •
KUNSTHISTORISCHES MUSEUM, VIENNA

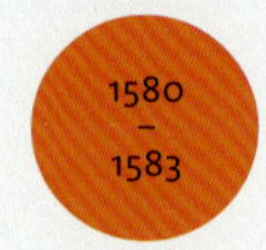

**PAOLO VERONESE
(1528–1588)**
Veronese left his mark on the history of art through his bold use of color and his flair for composition. A true expert in the Mannerist and Venetian styles of painting, he favored dazzling colors and contrasts, some jarring, arranged in a series of planes, as demonstrated in his most famous painting, *The Wedding at Cana* (1562–63, Musée du Louvre, Paris), which is enlivened with myriad bright splashes of color.

Lucretia, the wife of Tarquinius Collatinus—one of the founders of the Roman Republic (753–509 BCE)—was raped by Sextus Tarquinius, one of the sons of the Roman king Tarquinius Superbus, when he was a guest in her home. She refused to live with the violation and, after asking her father to avenge her, committed suicide. In retaliation, the population rose up against the royal family: the monarchy was overthrown and replaced by the Republic. This tragedy, especially as recounted by the Roman author Titus Livius (c. 59–17 BCE) was considered an *exemplum virtutis* (example of virtue).

Veronese depicted Lucretia alone, with pale complexion and reddened eyelids. She stands bare-shouldered, wearing ornate accessories and attire, and enveloped in luxurious fabrics. She holds a dagger with a finely crafted gold hilt with which she intends to end her life. The composition is dominated by an unusual monochrome palette in shades of deepest to brightest green, pigments traditionally feared for their toxicity. There was nothing coincidental about the artist's choice: green, an ambiguous color if ever there was one, symbolizes fate—the young woman is about to meet hers—and the brevity of earthly existence. Although this conception of colors was not formalized until the sixteenth century, green happens to be the complement of red—the color of the blood the dagger will spill. In *Judith with the Head of Holofernes* (1582, Kunsthistorisches Museum, Vienna), the twin to this *Lucretia*, blood is indeed spilled and the color red appears alongside green.

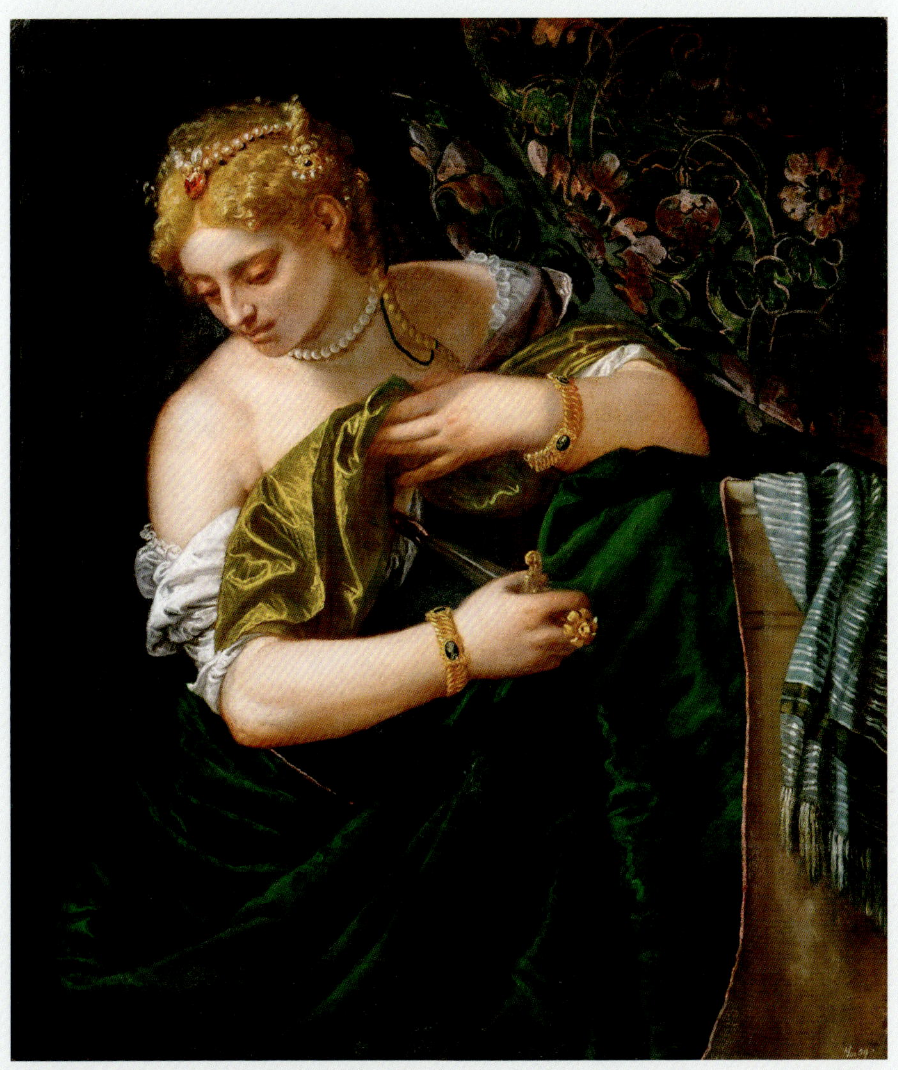

Other important works
The Wedding at Cana, 1562–63. Musée du Louvre, Paris.
The Feast in the House of Levi, 1573. Gallerie dell'Accademia, Venice.
Venus and Adonis, 1582. Museo del Prado, Madrid.

GREEN PIGMENTS **p. 195**

The Repentant Magdalen

GEORGES DE LA TOUR • OIL ON CANVAS • 3 FT. 8½ IN. × 3 FT. ½ IN.
(113 × 92.7 CM) • NATIONAL GALLERY OF ART, WASHINGTON, DC

1635
–
1640

GEORGES DE LA TOUR (1593–1652)

About fifty works have been attributed to Georges de la Tour, a painter from Lorraine in northeastern France, whose life and work is shrouded in mystery. Although he was belatedly rediscovered after a successful career, little is known about his training, and his apparently violent character contrasts strangely with the spirituality emanating from his art. His work can be categorized into two main groups: daytime scenes, probably painted during the first part of his career, and masterful nocturnal scenes.

In the Christian tradition, Mary Magdalene represents the repentant sinner, absolved of her sins by Christ, symbol of unconditional love. She appears in several paintings by La Tour, who was fascinated by the complex character of the former prostitute and disciple of Jesus.

In this version, held at the National Gallery of Art in Washington, DC, a bare-headed Mary Magdalene is deep in reflection, her chin resting on her palm in a quintessential gesture of melancholy. The scene is illuminated by a single candle, which enabled the painter to use one of his preferred techniques—chiaroscuro—and to symbolize divine light and the hope that guides believers. With her fingertips, Mary Magdalene caresses a skull whose reflection is visible in the mirror placed before her, a suggestion of mournful foreshadowing. This iconography drawn from vanitas paintings, accentuated by the model's beauty and youth, underscores the brevity of earthly existence.

A master of candlelight, La Tour used a subtle palette of pale yellow to dark brown ocher, including reddish hues, that he paired with solid, monumental, austere, and simplified forms. These muted shades are associated with moral rigor and repentance. La Tour would certainly have been familiar with the work of Caravaggio, whose violent realism and use of chiaroscuro attracted many followers throughout seventeenth-century Europe.

Other important works
The Fortune-Teller, c. 1630. The Metropolitan Museum of Art, New York, NY.
The Cheat with the Ace of Diamonds, c. 1636–38. Musée du Louvre, Paris.
The Magdalen with the Smoking Flame, c. 1640–45. Musée du Louvre, Paris.

CHIAROSCURO **p.24** RED **p. 46** YELLOW **p. 47** BROWN **p. 52**

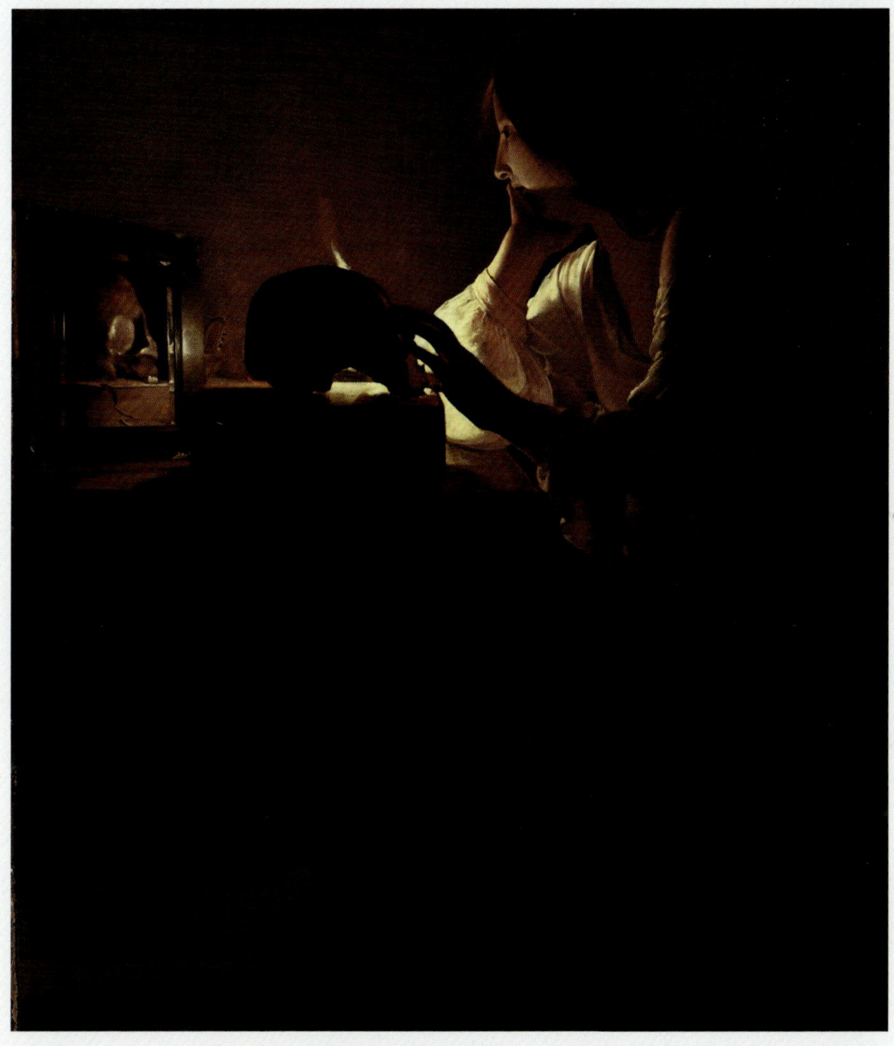

Woman in Blue Reading a Letter

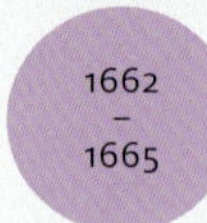

JOHANNES VERMEER • OIL ON CANVAS • 1 FT. 6 IN. × 1 FT. 3½ IN. (46.5 × 39 CM) • RIJKSMUSEUM, AMSTERDAM

JOHANNES VERMEER (1632–1675)

Only thirty-four paintings have been attributed to Vermeer, each of them characterized by an exceptional mastery of the methods of paint application (applying paint to canvas). In keeping with Dutch tradition, he specialized in interior scenes, which provided an opportunity to strip down the composition and focus on details. He was very mindful of the effects of light and their depiction through color.

Other important works
The Milkmaid, 1657–58. Rijksmuseum, Amsterdam.
Girl with a Pearl Earring, 1665. Mauritshuis, The Hague.
The Lacemaker, c. 1669–70. Musée du Louvre, Paris.

A young woman, in the intimacy of her home, stands in profile, immersed in a letter. As in other paintings, Johannes Vermeer illuminates the scene from the left; but unlike other paintings, he does not depict the window through which the light filters. The soft, meticulous way this light models the forms attests to the painter's talent for rendering the brightness of the dawning day. He pairs the effects of light with finely rendered textures: smooth skin, a silky garment, bright gold upholstery studs, and matte paper.

Vermeer's fondness for ultramarine, present in many of his compositions, is well known—the color is even referred to as "Vermeer blue"—but in this work, it is used with unequaled abundance. From the model's bed jacket, it spreads throughout the canvas, from the fabric covering the chairs to the table to the turned wood sphere that secures the dowel beneath the map on the wall—to justify the color's dominance, art historians point to the oxidation of certain pigments. But Vermeer was passionate about lapis lazuli, which he paired here with yellow ocher in what is almost a two-tone work. The symbolic meaning of blue, traditionally associated with the Virgin Mary and one of the few colors accepted in an austere Protestant society, adds to the contemplative atmosphere of this harmonious domestic scene. Within this private space, the outside world is suggested by the map of Holland and West Friesland hanging on the wall.

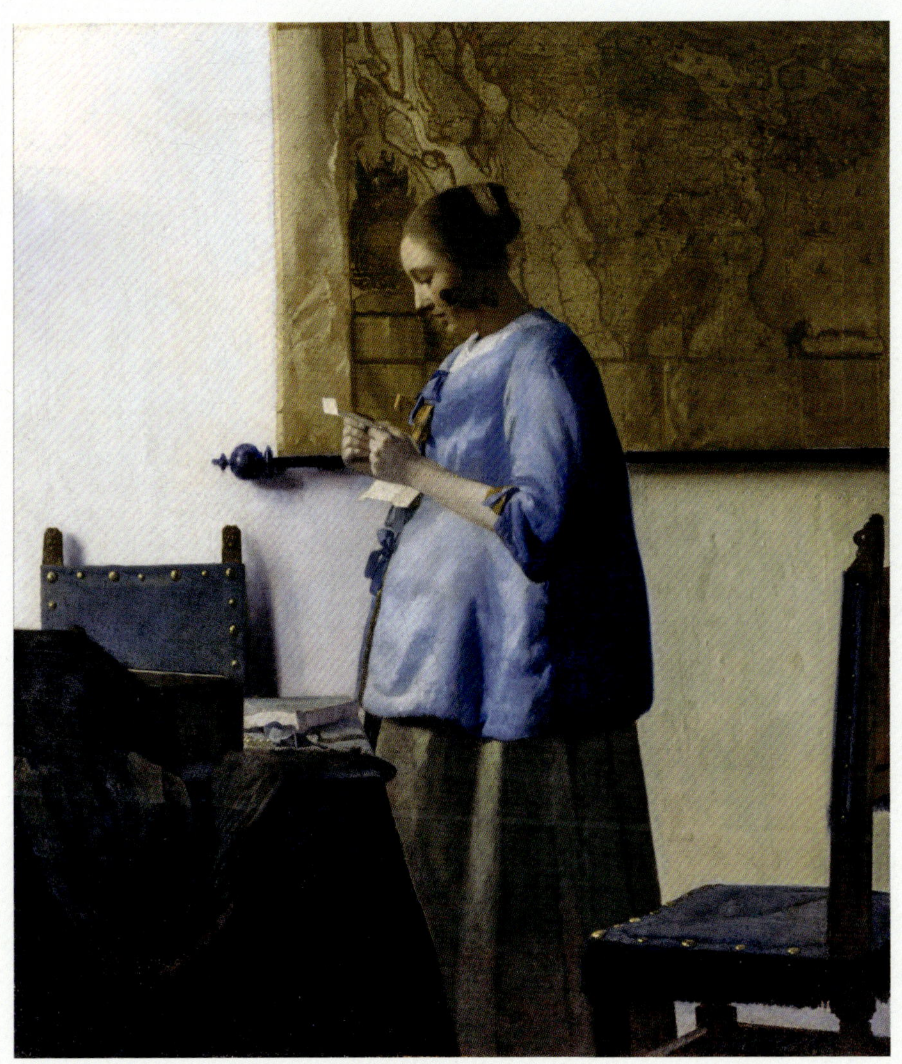

→ BLUE PIGMENTS **p. 194**

Portrait of Louis XIV

HYACINTHE RIGAUD • OIL ON CANVAS • 9 FT. 1 IN. × 6 FT. 4 IN.
(277 × 194 CM) • MUSÉE DU LOUVRE, PARIS

HYACINTHE RIGAUD (1659–1743)

Rigaud was one of the most important portrait artists at the court of Louis XIV. He excelled at creating lavish portraits of his models and masterfully rendered fine fabrics and clothing, furniture, and interior decoration. For formal and iconographic reasons, he intensified the effects of brightness and shimmering colors.

Other important works
Philip V, King of Spain, 1701. Musée National du Château de Versailles, Versailles.
Philippe de Courcillon, Marquis de Dangeau, 1702. Musée National du Château de Versailles, Versailles.
Louis XV as a Child, 1715–17. Musée National du Château de Versailles, Versailles.

In this ceremonial portrait of Louis XIV intended for the monarch's grandson, Philippe V of Spain (1683–1746), the king appears grandiose and elegantly dressed, his legs slender and muscular, as though ready to dance—an art form he loved. Nearly all of the emblems of royalty are depicted: the fleur-de-lys coronation robe; the collar of the Order of the Holy Spirit, of which he was the Grand Master; the Charlemagne sword marking the continuity with the Carolingian Empire; the scepter (held upside down); Henry IV's hand of justice; and the closed crown. Other symbols of the monarchy are also visible: the throne; a marble column (linking the heavenly and earthly realms); the goddess Themis on the stylobate, representing justice; and red-heeled shoes, a fashion Louis XIV had started in the royal court. The red heels, a sign that the high nobility kept its feet clean and out of the mud, declare the authority of the wearer and their will to trample any opponent of the regime.

More broadly, the four dominant colors—red, blue, white, and gold—represent different aspects of the king's dominance: red, a symbol of power as old as antiquity; blue, symbol of the French monarchy since the thirteenth century; white, symbol of sainthood and superiority (strengthened by the ermine fur), and also the color of the royal commander in chief; and gold, by nature luxurious and associated with the Sun King. Finally, the low-angle view, creating the illusion of height, and the dramatic setting complete the glorification of the king.

WHITE **p. 45** RED **p. 46** BLUE **p. 48** GOLD **p. 56**

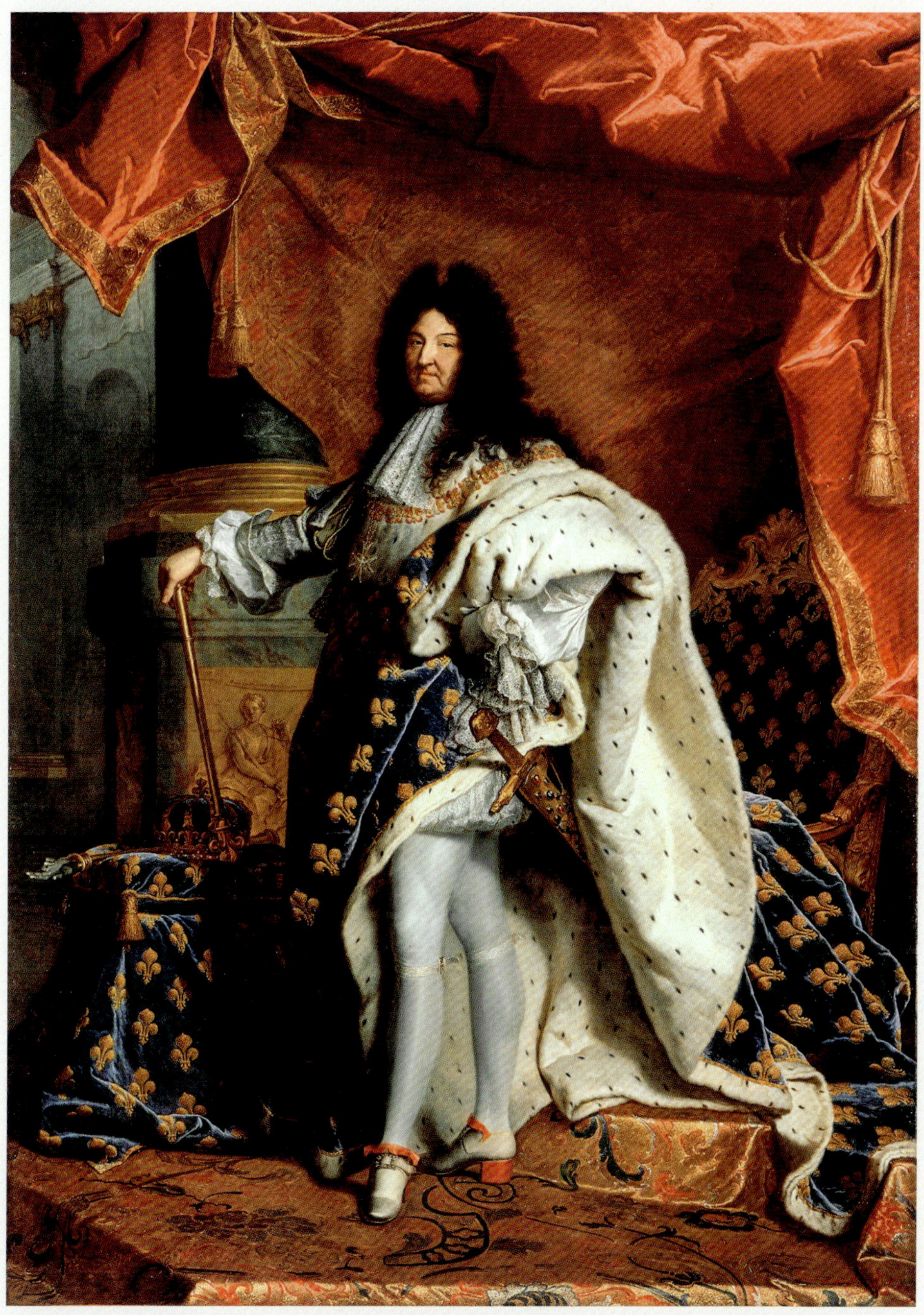

Witches' Sabbath

FRANCISCO DE GOYA • OIL ON MURAL TRANSFERRED TO CANVAS •
4 FT. 7 IN. × 14 FT. 4½ IN. (140 × 438 CM) • MUSEO DEL PRADO, MADRID

c. 1819
–
1823

Other important works
The Third of May 1808, 1814.
Museo del Prado, Madrid.
Saturn Devouring His Son,
1819–23. Museo del Prado, Madrid.
Judith and Holofernes, 1819–23.
Museo del Prado, Madrid.

Around 1819, Francisco de Goya began decorating the
Quinta del Sordo, his newly acquired residence. Perhaps
influenced by the serious illness he had recently endured
or the restoration of the absolute monarchy, he created a
bleak decorative cycle of fourteen frescoes called the
Black Paintings that reflect his metaphysical malaise.

Instead of the bucolic landscapes that typically
adorned bourgeois country homes, he created nocturnal
scenes characterized by gloomy iconography and a muted
palette enhanced with chiaroscuro lighting. The main
themes Goya chose for the walls of his house were Saturn
devouring one of his children, Judith about to decapitate

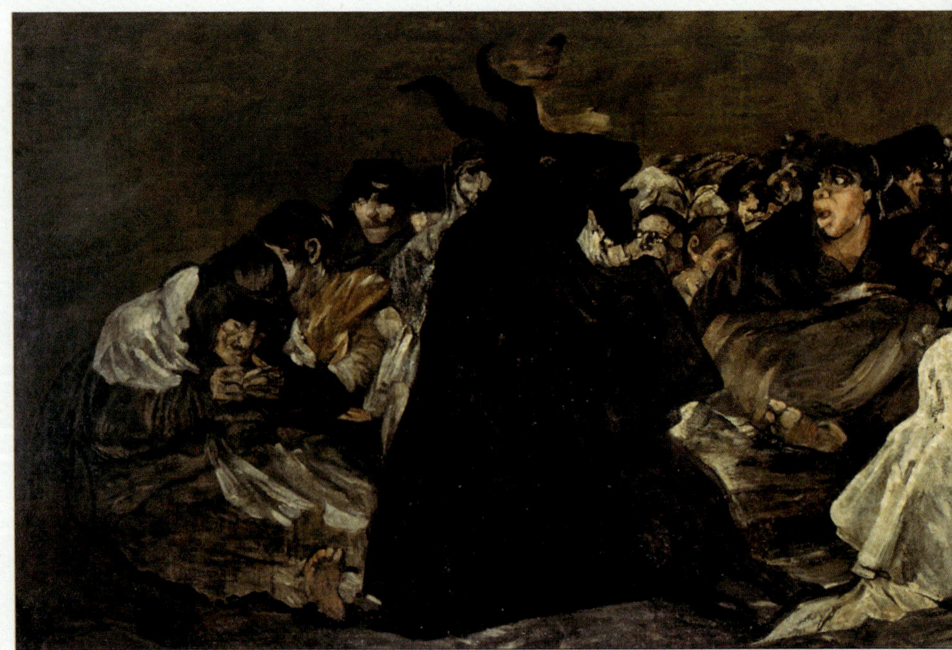

CHIAROSCURO **p. 24** BLACK **p. 44** WHITE **p. 45** YELLOW **p. 47**

Holofernes, the Fates deciding a man's destiny, and witches celebrating the sabbath. Goya strove to express the pathos, tragedy, and cruelty of life with a hint of black humor. He exaggerated the expressiveness of his figures to the point of ugliness, deformation, and bestiality using a strong play of contrasts between dark and light values, from black to white, including ochers, enhanced in places with blue or red.

This set of paintings depicts the death of light and the onset of old age and political decline with a remarkable philosophical and visual boldness. In 1824, Goya left Spain to settle in France.

FRANCISCO DE GOYA (1746–1828)
Goya was a lucid observer of his time. He invented an aesthetic language that paved the way for modern painting. Appointed painter to the king, he became the preferred portraitist of Charles IV (1748–1819). But rampant corruption in the circles of power soon drove him from that frivolous world. Freed from society life, and deaf as of 1792, he began inventing a troubling world populated by grotesque and monstrous creatures, a reflection of a cruel reality.

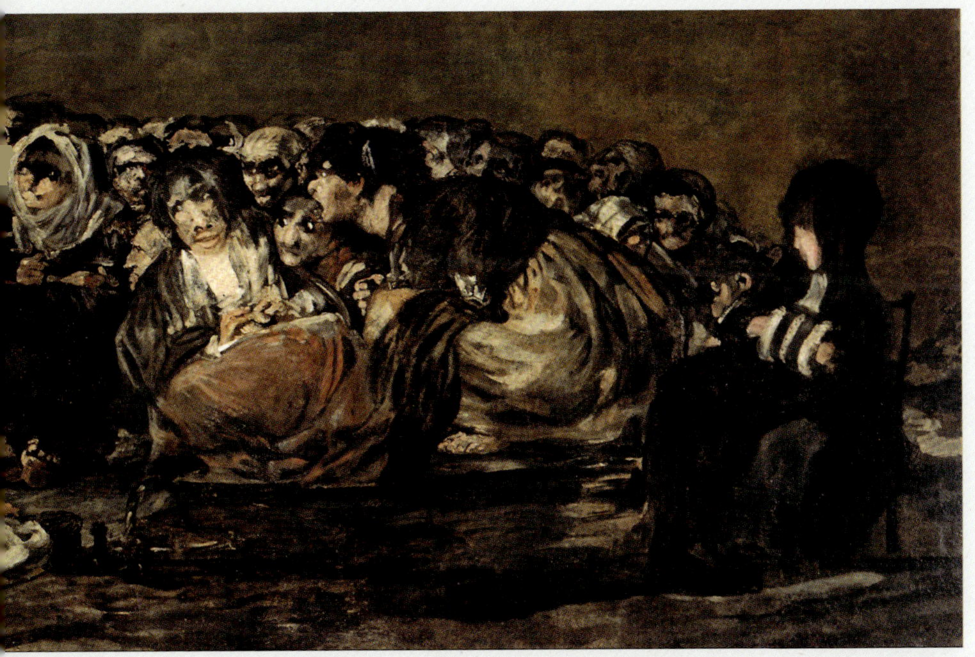

The Death of Sardanapalus

EUGÈNE DELACROIX • OIL ON CANVAS • 12 FT. 10½ IN. × 16 FT. 3½ IN. (392 × 496 CM) • MUSÉE DU LOUVRE, PARIS

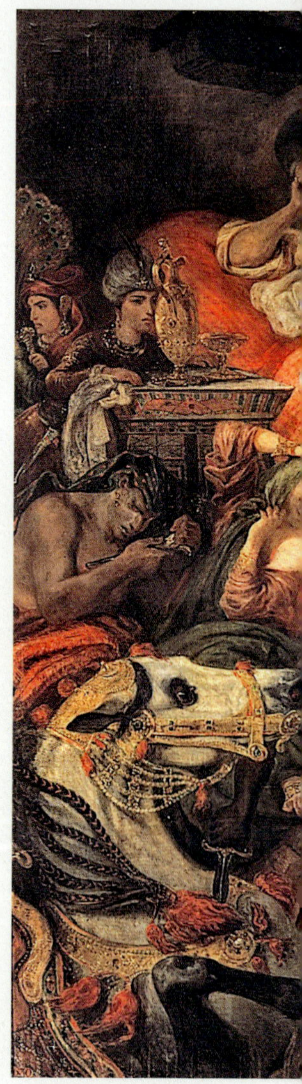

A young Eugène Delacroix caused a scandal at the Salon of 1827–28 with his latest painting, *The Death of Sardanapalus*. Drawing inspiration from the recently published dramatic poem *Sardanapalus* by Lord Byron (1788–1824) and ancient sources like Diodorus Siculus's *Bibliotheca Historica* (100 BCE), the painter depicted the death of the Assyrian ruler Sardanapalus (685–631 BCE or 628 BCE), whom the Ancients associated with depravity. According to the legend as told by Ctesias of Cnidus (500 BCE), the ruler, besieged in his palace during the sacking of Nineveh, chose immolation over surrender, surrounded by his possessions, eunuchs and concubines, and stallions and guard dogs. In the Salon catalog, Delacroix writes, "Lying on a magnificent bed, atop a huge pyre, Sardanapalus orders his slaves and palace officers to slit the throats of his wives, his pages, even his horses and his favorite dogs; none of the objects that had given him pleasure were to survive him."

Delacroix imagined a scene dominated by Sardanapalus, lying on a sumptuous sculpted bed featuring elephant heads and draped in scarlet velvet, and indifferent to the chaos around him. Luxurious possessions, naked women, and muscular slaves seem swept away in a tragic whirlwind while fire rages in the background.

The primacy of color—dominated by the red of the blood soon to be spilled—and the turbulent composition shocked defenders of academic beauty and neoclassical virtue.

Other important works
The Massacre at Chios, 1824. Musée du Louvre, Paris.
Liberty Leading the People, 1830. Musée du Louvre, Paris.
Women of Algiers in Their Apartment, 1834. Musée du Louvre, Paris.

ROMANTIC COLOR **p. 29** RED **p. 46** YELLOW **p. 47**

EUGÈNE DELACROIX (1798–1863)
Delacroix was full of contradictions. He mystified his contemporaries with bold workmanship and a liberated style while remaining mindful of tradition. His remarkable submissions to the Salon quickly earned him a certain notoriety. Associated with the Romantic movement, he often painted literary themes and was indebted to the work of great colorists like Titian, Veronese, and Rubens. Later in his career, he was given large commissions for decorative cycles and with them gained institutional recognition.

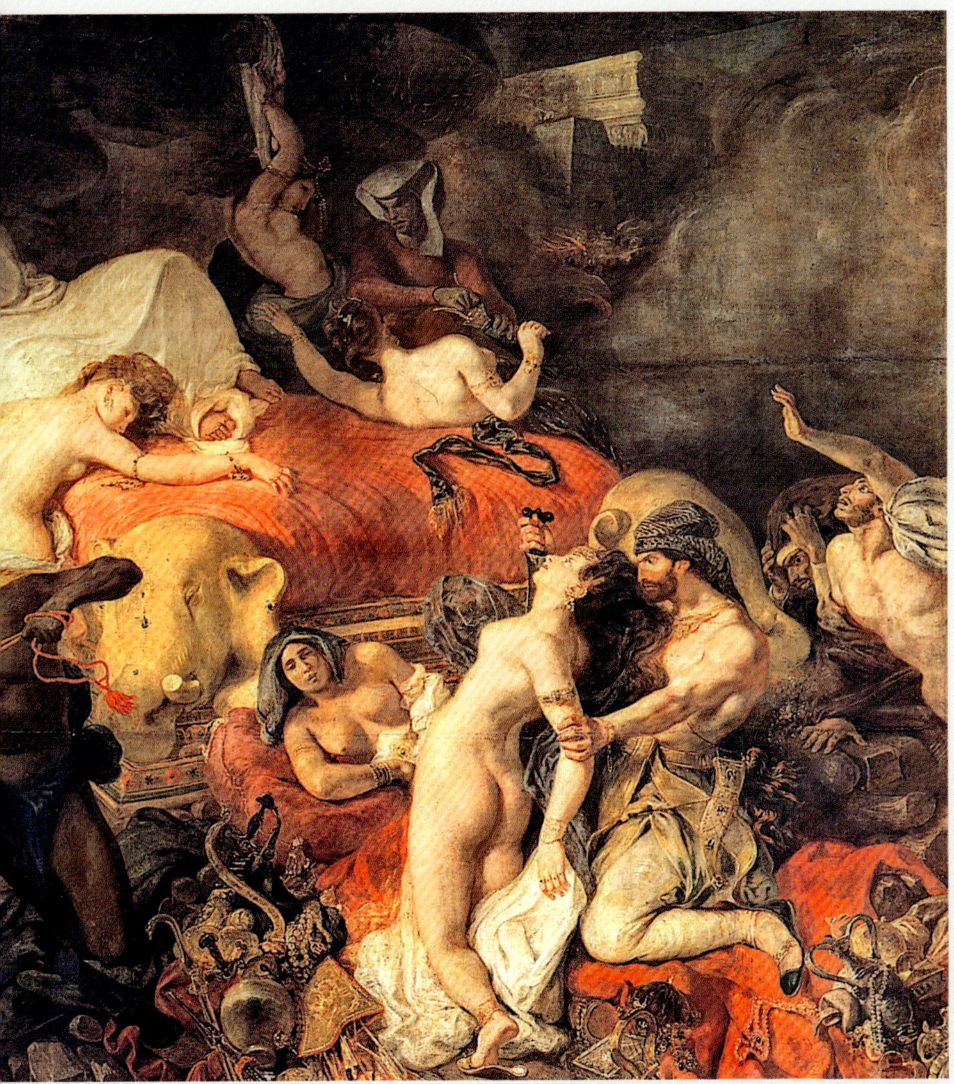

Light and Colour (Goethe's Theory)

JOSEPH MALLORD WILLIAM TURNER • OIL ON CANVAS • 40 × 40 IN. (78.7 × 78.7 CM) • TATE BRITAIN, LONDON

JOSEPH MALLORD WILLIAM TURNER (1775–1851)
Turner was one of the greatest English painters, considered a forerunner of the impressionists for his work with color, light, and brushstroke, although he executed all of his landscape paintings in the studio. He painted from preparatory studies made during his many travels. From the late 1820s, his landscapes grew increasingly atmospheric and innovative, dominated by large, expressive expanses of color made luminous by the use of a white primer.

As indicated by the title, this work is a reference to Goethe's *Theory of Color* (1810), which Turner owned in translation. In the book, the German writer theorized an idea that was already present in eighteenth-century culture: the opposition between warm, active reds, oranges, and yellows and their complements—cool, passive greens, blues, and violets. Here, the painting is dominated by warm colors; its twin, *Shade and Darkness: The Evening of the Deluge* (1843, Tate, London) is dominated by cool colors. Turner sought to equalize shadow and light. However, he had no illusions—the lines of poetry he penned to accompany an exhibition of the two paintings at the Royal Academy of London in 1843 announce light's demise: "Hope's harbinger, ephemeral as the summer fly / Which rises, flits, expands, and dies."

In an explosion of light, the centrifugal composition, perhaps influenced by the many cupolas Turner saw in Rome, celebrates God's alliance with man on the morning after the biblical flood. Moses writes the Book of Genesis; the bronze serpent he used to cure those bitten by the plague of snakes represents redemption—ordinarily, the snake symbolizes evil in Turner's work. The lower portion of the composition stirs with pale figures emerging from the torrent of light, who, through Christ's action, fight the darkness.

Other important works
The Fighting Temeraire, 1838. National Gallery, London.
Slave Ship, 1840. Museum of Fine Arts, Boston, MA.
Norham Castle, Sunrise, 1845. Tate, London.

CONTRASTS **p. 25** PRIMARY AND COMPLEMENTARY COLORS **p. 27** IMPRESSIONISM AND PLEIN AIR PAINTING **p. 32**
RED **p. 46** YELLOW **p. 47** ORANGE **p. 50**

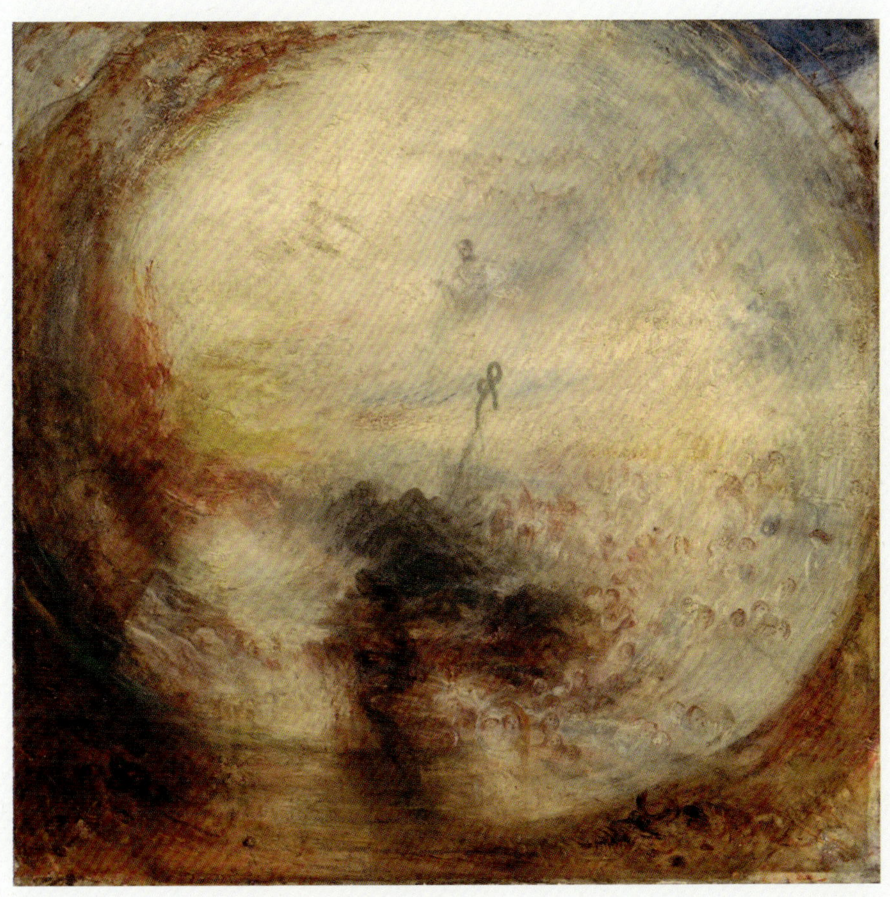

Thunder God

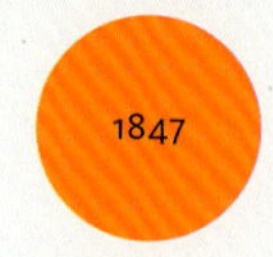

HOKUSAI • INK AND COLOR ON PAPER • 4 FT. 2 IN. × 1 FT. 9 IN. (126.9 × 53.8 CM) • NATIONAL MUSEUM OF ASIAN ART, WASHINGTON, DC

Other important works
Under the Wave off Kanagawa, c. 1830–32. The Metropolitan Museum of Art, New York, NY.
South Wind, Clear Sky, also known as *Red Fuji*, c. 1830–32. The Metropolitan Museum of Art, New York, NY.
Kajikazawa in Kai Province, c. 1830–32. The Metropolitan Museum of Art, New York, NY.

HOKUSAI (1760–1849)
Hokusai is the most well-known Japanese artist of the nineteenth century, and the most prolific: he produced more than 13,500 illustrated plates, in addition to the three thousand prints and one thousand paintings to his name. Hokusai's wood prints fascinated Eastern and Western artists and writers for their realism and for the harmonious and decorative use of color, which Hokusai achieved with mineral- and plant-based pigments (lead oxide, saffron, indigo, oyster powder, etc.).

Toward the end of his life, the painter and printmaker Hokusai created a striking representation of Raijin, the god, or *kami*, of thunder and lightning in Japanese mythology since at least the fourteenth century. The fiery god looms from within a black cloud that conveys the storm's violence, partially rendered using the crachis technique. On his back is a wheel of drums, or *taiko*, that he strikes with his drumsticks, producing the rumbling of thunder. Scarlet bolts of lightning erupt around Raijin: in Japanese, the word "red" (*aka*) also means "brightness." The god's monstrous appearance is reinforced by a muscular silhouette; puffy skin, as though burned alive; clawed hands and feet; and a malicious smile.

The painting is dominated by the contrast between red, and black and gray. The energy emanating from the curling, uncentered composition is a remarkable depiction of the power of disruption, characterized by the natural phenomena of thunder and lightning, and by often heavy wind and rain. In Shintoism and Buddhism, the symbolism associated with Raijin can be positive or negative, changeable as a storm.

Protector of temples, he brings rain to farmers, but can also bring terrible destruction. This ambiguity also influenced Hokusai's choice of colors: red for vitality and energy, and black for destruction.

IN PRAISE OF SHADOWS IN JAPAN **p. 30** BLACK **p. 44** RED **p. 46** GRAY **p. 54**

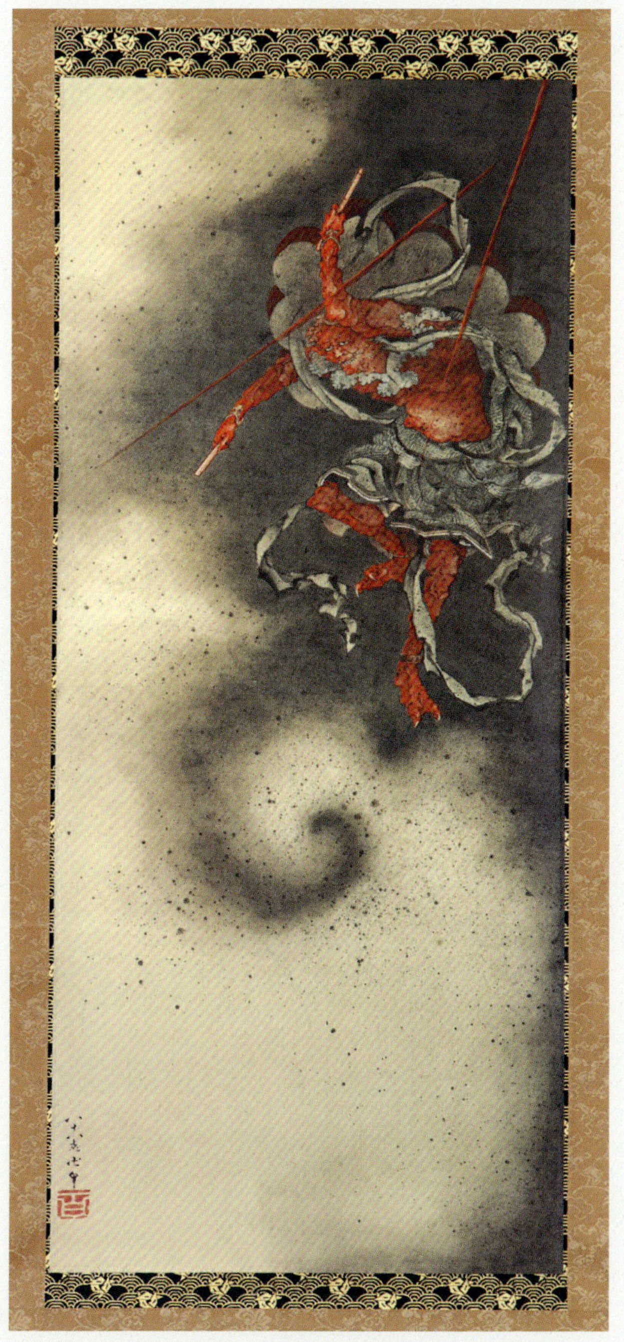

COLOR PRINTMAKING **p. 208**

Olympia

ÉDOUARD MANET • OIL ON CANVAS • 4 FT. 3½ IN. × 6 FT. 3 IN.
(130.5 × 191 CM) • MUSÉE D'ORSAY, PARIS

1863

The bouquet, rendered in loose, colorful brushstrokes, fueled the scandal that erupted among viewers and critics alike at the sight of Olympia's forthright gaze. The flowers—a gift from a client—underscore the fact that this woman is indeed someone's richly kept mistress.

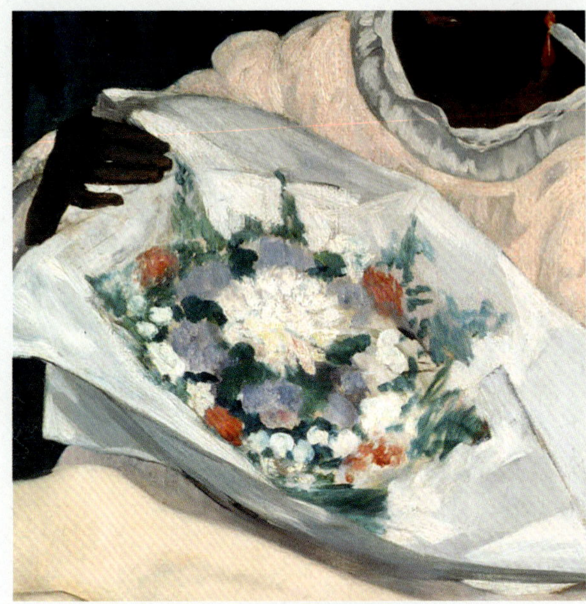

Other important works
Dejeuner sur l'Herbe, 1863.
Musée d'Orsay, Paris.
The Balcony, 1868–69.
Musée d'Orsay, Paris.
A Bar at the Folies-Bergère,
1881–82. Courtauld Institute of Art,
London.

In 1863, Édouard Manet transposed a pictorial theme inherited from the Renaissance—the reclining nude woman—into Second Empire Paris. Instead of the traditional sublimated goddess, he presented a naturalistic rendering of a young, nude prostitute. The painting caused a scandal when it was shown at the Salon two years later. What was shocking was not the nudity of the model, Victorine Meurent (1844–1927), but the artist's approach and the absence of mythological or literary anecdote—not to mention the model's direct, shameless gaze. Contemporary viewers were accustomed to the idealized forms of academic art, like the pearly, plump, smooth-bodied Venuses painted by Alexandre Cabanel (1823–1889). They were the very opposite of this Olympia, deplored a majority of critics, including Jules Claretie writing in the May 15, 1865 edition of the review *L'Artiste*: "What is this odalisque with the yellow chest, an ignoble model picked up who knows where and who has the pretention to represent Olympia? What Olympia? A courtesan no doubt. Manet cannot be accused of idealizing the foolish virgins, he who turns them into degraded virgins."

What the modern eye does not perceive—this "dirty" and "yellow" skin—is precisely what struck the contemporary observer. Théodore Duret, one of Manet's defenders, saw this rejection as a response to the artist's innovative use of color and light: "This picture was painted in a luminous note throughout. It burst with an almost painful shock upon eyes that were habituated to the deadness and gloom of the pictures of the period. The effect of the different planes was obtained without the use of shadow to give them prominence or distance, light on light; the boldest colors were juxtaposed without any half-tones or gradations." (*Manet and the French Impressionists*, 1910.)

ÉDOUARD MANET (1832–1883)
Manet is a legendary figure in the history of art and of modernity. Focused on real-world subjects, he invented a new form of painting: one concerned with realism, uninterested in slick finishes, composed with flat areas of contrasting colors, sometimes with dark outlines, and an absence of modeling and color perspective. These aesthetic upheavals paved the way for impressionism, although Manet cannot be considered part of the movement.

The white, unmade sheets that occupy the lower portion of the painting and frame the unashamedly nude body are exquisitely rendered. The fabric is creased with evocative folds in shades of gray, blue, yellow, and brown.

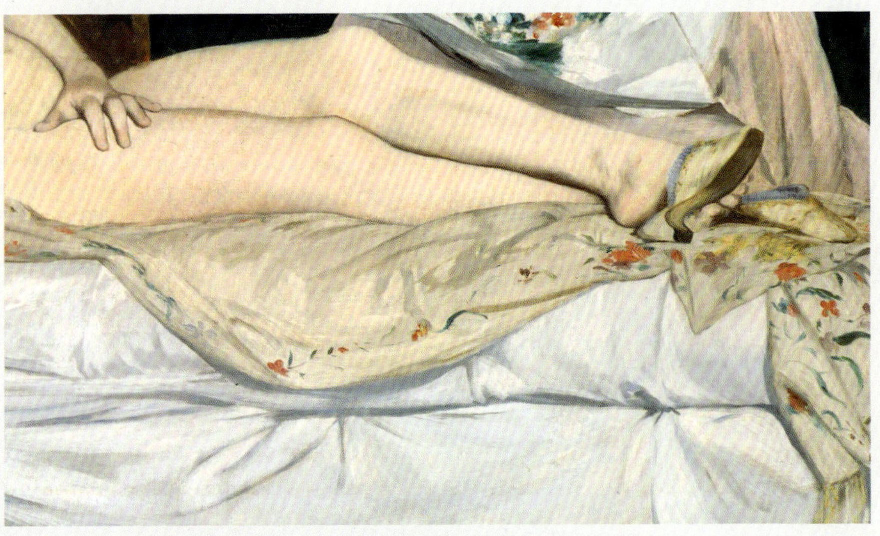

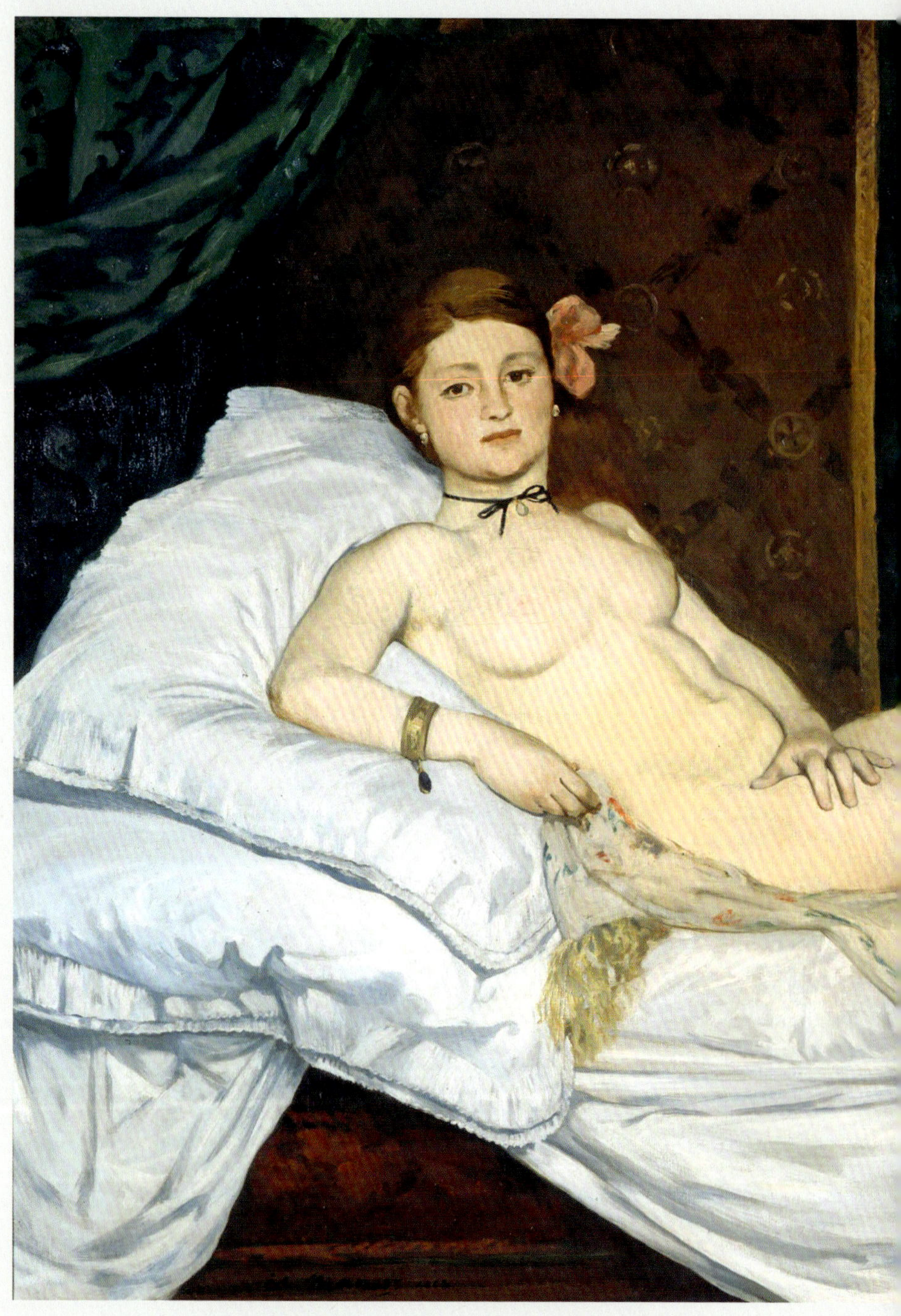

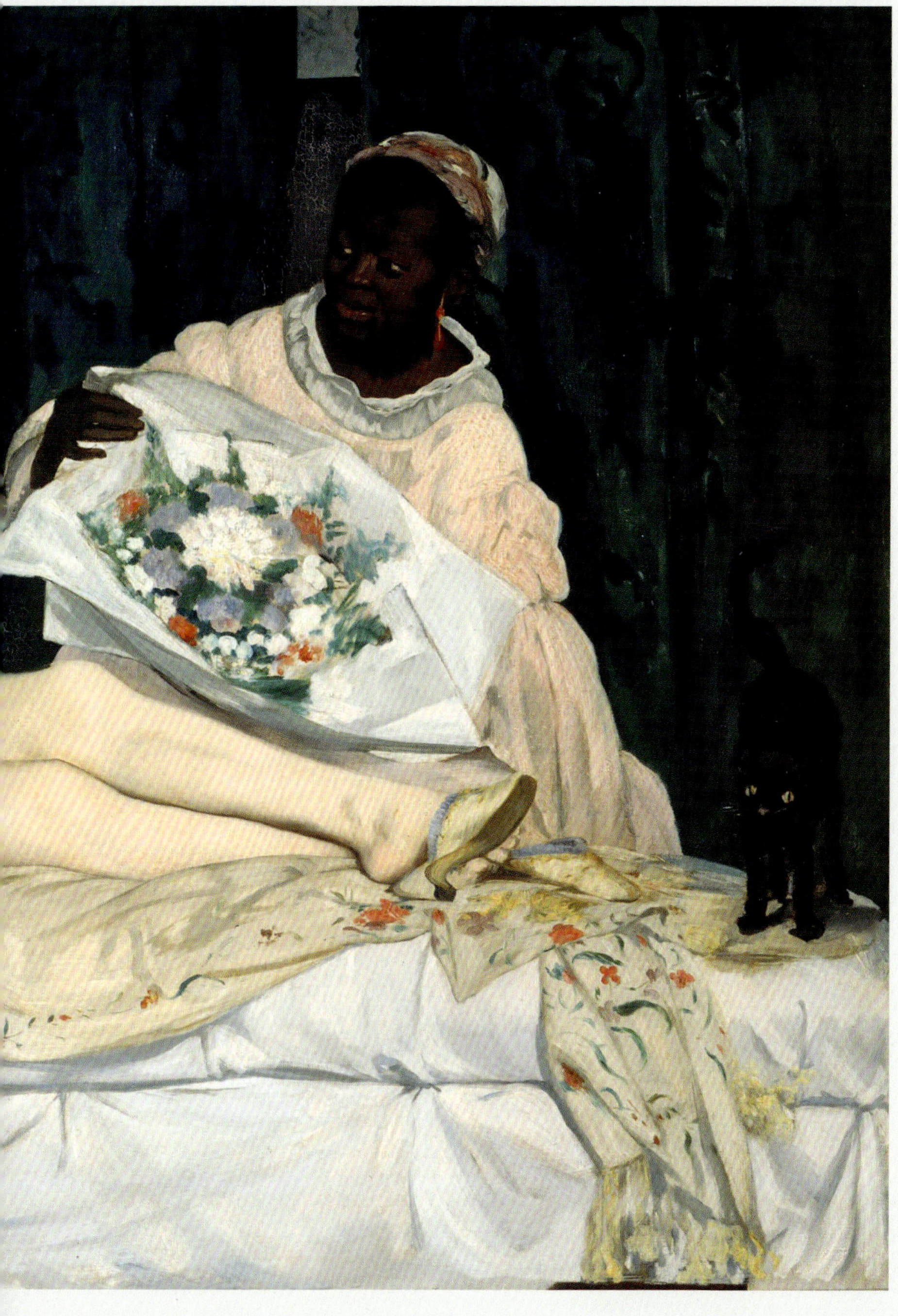

Symphony in Flesh Colour and Pink: Portrait of Mrs. Frances Leyland

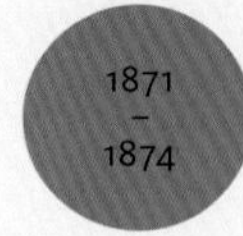

JAMES ABBOTT MCNEILL WHISTLER • OIL ON CANVAS • 6 FT. 5 IN. × 3 FT. 4 IN. (195.9 × 102.2 CM) • THE FRICK COLLECTION, NEW YORK, NY

JAMES ABBOTT MCNEILL WHISTLER (1834–1903)
Born in the United States, Whistler lived and worked primarily between London and Paris. Moving in pre-Raphaelite and then symbolist circles, he produced literary paintings influenced by Renaissance and Japanese art. Color, a poetic path to harmony, is central to his work and takes precedence over motif. Using a synesthetic approach, he often associated color with a musical vocabulary ("symphony," "arrangement," "nocturne," etc.). To intensify the effects of color, he prepared his canvases with a light, yellow or white primer and stretched them on large gilded frames that he designed himself.

Whistler liked to provide color indications in the titles of his paintings. Employing musical terminology, he creates here a "symphony" of thrumming pink and creamy tones.

In the fall of 1871, one of the artist's primary patrons, the shipowner Frederick R. Leyland, commissioned a portrait of his wife, Frances Dawson Leyland (1834–1910). Whistler chose an unusual composition, with the woman seen from the back in a nearly three-quarter pose. In this way, her diaphanous dress becomes the main subject of the work. The viewer's gaze is only later drawn to the model's face, depicted in profile, following High Renaissance tradition.

The dress, a unique cross between a kimono and a medieval tunic, was designed by Whistler himself. The embroidered reddish-brown flowers resemble the color of the woman's hair, arranged in a thick bun, and echo the flowering cherry branch to the left, another nod to Japanese culture. The format of the painting is similar to the kakemono: a Japanese painted silk or paper wall scroll. The use of pink and beige monochrome balances and accentuates the rich red hair. Even the painter's emblematic signature—a butterfly with outstretched wings (mid-right)—is rendered in these colors.

Other important works
Arrangement in Grey and Black No. 1 (Portait of the Artist's Mother), 1871. Musée d'Orsay, Paris.
Nocturne: Blue and Gold—Old Battersea Bridge, 1872–75. Tate, London.
Harmony in Blue and Silver: Trouville, 1865. Isabella Stewart Gardner Museum, Boston, MA.

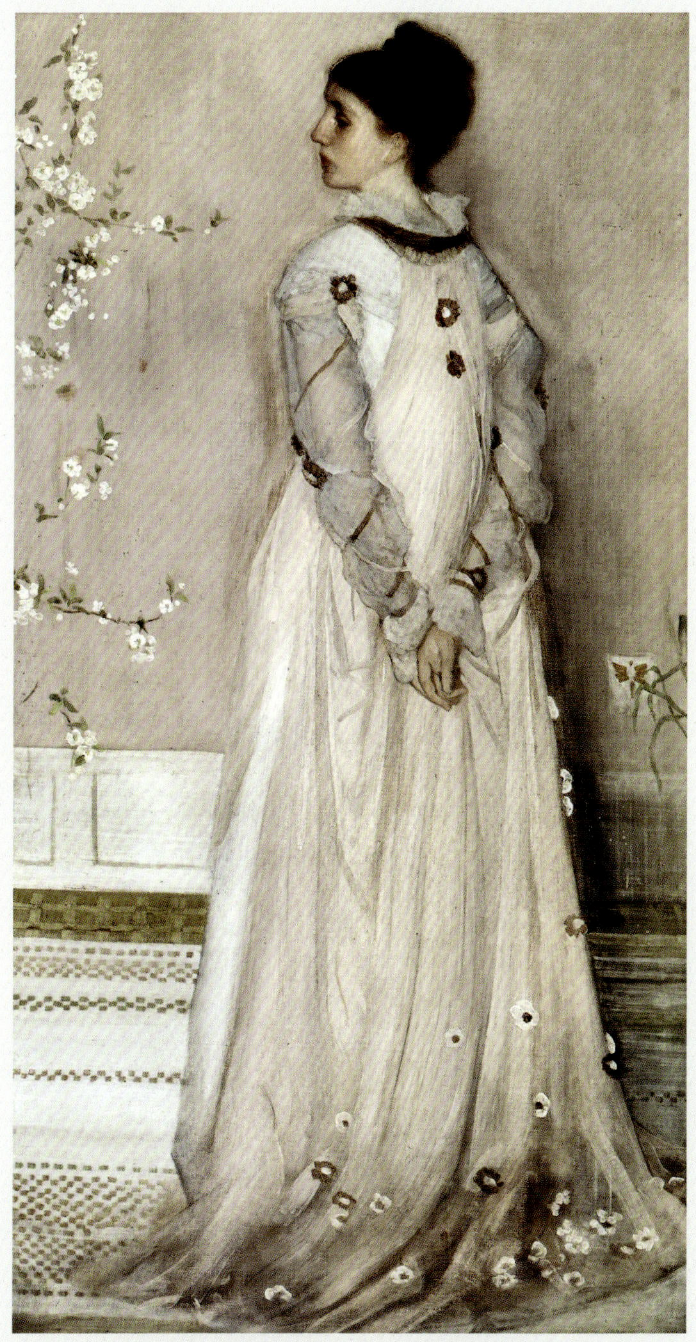

PRIMER, UNDERCOAT, AND VARNISH **p. 206**

Hopi Kachina Figure: Angwusnasomtaka

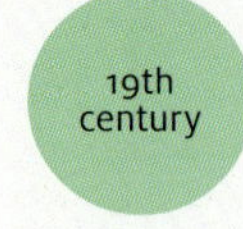

HOPI PUEBLO • PAINTED WOOD, COTTON STRING • 6¼ × 2 × 1¾ IN. (16 × 5.3 × 4.7 CM) • MUSÉE DU QUAI BRANLY-JACQUES CHIRAC, PARIS

The Hopi people, who settled in the region between Arizona, Utah, Colorado, and New Mexico, use the word *kachina* to describe spiritual messengers who appear in daily life, and for ceremonies and rituals. They act as moral guides and intercessors with the past and the gods, and can bring the rain. During ceremonies, Hopi dancers wearing costumes and masks embody these messengers.

There are 250 different kinds of small statues known as kachina dolls—more accurately termed *tithu* statuettes— which represent these messengers and are often used to educate children about spiritual traditions. Each type has a name and is painted with specific colors. Older *tithu* are often more geometric in form than pieces produced after the first decades of the twentieth century.

The colors used by the Hopi people, in this case mineral or plant-based pigments, are associated with the cardinal directions and can be used to identify provenance, function, and the group of kachina to which the figure belongs: in this example, black is used to represent the nadir or underworld (the direction opposite the zenith or heaven and oriented toward the center of the Earth), red for south (or south-west), and white for north (or north-east). Blue and green may also be used to represent west (or south-west), yellow for north (or north-west), and all the colors together for the nadir.

This kachina figure dates from before 1885. The schematic form (a flat body and minimal features) is typical of older pieces. Intended as an educational aid for children, the kachina doll represents Angwusnasomtaka, "Crow Mother," the mother of all kachinas, who is recognizable by the black geometric forms depicting her face and her hands placed in front of her. She appears in February, during the Powamu ceremony (or bean-planting festival) to initiate young boys into tribal rituals.

BLACK **p. 44** WHITE **p. 45** RED **p. 46** YELLOW **p. 47** BLUE **p. 48** GREEN **p. 49**

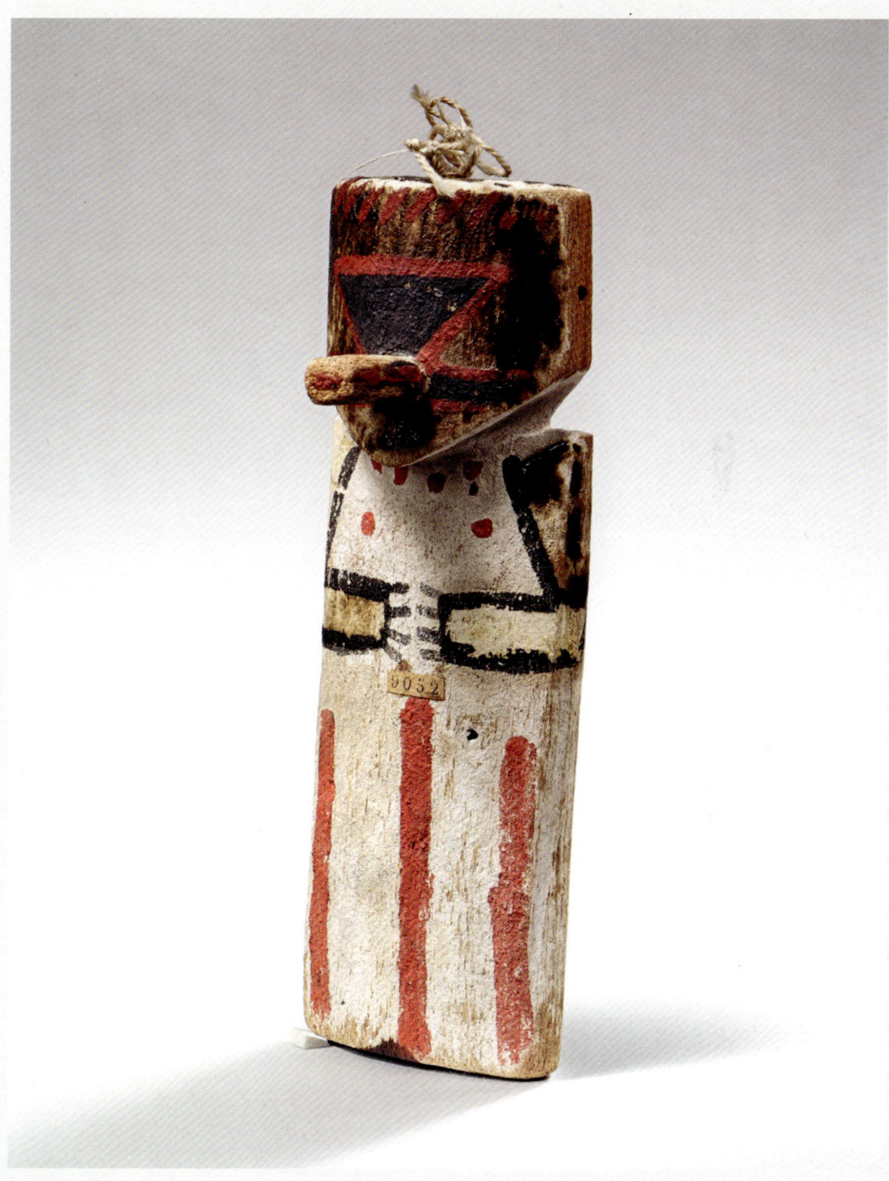

NATURAL AND SYNTHETIC PIGMENTS **p. 190**

Impression, Sunrise

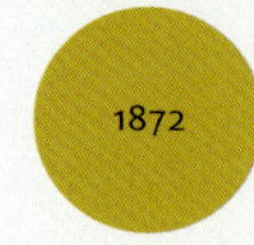

CLAUDE MONET • OIL ON CANVAS • 19 × 24¾ IN. (48 × 63 CM) •
MUSÉE MARMOTTAN MONET, PARIS

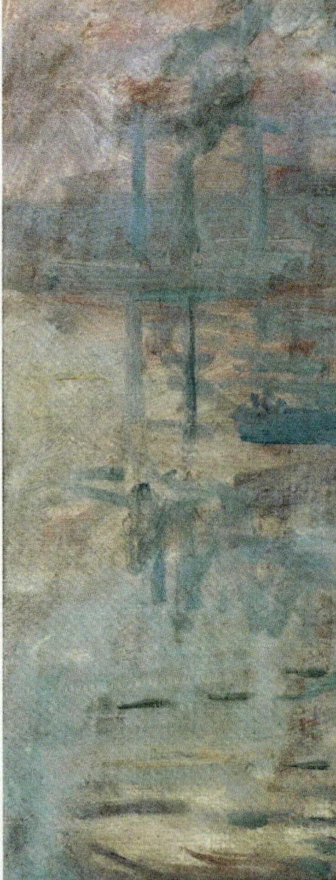

Claude Monet painted *Impression, Sunrise* in 1872. At the
first exhibition of the Société Anonyme des Artistes
Peintres, Sculpteurs et Graveurs, the title inspired one
derisive journalist, Louis Leroy, to coin the term
"impressionist" in an article published in *Le Charivari* on
April 25, 1847: "Impression—I was certain of it. I was just
telling myself that, since I was impressed, there had to be
some impression in it . . . and what freedom, what ease of
workmanship! Wallpaper in its embryonic state is more
finished than that seascape." Paradoxically, the word
stuck as a label for one of the most innovative movements
in modern art, which would go on to become one of the
most popular styles with the general public.

The painting depicts a small boat at dawn in the old
outer harbor of Le Havre; in the background, ships'
masts, port cranes, and smoking chimneys are barely
visible through the enveloping fog. Monet's
contemporaries were perplexed by the work's unusual
style. Using loose brushstrokes, the painter employed a
bold new color palette to express, in painting, a fleeting
sunrise. The sky illuminated by the reflections of the
orange sun, and the way the colors of the atmosphere and
the mauve sea peppered with green blend together,
prophesied the wealth of color experiments that the
impressionists would undertake in the 1870s and 1880s.
Despite his innovation, Monet also drew inspiration from
certain historical works, including Turner's extraordinary
hazy and colorful seascapes, painted around 1830.

Other important works
Poppy Field, 1873. Musée d'Orsay, Paris.
Bridge over a Pond of Water Lilies, 1899. The Metropolitan Museum of Art, New York, NY.
The Houses of Parliament, Sunset, 1903. National Gallery, London.

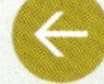

CLAUDE MONET (1840–1926)
Considered the leader of the impressionists, Monet was one of the first artists to give precedence to his subjective vision by privileging the effects of light and color, enhanced by his energetic painting style. Monet favored plein air painting, which gave him many opportunities to translate the seasonal and atmospheric variations of light into unmixed colors squeezed straight from the tube.

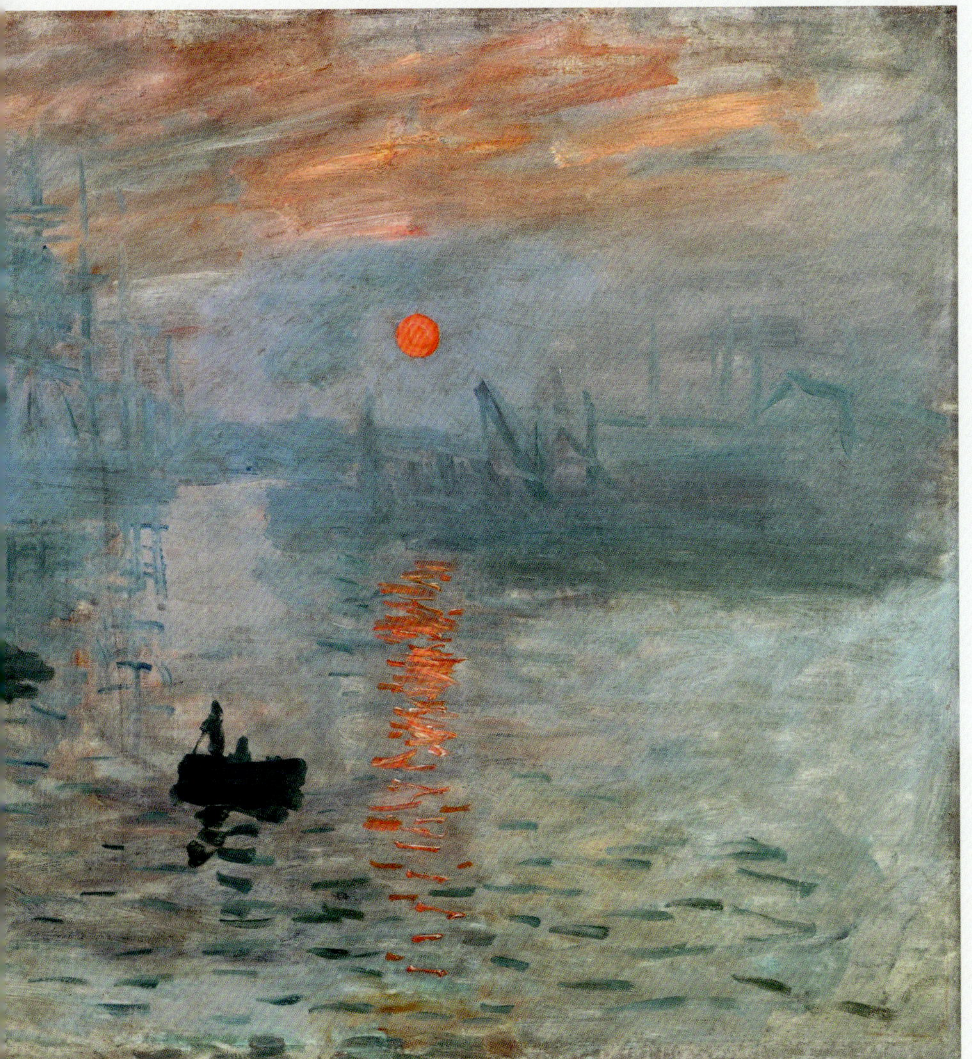

PAINT IN TUBES **p. 204**

Field with Irises Near Arles

VINCENT VAN GOGH • OIL ON CANVAS • 21¼ × 25½ IN. (54 × 65 CM) •
VAN GOGH MUSEUM, AMSTERDAM

1888

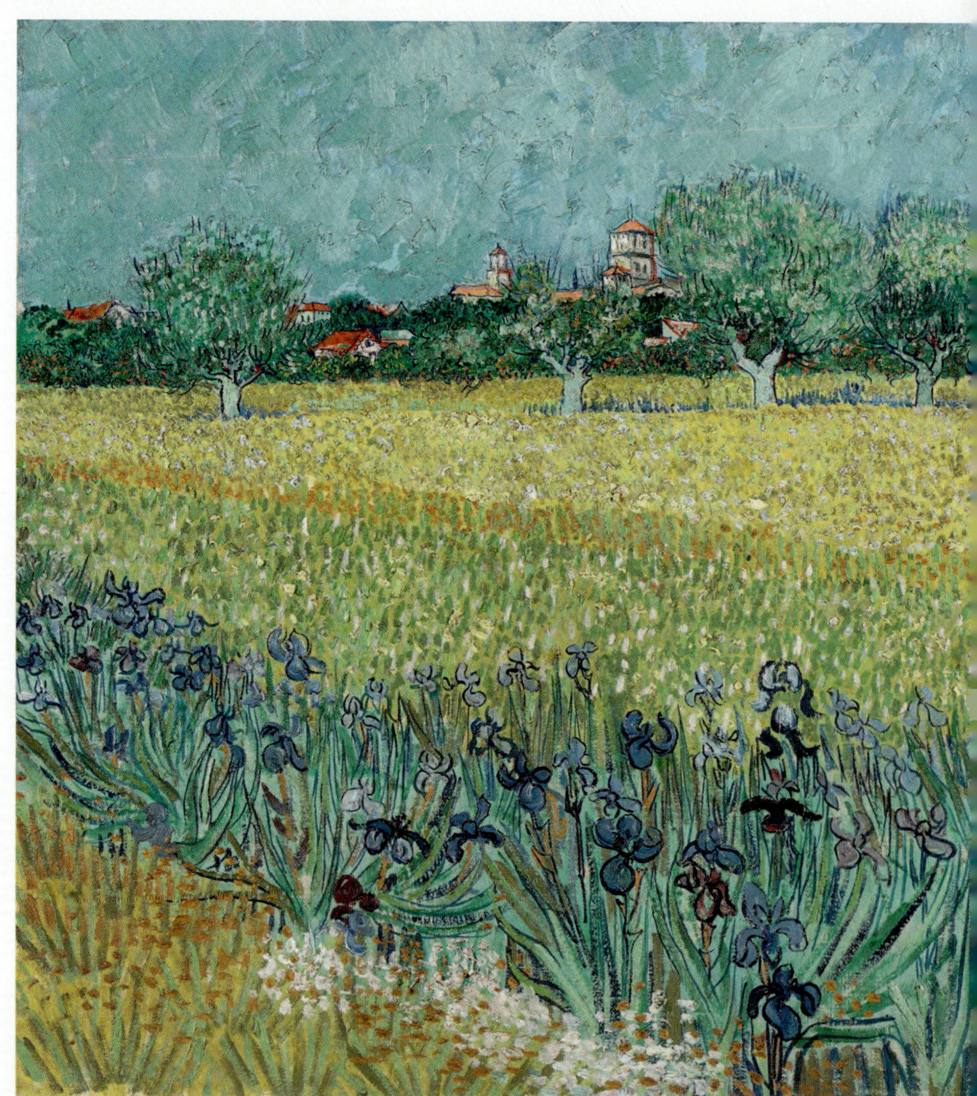

VINCENT VAN GOGH (1853–1890)

Van Gogh began painting at the age of twenty-seven. Initially influenced by the Dutch realist tradition, he adopted color after discovering the works of Peter Paul Rubens and Japanese woodcuts. Through Camille Pissarro and Paul Signac, he became acquainted with new theories about color and light. From then on, his vivid and often contrasting palette took on a new symbolic value that, combined with sinuous brushstrokes, foreshadowed expressionism.

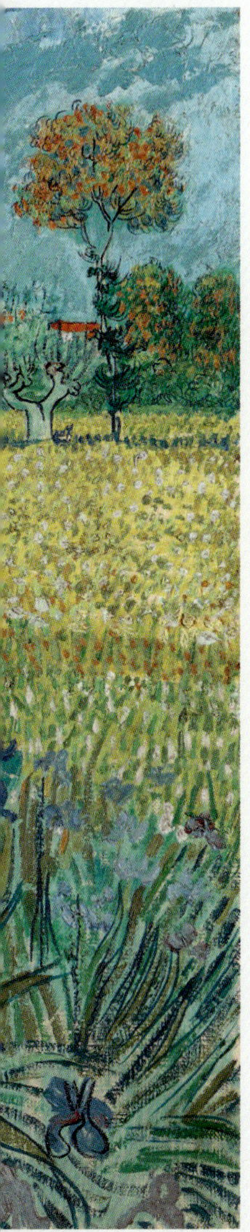

When he settled in Arles in February 1888, Van Gogh was exhilarated by the southern light, which he associated, surprisingly, with Japan. An enthusiastic collector of Japanese prints, Van Gogh appreciated the art form for its strong palette, flat fields of color, and asymmetrical compositions. The artist explicitly mentions this unexpected merging of Provence and Japan in a letter to the painter Émile Bernard dated March 18, 1888, written soon after Van Gogh arrived in the region: "This part of the world seems to me as beautiful as Japan for the clearness of the atmosphere and the gay color effects. The stretches of water make patches of a beautiful emerald and a rich blue in the landscapes, as we see it in the Japanese prints. Pale orange sunsets making the fields look blue—glorious yellow suns."

In the spring, Van Gogh painted in the countryside around this field bordered by purple irises. The dazzling palette is dominated by greens and yellows enhanced with blue and violet, as well as a few touches of orange-red—colors that appear in many of Van Gogh's paintings from this period. The rhythm of his brushstrokes, which is ample in the sky, becomes lively and tight in the landscape, and sinuous, with darkly outlined forms, in the flowers. The energy of the composition is intensified by strong diagonals. In this painting, Van Gogh applied features of Japanese prints, such as large colored areas, diagonal lines, and details in the foreground.

Other important works
The Starry Night, 1889. Museum of Modern Art, New York, NY.
The Bedroom, 1888. Van Gogh Museum, Amsterdam.
Wheatfield with Crows, 1890. Van Gogh Museum, Amsterdam.

COLOR PRINTMAKING **p. 208**

The Circus

GEORGES SEURAT • OIL ON CANVAS • 6 FT. 1 IN. × 5 FT. (186 × 152 CM) •
MUSÉE D'ORSAY, PARIS

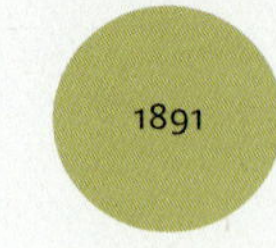

The Circus is the third and final painting in a small series that Georges Seurat dedicated to modern entertainments (*Circus Sideshow*, 1888, The Metropolitan Museum of Art, New York; and *Le Chahut*, 1889–90, Kröller-Müller Museum, Otterlo). It depicts the climax of the show—an act by the trick rider Fernando. The composition's unusual framing, inspired by the Japanese prints that were so popular with artists at the time, structures the work into two distinct spaces: the arena, which is full of movement, and the stands, which are straight, rigid, and unmoving.

Here, Seurat applied his method of pointillism, which grew out of his scientific readings. Following the laws of optical mixing, he applied color in a multitude of small dots that seem to vibrate in the viewer's eye. The palette is made up of white (the color of pure light according to the physicist Isaac Newton) and the three primary colors—yellow, red, and blue. Seurat associated this scientific approach to color with a psychological interpretation of the lines that structure the canvas (ascending lines and arabesques, synonymous with joy and enthusiasm), which reinforce the impression of vitality, energy, or even instability at the center of the painting. The forms themselves are very stylized. Finally, he painted a border—in addition to adding a flat wood frame—around the edge of the canvas using countless dark blue dabs that enhance the colors in the painting itself.

PRIMARY AND COMPLEMENTARY COLORS **p. 27** ART AND SCIENCE **p. 28**
POINTILLISM AND OPTICAL MIXTURES **p. 33** WHITE **p. 45** RED **p. 46** YELLOW **p. 47** BLUE **p. 48**

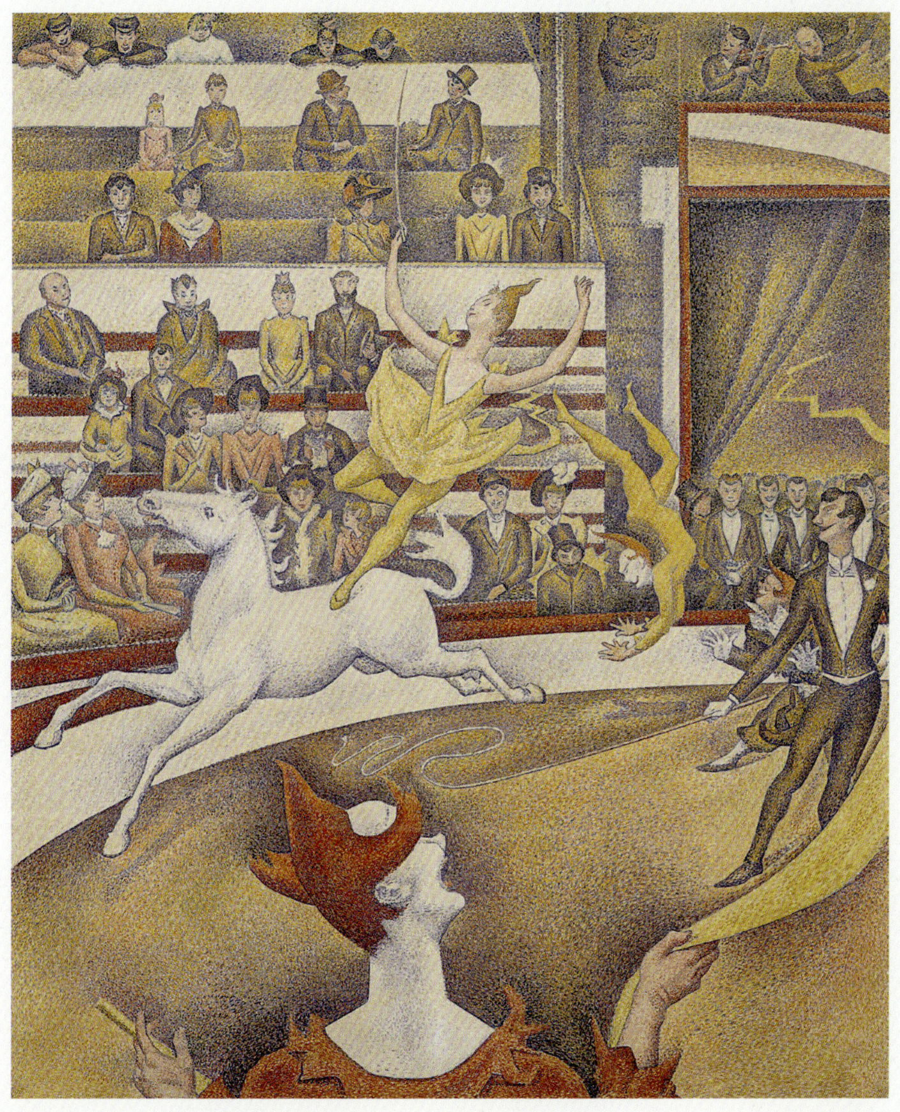

GEORGES SEURAT (1859–1891)
As an adolescent, Georges Seurat read books by art historians and scientists (Charles Blanc, Michel Eugène Chevreul, Ogden Rood, and Charles Henry) on color contrasts and how they are perceived. These texts enabled him to develop what was both a method and a style: pointillism, also called divisionism. Contrary to the more intuitive impressionists, he took a rigorous approach, painting tight dots of unmixed color that interact with each other to blend in the eye of the viewer.

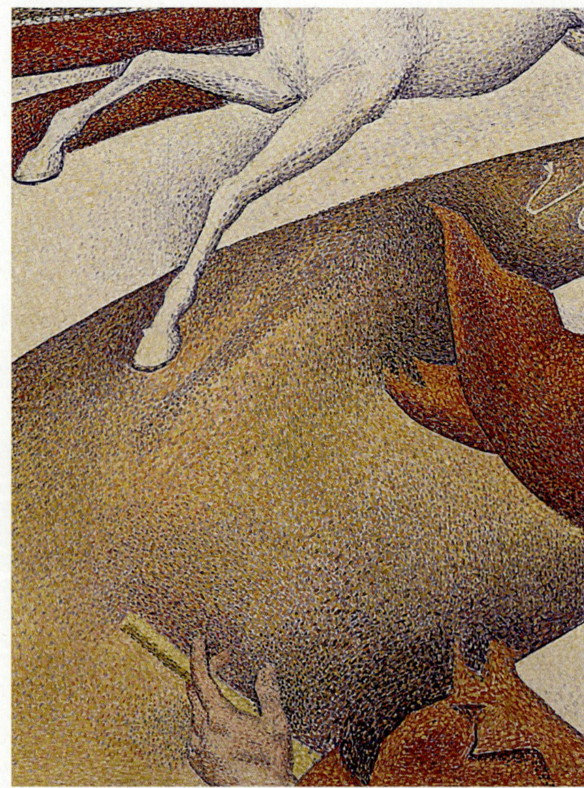

The painter placed colors directly on the canvas in tight groupings of dots, creating a stronger contrast and bringing light into the painting.

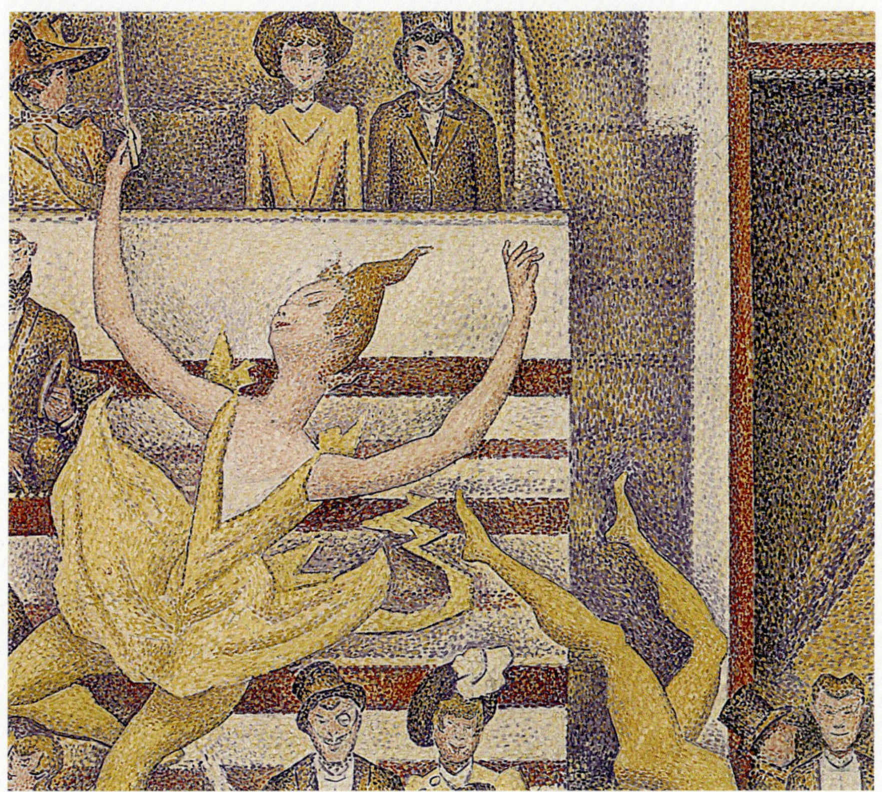

The curved movements in the
foreground, in the circus ring, contrast
with the rectilinear background.

Other important works
Bathers at Asnières, 1884. National Gallery, London.
A Sunday on La Grande Jatte, 1884–86. The Art Institute of Chicago, Chicago, IL.
Eiffel Tower, 1889. Fine Arts Museums of San Francisco, San Francisco, CA.

Sunbeams or Sunlight.
Dust Motes Dancing
in Sunbeams

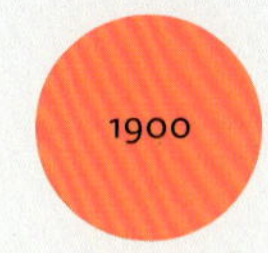

VILHELM HAMMERSHØI • OIL ON CANVAS • 29½ × 23 IN. (70 × 59 CM) •
ORDRUPGAARD MUSEUM, COPENHAGEN

**VILHELM HAMMERSHØI
(1864–1916)**
Hammershøi is considered one of the most important Danish painters of the late nineteenth century. Four themes dominate his work: figures, often nudes; landscapes; architecture; and interiors, for which he is most well known today. He developed a contemplative and austere style of painting using exceptionally muted tones, and a preference for the neutrality of gray, which imparts an air of tension and mystery.

Between 1898 and 1909, Vilhelm Hammershøi lived with his wife in an apartment at 30 Strandgade in Copenhagen. In many of his paintings, he depicts their quiet home, in which a figure sometimes appears seated or viewed from behind. Simple depictions of the domestic realm quickly became a central theme in his work.

To represent this peaceful atmosphere, Hammershøi chose a monochromatic palette of gray, ocher, and brown—one of his favorites—applied in subtle shades that soften the space, structured by a series of vertical and horizontal lines. The principal character of the painting is the sunlight streaming in through the window. Ordinarily, Hammershøi liked to create enclosed interior spaces, but here he depicts the exterior: the roof and facade of the neighboring house are visible. The light creates bright reflections on the casement and on the flooring which produce diagonal lines. These areas, rendered in a radiant pale yellow, seem to open up the room. But the dust in the air also gives the beams of sunlight a strong and geometric materiality. The painting is absent of anecdote or iconographic narrative. To the contrary: it celebrates a form of simple mysticism, a spirituality deeply anchored in daily life.

Other important works
Interior of Courtyard, Strandgade 30, 1899. Toledo Museum of Art, Toledo.
Interior with a Reading Lady, 1900. Nationalmuseum, Stockholm.
Self-Portrait at Spurveskjul, 1911. The Metropolitan Museum of Art, New York, NY.

WHITE **p. 45** BROWN **p. 52** GRAY **p. 54**

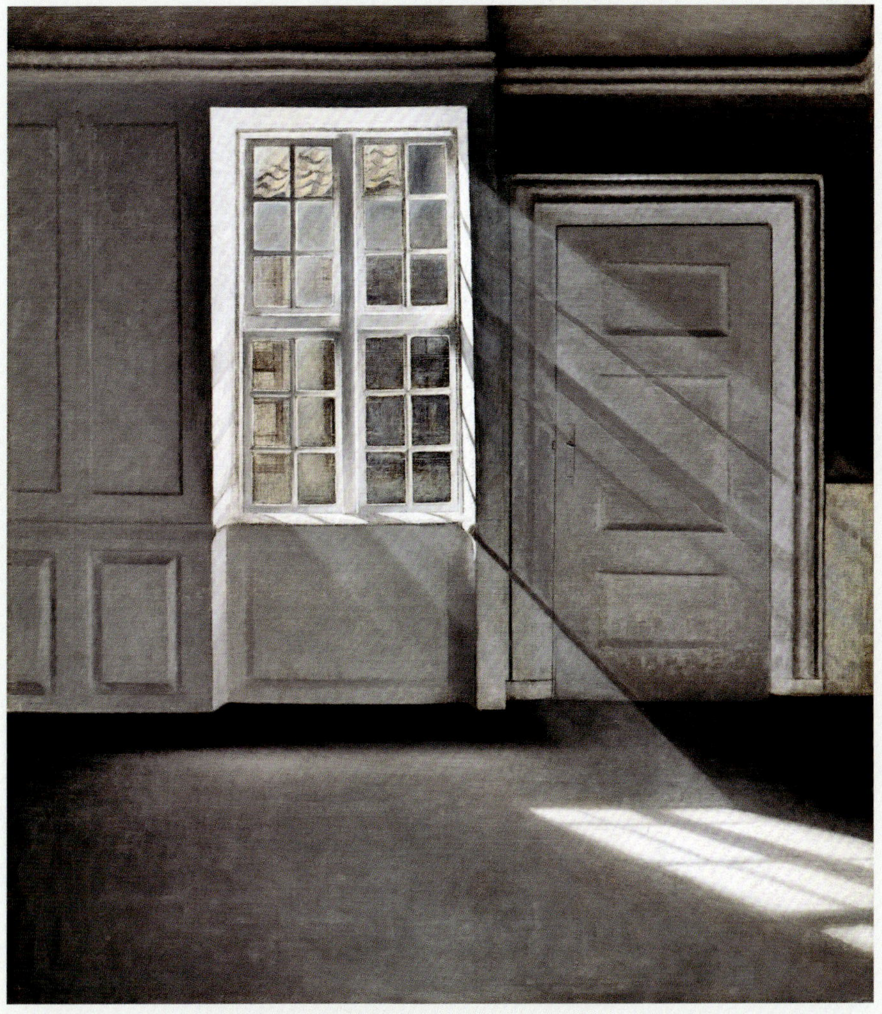

Mukudj Mask

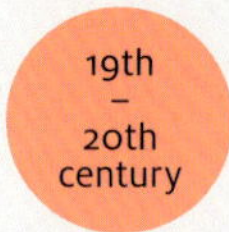

WOOD, PIGMENT, KAOLIN • 13½ × 7½ IN. (34.3 × 19.1 CM) •
THE METROPOLITAN MUSEUM OF ART, NEW YORK, NY

Other important works
Punu mask, early 20th century.
Musée du Quai Branly-Jacques
Chirac, Paris.
Okuyi mask, date unknown. Museu
Oscar Niemeyer, Curitiba (Brazil).
Punu mask, 20th century.
Nationaal Museum van
Wereldculturen, Amsterdam.

Sculptors of Punu masks are
exclusively men, and although they
remain anonymous, they are
considered by the community to be
exceptional craftsmen. The whitened
faces of these masks captivated
Westerners from the late nineteenth
century onward and fueled a quest for
authenticity pursued by many modern
artists like Pablo Picasso, who
acquired a mask in 1910.

Anthropomorphic masks such as this one—sculpted in Ricinodendron, a light wood, whitened with kaolin, decorated with scarification motifs on the forehead and temples, and defined by a bi-lobed coiffure—are common among communities in Gabon and the Democratic Republic of Congo.

Kaolin, called *pembi* in the Punu language, is a ritual paint used to embellish masks or statues, as well as the faces of initiates and officiants during large collective ceremonies such as births, funerals, wakes, and initiations. Historically this white color was obtained by mixing white clay and the ashes of human bones, explain Louis Perrois and Charlotte Grand-Dufay in *Punu* (2008). In Punu tradition, the color is associated with the realm of spirits and ancestors, with the sources of life. In some ritual circumstances, the white mask is painted brown or black and displayed at dusk as a keeper of the peace or upholder of law.

These masks are generally considered female (they take on male attributes when painted black/brown). The almond eyes and high cheekbones, the prominent and often painted mouth common to this typology, are those of the "woman ancestor." They are worn for traditional, acrobatic dances, primarily the *okuyi* dance, performed on high stilts during communal ceremonies. Pragmatically speaking, the masks hide the identity of the dancers who, as *okuyi*, cannot be mortal. From a spiritual perspective, they link the worlds of the living and the dead, and attract magical powers.

BLACK **p. 44** WHITE **p. 45**

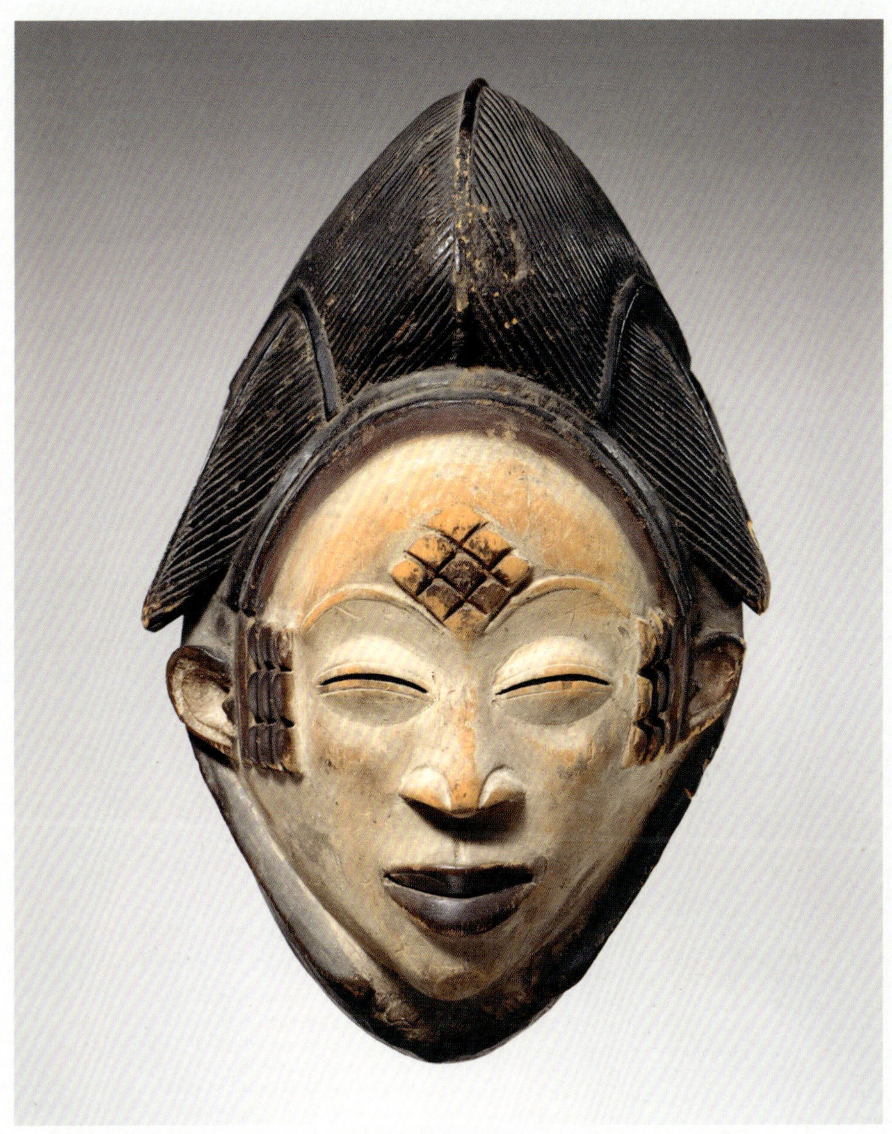

WHITE PIGMENTS **p. 191** BLACK AND BROWN PIGMENTS **p. 196**

La Vie

PABLO PICASSO • OIL ON CANVAS • 6 FT. 5½ IN. × 4 FT. 3 IN.
(196.5 × 129.2 CM) • CLEVELAND MUSEUM OF ART, CLEVELAND, OH

1903

**PABLO PICASSO
(1881–1973)**
An emblematic figure of modern art, Picasso left behind a vast, rich body of work. He painted *La Vie* during his "blue period" (1901–4), early in his career, when he was affirming himself as an artist. This was followed by the "pink period" (1904–6), when Picasso's palette grew warmer, but less monochrome—pink appeared alongside blue, red, orange, green, and mauve. His iconography also changed, shifting to the world of the circus and the cabaret.

Other important works
The Blue Room, 1901. The Phillips Collection, Washington, DC.
Self-Portrait, 1901. Musée National Picasso-Paris, Paris.
Acrobat and Young Harlequin, 1905. Fondation Beyeler, Riehen (Switzerland).

In 1901, Picasso's roommate and friend, the painter Carlos Casagemas (1880–1901), committed suicide in a Parisian café, sending the young artist into depression. The experience prompted what is now one of Picasso's most famous cycles. Known as the "blue period," it is characterized by the nearly monochrome palette the artist used until 1904. According to Picasso, blue symbolized melancholy and death, as well as night and mystery. He used it in paintings suffused with misery and alienation—he himself lived at the time in great poverty in Montmartre.

In May 1903, Picasso painted *La Vie*, an allegory of life from childhood to death that he worked on for many long months and which would prompt many interpretations. The young man has the features of Casagemas, and the young woman he embraces is probably Germaine Pichot (1880–1948), with whom he was obsessively in love. On the right, a woman stands holding a baby, inspired by sketches Picasso made at the Saint-Lazare prison—where women were imprisoned for prostitution—of hieratic figures in large tunics. Hunching figures occupy the center of the painting.

In a preparatory sketch, Picasso depicted a studio scene with the pair of models on the left, a bearded painter on the right, and an easel between them. These differences in iconography demonstrate the shift from visual anecdote to allegory. The composition is rendered in a blue monochrome palette that cloaks the entire painting in a deeply melancholy hue.

CONTRASTS **p. 25** BLUE **p. 48**

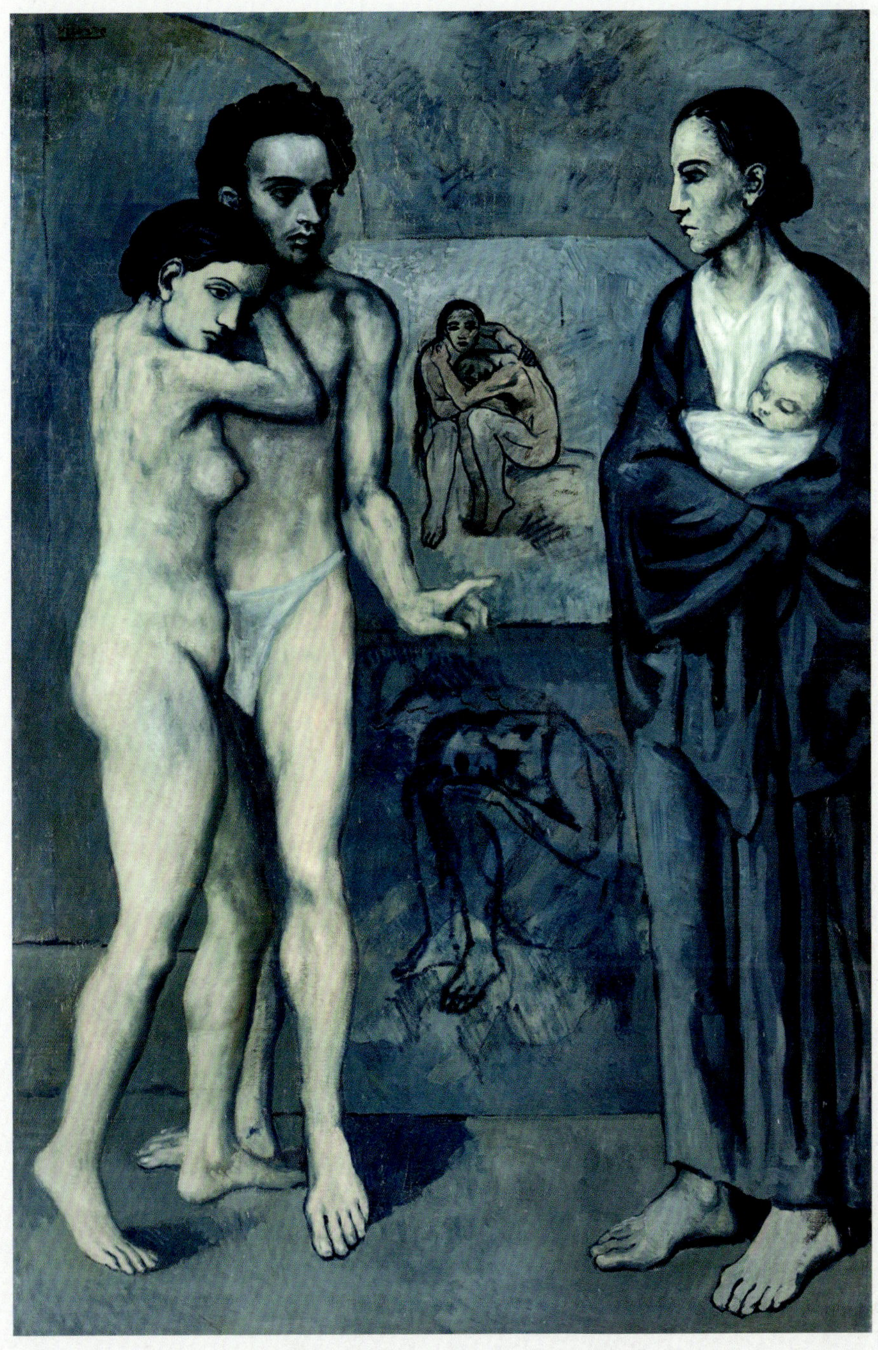

Portrait of Adele Bloch-Bauer I

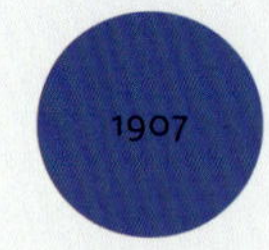

GUSTAV KLIMT • OIL, GOLD, AND SILVER ON CANVAS • 4 FT. 6½ IN. × 4 FT. 6½ IN. (138 × 138 CM) • NEUE GALERIE, NEW YORK, NY

GUSTAV KLIMT (1862–1918)
Klimt is the most well-known figure in the Vienna Secession, the first modern painting movement in Austria. In his portraits and allegories, Klimt's decorative sense, which broke down the boundaries between major and minor arts, baffled his contemporaries. He boldly combined the erotic and the uncanny, and made reference to Byzantine and Egyptian art. He also painted landscapes, which he often framed in innovative ways.

Other important works
The Three Ages of Woman, 1905. Galleria Nazionale d'Arte Moderna e Contemporanea, Rome.
The Kiss, 1908. Belvedere Palace, Vienna.
Death and Life, 1908–15. Leopold Museum, Vienna.

In 1903, the Viennese industrialist and collector Ferdinand Bloch-Bauer commissioned a portrait of his wife, Adele (1881–1925). The same year, Klimt discovered the Basilica of San Vitale in Ravenna, Italy, known for its splendid gilded mosaics—a revelation that would have a lasting influence on his work.

After meticulous preparation, Klimt combined different techniques to paint a portrait of his model. Her hair and face, décolletage, forearms, and hands are rendered sensually and naturalistically in dark and pale shades of oil paint; more intense pink is used to highlight her cheeks and mouth. The gown and cloak, and the armchair she appears to be leaning on, as well as the rest of the space are primarily executed in gold or silver leaf, with dabs of red and indigo paint, and form a sweeping backdrop for the figure. A web of motifs—eyes, triangles, arabesques, circles, and chevrons—rendered in low relief using an impasto technique adorn the surface of the work.

Gold dominates the composition, giving the portrait a quality of preciousness and immortality, while the reflective qualities of metal create a literally dazzling effigy. Symbolic of warmth and joy, the metal channels these virtues to the beautiful Adele Bloch-Bauer. The model seems to emerge from a dream in a hallucinatory union of reality and imagination.

This work, emblematic of Klimt's "golden phase," was seized by the Nazis after the Anschluss and was not returned to Ferdinand and Adele Bloch-Bauer's heirs until 2006.

GOLD **p. 56** SILVER **p. 57**

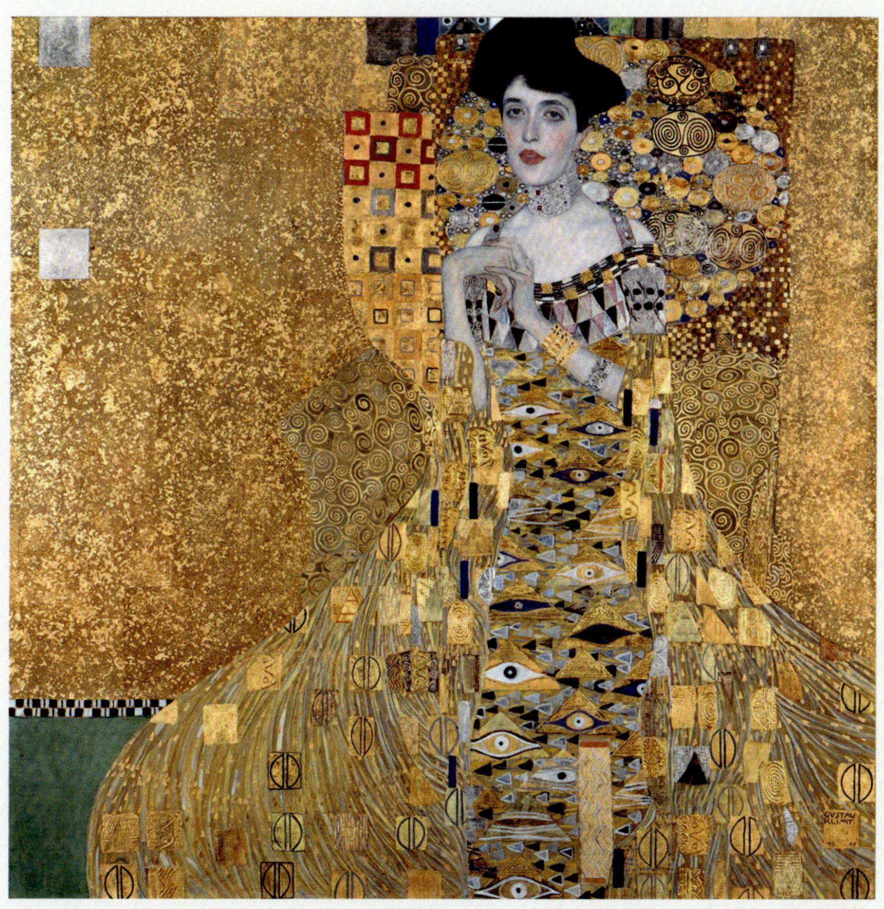

BLUE PIGMENTS **p. 194** WORKING WITH GOLD **p. 199** OIL PAINT **p. 203**

Street Light

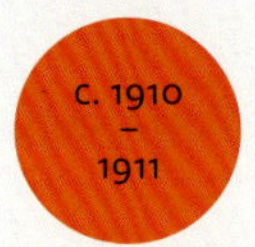

GIACOMO BALLA • OIL ON CANVAS • 5 FT. 9 IN. × 3 FT. 9 IN.
(174.7 × 114.7 CM) • MUSEUM OF MODERN ART, NEW YORK, NY

Other important works
Dynamism of a Dog on a Leash, 1912. Albright-Knox Art Gallery, Buffalo, NY.
The Hand of the Violinist, 1912. Estorick Collection of Modern Italian Art, London.
Girl Running on a Balcony, 1912. Museo del Novecento, Milan.

In *Street Light*, Giacomo Balla depicts a mundane subject: an electric lamppost recently installed outside the Termini train station in Rome. A symbol of technological progress, the street lamp produces an intense white light that eclipses the weak glow of the crescent moon depicted on the right. In a letter dated 1954 to the curators at the Museum of Modern Art in New York, the artist wrote that his painting "demonstrated how romantic moonlight had been surpassed by the light of the modern electric street light. This was the end of Romanticism in art. From my picture came the phrase (beloved by the Futurists): 'We shall kill the light of the moon.'"

The light spreading outward in a multitude of brushstrokes—yellow, white, green, red, mauve, and blue—shaped like arrowheads or beams of light and inspired by Georges Seurat's and Paul Signac's pointillism, conveys the urgency of modern life. The halo is abruptly interrupted, giving way to the darkness rendered in intertwining curls of black, midnight blue, and dark green. The colors radiating outward from light to dark values could almost be seen as a proposal for a new color wheel. Balla contrasts the moon, which the futurists associated with historical Rome and art of the past, with electricity, the new city, and the avant-garde.

GIACOMO BALLA (1871–1958)
Balla was a founding member of Italian futurism, along with Umberto Boccioni (1882–1916), Carlo Carrà (1881–1966), Luigi Russolo (1885–1947), and Gino Severini (1883–1966). After using optical mixtures to divide hues into small dabs of pure color, he turned his attention to space and deconstructing movement. In the 1920s, he developed ties with the Fascist party before becoming one of its official artists.

CONTRASTS **p. 25** POINTILLISM AND OPTICAL MIXTURES **p. 33** BLACK **p. 44** WHITE **p. 45** RED **p. 46** YELLOW **p. 47** BLUE **p. 48** GREEN **p. 49** VIOLET **p. 51**

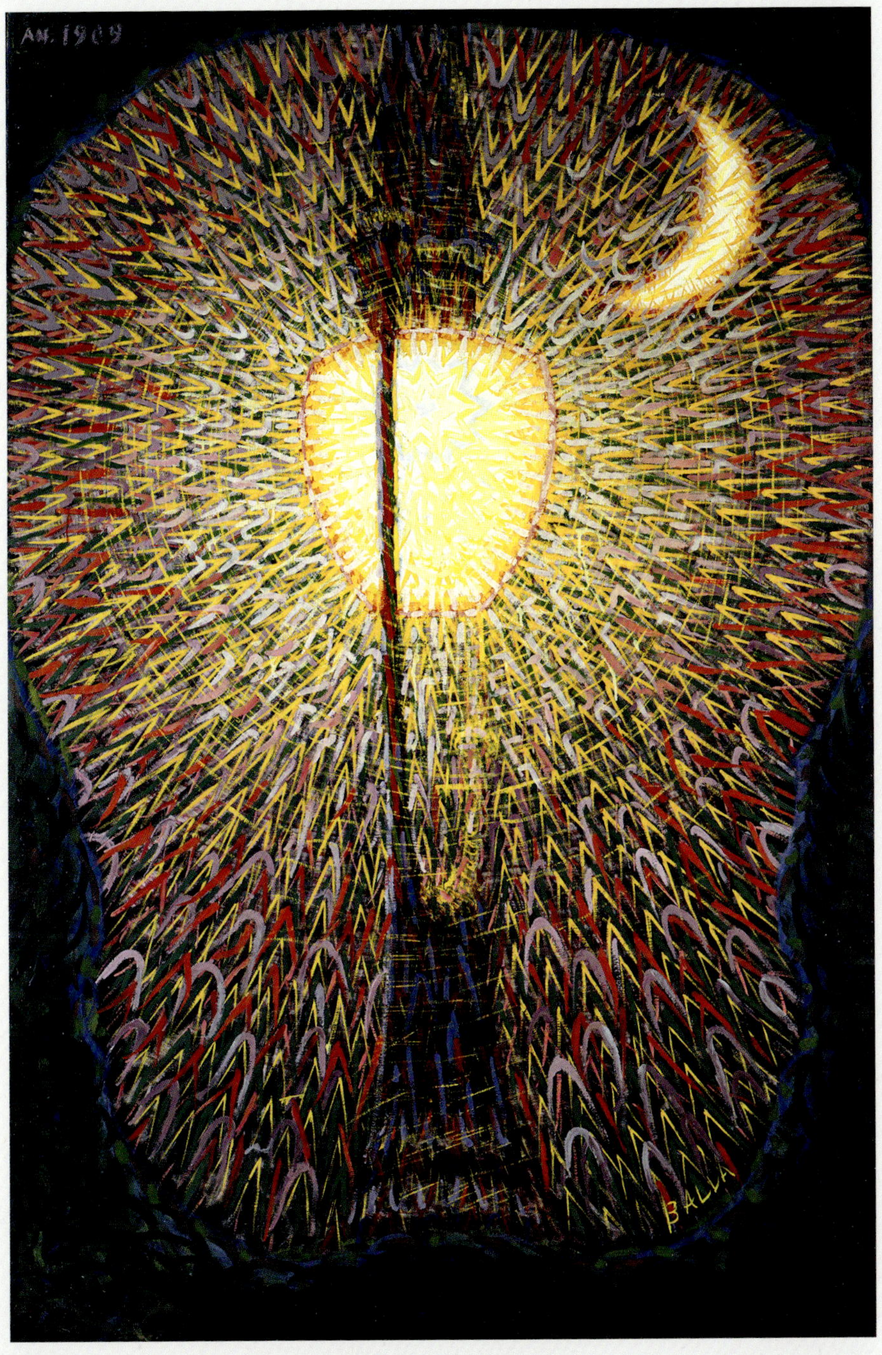

Disks of Newton (Study for "Fugue in Two Colors")

FRANTIŠEK KUPKA • OIL ON CANVAS • 3 FT. 3½ IN. × 2 FT. 5 IN. (100.3 × 73.7 CM) • PHILADELPHIA MUSEUM OF ART, PHILADELPHIA, PA

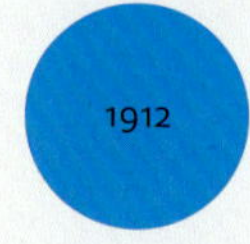

FRANTIŠEK KUPKA (1871–1957)
Kupka studied in Prague and Vienna before settling in France in 1897. An acerbic caricaturist and an observer of social rituals, he developed a growing interest in color, although he deplored what he considered the lie of realism. In 1911 he painted his first "abstract" works (a qualification he rejected), guided by an organic vitality specific to each painting, which resonated with a cosmic rhythm.

Other important works
Mme Kupka among Verticals, 1910–11. Museum of Modern Art, New York, NY.
Woman Picking Flowers, 1910–11. Centre Pompidou, Paris.
The Cathedral, 1912–13. Museum Kampa, Prague.

In 1911–12, František Kupka, considered a pioneer of abstract art, painted several works composed of large, broken rings of color that allude to Isaac Newton's discoveries about the composition of light. The British physicist had established that white light refracted in a prism is composed of a spectrum comprising six colors—violet, blue, green, yellow, orange, and red. Conforming to the era's conventions, Newton added a seventh color—indigo (a second shade of blue)—to obtain seven essential colors based on the musical scale. Kupka chose precisely these seven colors, with the addition of white, for this painting. Around 1910, the painter proposed his own version of Newton's color wheel, which consisted of nine main colors ordered clockwise from orange to yellow. This work helped him liberate color from all realist and descriptive functions.

The formal use of radiating circles gives *Disks of Newton* a vibratory quality reminiscent of a burst of light. Kupka's interest in astronomy shines through in what could be a depiction of the sun, or of the solar system and planetary movements. Finally, aware of the synesthetic relationship between painting and music, Kupka, like Newton, alluded to the seven notes of the musical scale by giving the work a music-themed subtitle: "I am still groping in the dark," he told a *New York Times* journalist in 1913. "But I believe I can find something between sight and hearing and I can produce a fugue in colors as Bach has done in music. At any rate, I will no longer be content with slavish copy."

NEWTON'S COLOR WHEEL **p. 26** THE RAINBOW **p. 59**

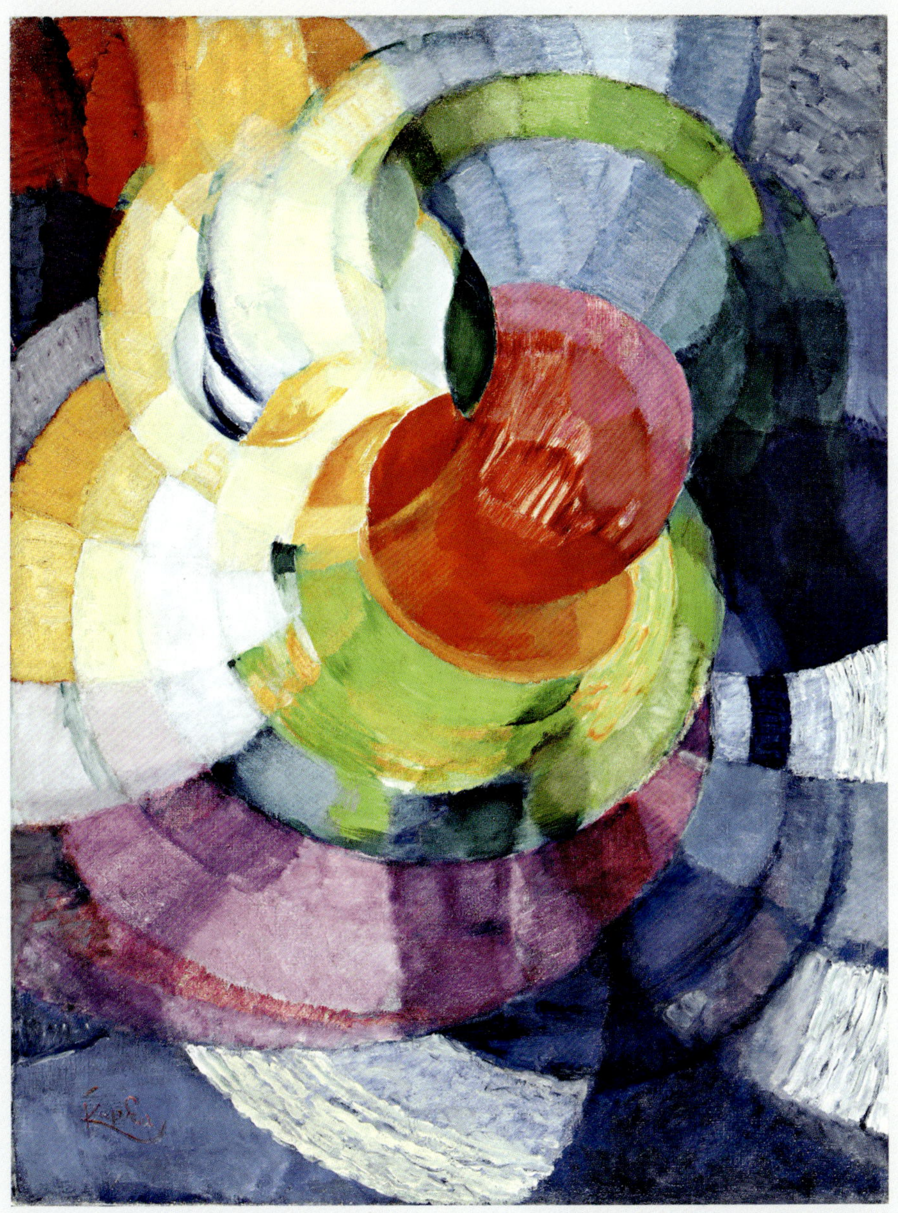

Electric Prisms

SONIA DELAUNAY • OIL ON CANVAS • 8 FT. 2½ IN. × 8 FT. 2½ IN.
(250 × 250 CM) • CENTRE POMPIDOU, PARIS

SONIA DELAUNAY (1885–1979)

Sonia Delaunay's work was long overshadowed by that of her husband, Robert Delaunay, although both artists worked together to define a new mode of art. In addition to painting, Delaunay explored the applied arts (textiles, clothing, tableware, jewelry, bookbinding, among others) using a very modern approach to break the boundaries between the major and minor arts, between fine art and craft.

A year after Sonia Terk arrived in France in 1906, she met Robert Delaunay (1885–1941). They both developed a fascination for Michel Eugène Chevreul's work on the contrast of colors and together undertook artistic explorations that would lead to simultanism. According to the two artists, color, when correctly used, has a dynamic power that can convey the energy of modern life: "[W]e had been led to a new conception of painting through the observation of light," explained Sonia Delaunay in 1963, in the review *XXe siècle*. "The rupture of objects and forms by light, and the birth of colored surfaces brought new structure to painting. The ties with traditional art as they had been defined are definitively broken; color has been unleashed—no longer an element used to describe a subject, it now has a life of its own. It becomes the subject." From this perspective, *Electric Prisms* translates Delaunay's fascination with artificial light.

She creates vibrant, active contrasts between primary and secondary colors, arranged in arcs, quadrants, and stripes on the canvas, in a similar disposition to the color wheels popularized by artists and scientists since Isaac Newton in the seventeenth century. A cartouche on the left makes reference to *La Prose du Transsibérien et de la petite Jehanne de France* by Blaise Cendrars (1887–1961), a poem celebrating the steady rhythm of train travel that Sonia Delaunay illustrated in 1913.

Other important works
Le Bal Bullier, 1913.
Centre Pompidou, Paris.
Market at Minho, 1915.
Private collection.
Rhythm Colour No. 1076, 1939.
Palais des Beaux-Arts, Lille.

NEWTON'S COLOR WHEEL **p. 26** ART AND SCIENCE **p. 28** THE RAINBOW **p. 59**

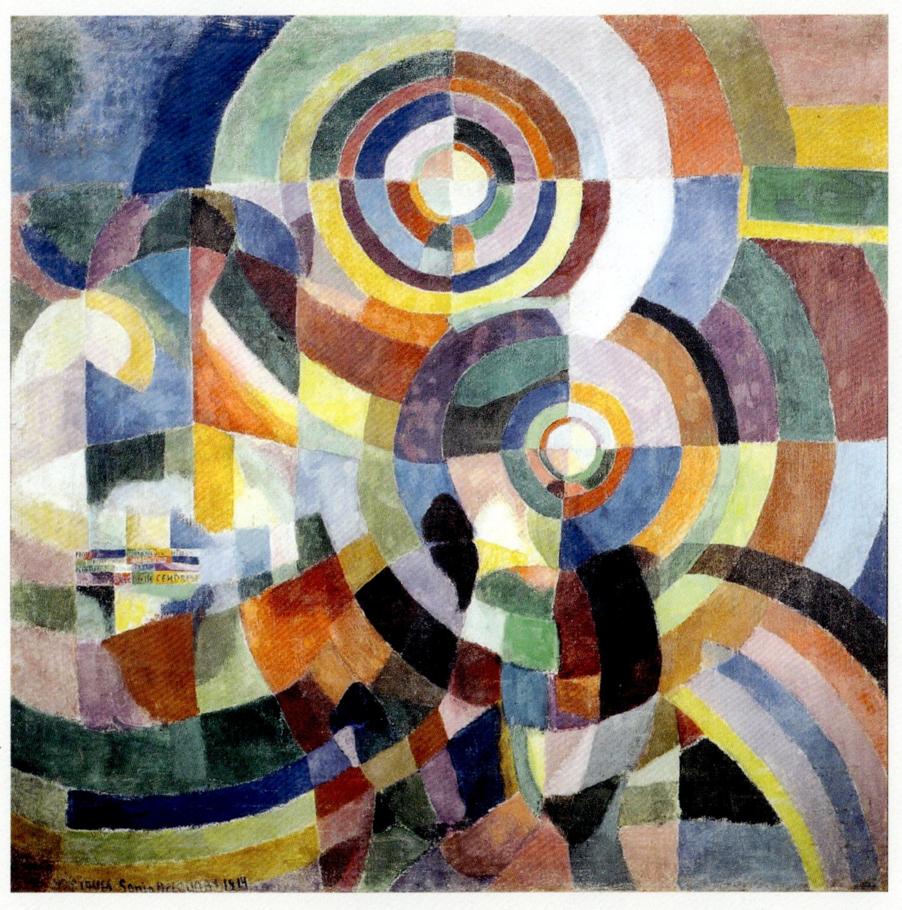

Group X, Altarpiece No. 1

1915

HILMA AF KLINT • OIL AND METAL LEAF ON CANVAS • 7 FT. 9½ IN. × 5 FT. 11 IN. (237.5 × 179.5 CM) • HILMA AF KLINT FOUNDATION, STOCKHOLM

HILMA AF KLINT (1862–1944)
Today, Swedish artist Hilma af Klint is considered a forerunner of abstract art. And yet her work, rooted in the mystic and the occult, was not discovered and appreciated until the 1980s. After studying at the Royal Academy of Fine Art in Stockholm, she painted landscapes and portraits, before her spiritual practice as a medium drew her onto a parallel, bold and colorful, non-representational path.

Altarpiece No. 1 belongs to a series of three paintings executed in 1915, nine years after Hilma af Klint turned to abstraction. This series is part of *The Paintings for the Temple* (1906–8, then 1913–15), a set of 193 paintings intended to adorn a theosophic temple of her own design. Af Klint received the command to design this temple and its decor during a Spiritist séance with fellow artists.

Under the title *Altarpieces*, in reference to medieval altar paintings, she chose to represent the evolutionary theories of the Theosophical movement, to which she belonged. According to these teachings, the world is animated by a dual movement from the physical world to the divine, and vice versa, a movement af Klint depicted as the pyramid-shaped construction. The colors grow lighter as the triangle approaches the golden circle, creating an illusion of perspective that is strengthened by the geometric forms growing progressively smaller. To the left are warm, feminine colors; to the right, cool, masculine ones. In addition, af Klint used metal leaf to create reflections and intensify the symbolic impact of this pictorial and spiritual grouping.

The altarpieces were to be displayed in the center of the temple; the altar would stand at the top of a spiral staircase connecting the three floors of the nearly round structure. In a notebook dated 1931, af Klint wrote that "a certain power and calm" must emanate from the building and its decor.

Other important works
Group IV, The Ten Largest, No. 7, Adulthood, 1907. Hilma af Klint Foundation, Stockholm.
Group IV, The Ten Largest, No. 2, Childhood, 1907. Moderna Museet, Stockholm.
The Dove series, 1915. Hilma af Klint Foundation, Stockholm.

GOLD **p. 56** THE RAINBOW **p. 59**

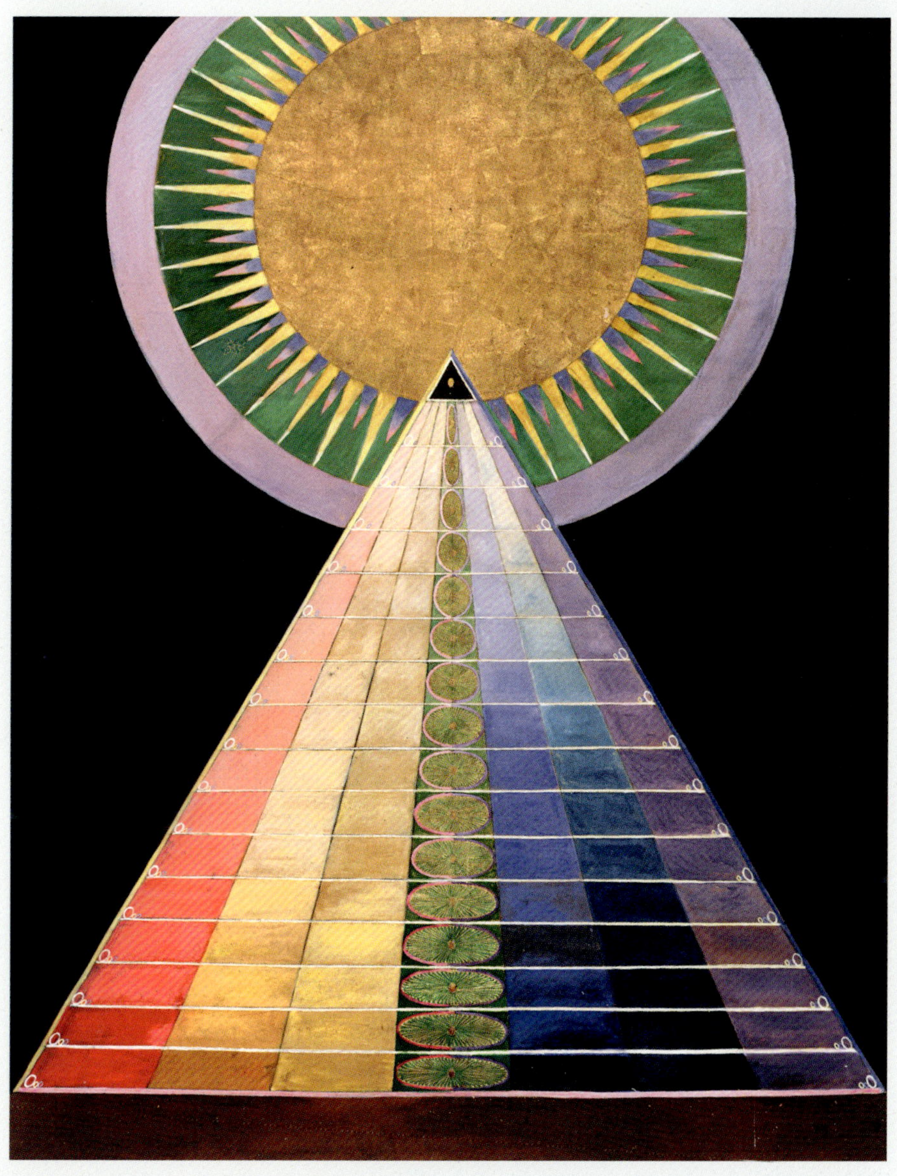

Composition with Triangles, Rectangles, and Half-Rings

1916

SOPHIE TAEUBER-ARP • WOOL TAPESTRY • 16 × 16 IN. (41 × 41 CM) • CENTRE POMPIDOU, PARIS

SOPHIE TAEUBER-ARP (1889–1943)

Sophie Taeuber-Arp was raised by a feminist mother who introduced her to artistic creation from an early age. Trained in the applied arts, Taeuber-Arp joined the Dada movement alongside Hans Arp (1886–1966), Francis Picabia (1879–1953), and Tristan Tzara (1896–1963), and explored different artistic practices. In the late 1920s, her work became increasingly geometric—boldly colored squares, rectangles, and circles—foreshadowing the concrete art theorized by Theo Van Doesburg (1883–1931) in 1930.

Other important works
Composition of Circles and Overlapping Angles, 1930.
Museum of Modern Art, New York, NY.
Composition of Circles, 1938.
Centre Pompidou, Paris.
Composition in a Circle, 1938.
Centre Pompidou, Paris.

In 1916, Sophie Taeuber-Arp was hired to teach at the School of Arts and Crafts in Zurich. The same year, she created her first tapestries featuring geometric motifs, which included circles, lines, rectangles, herringbone patterns, and squares. Although she used simple forms, she eschewed symmetry and created a dynamic rhythm by slightly off-centering or inverting them. This rhythm is reinforced by the use of colors that are bold (red and orange), acidulous (pink, pale blue, mauve), and muted (gray, taupe, brown). These were sometimes applied in several shades that stand out strikingly from the cream ground.

Taeuber-Arp's Dada tapestry offers a reinterpretation on two levels. She created a bold abstract composition using not the traditional and almost sacred tools of the easel painter (canvas, oil paint, and brush), but with a loom, generally used for decorative pieces. Taeuber-Arp's ambition was to eliminate the hierarchy between major and minor arts, and between fine art and craft. She developed a multi-disciplinary practice that indiscriminately combined tapestry, theater costumes, furniture, interior design, sculpture, painting, relief, drawing, clothing and accessories, marionettes, and choreography: "The natural impulse toward the decorative," she wrote in a text dated 1927, "should not be elimination. It is one of humanity's primordial and deeply rooted needs. Primitive peoples decorated tools and objects used for worship out of a desire to beautify and enhance. . . . This is a feeling rooted in the desire for creative perfection and achievement."

PRIMARY AND COMPLEMENTARY COLORS **p. 27**

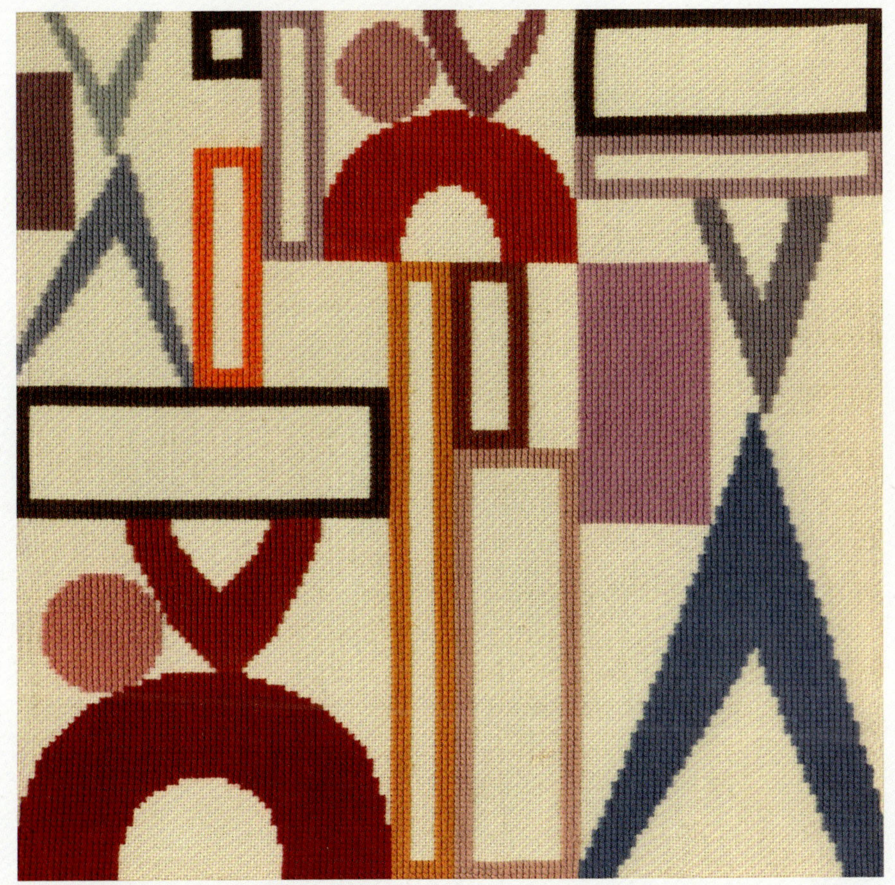

Composition with Large Red Plane, Yellow, Black, Gray, and Blue

PIET MONDRIAN • OIL ON CANVAS • 23½ × 23½ IN. (59.5 × 59.5 CM) • KUNSTMUSEUM DEN HAAG, THE HAGUE

PIET MONDRIAN (1872–1944)

Piet Mondrian's work can be divided into two major periods: the first, which lasted until the early 1910s, was characterized by a mastery of representational painting and the second by abstraction. As radically opposed as these periods may be, they share similarities such as frontality, the importance of verticality and horizontality, and seriality. In *Natural Reality and Abstract Reality* (1920), Mondrian explained his approach: "Everything is constituted by relation and reciprocity. Color does not exist other than by another color, the dimension is defined by the other dimension, there is only position in opposition to another position. That is why I say that rapport is the principal thing."

Other important works

Evening: The Red Tree, 1910. Kunstmuseum Den Haag, The Hague.
Composition with Red, Yellow and Blue, 1927. Kröller-Müller Museum, Otterlo.
Broadway Boogie-Woogie, 1942–43. Museum of Modern Art, New York, NY.

In the early 1920s, Piet Mondrian took his painting in a new direction. Since the revelation he experienced upon discovering Paul Cézanne and cubism in 1911, he had been seeking to liberate himself from pictorial illusionism, which had been practiced since the Renaissance. In his search for perfection, he abandoned realistic color in favor of pure color and gradually deconstructed tradition—the result would be neo-plasticism. Mondrian reduced painting to several binary elements that he considered universal: primary colors (red, blue, yellow) contrasted with non-colors (gray, black, white), all of them applied in flat areas of color, as well as straight horizontal lines contrasted with vertical lines; his infinite combinations of these elements were without hierarchy or center.

The square-format *Composition with Large Red Plane, Yellow, Black, Gray, and Blue* is one of the first neo-plastic paintings Mondrian produced. He underscored the flatness of the support with a network of black lines and white, yellow, red, blue, gray, and black quadrilaterals. He applied this method to many compositions into the 1930s, making several theoretical evolutions along the way. In 1940, he fled the war in Europe, seeking exile in the United States. This period was marked by the energy of New York and his discovery of jazz, which modified his approach to painting. He now favored a white ground with red, yellow, blue, or gray lines, some with segments of another one of these colors or magnified by rectangles of different colors.

PRIMARY AND COMPLEMENTARY COLORS **p. 27** THE ARTIST'S STUDIO AND THE EXHIBITION SPACE **p. 40** BLACK **p. 44** WHITE **p. 45** RED **p. 46** YELLOW **p. 47** BLUE **p. 48** GRAY **p. 54**

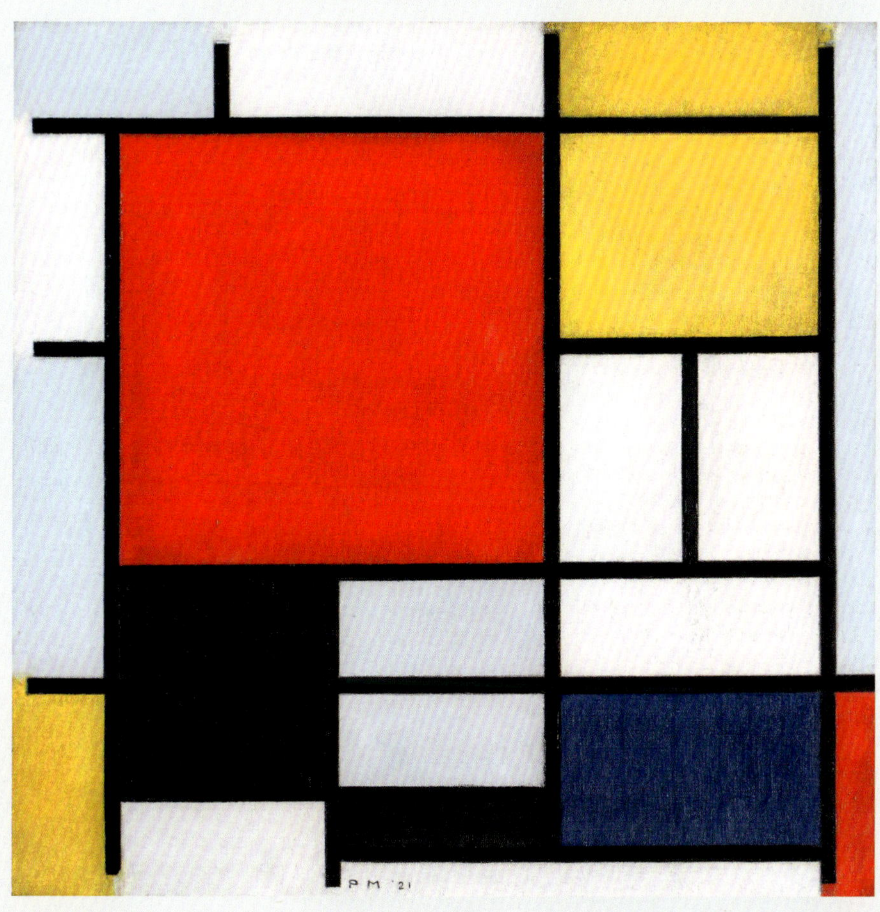

Bellboy

CHAÏM SOUTINE • OIL ON CANVAS • 38½ × 31¾ IN. (98 × 80.5 CM) •
CENTRE POMPIDOU, PARIS

1925

**CHAÏM SOUTINE
(1893–1943)**
Soutine left his native Russia for Paris in 1913. Heavily influenced by Rembrandt (1606–1669) then Vincent Van Gogh (1853–1890), he chose thickly applied color, meandering across the canvas, as his preferred language: "Everything depends on the way color is mixed, captured, and arranged," he declared. He painted the traditional themes of portraiture, still life, and landscape, but with an expressiveness so exaggerated that the paint became the very subject of the work.

In 1925, Chaïm Soutine painted the portrait of a bellboy tasked with opening and closing the doors of the famous Parisian restaurant Maxim's. It is one of a series of paintings featuring shop, domestic, or hotel workers that Soutine began several years earlier: anonymous pâtissiers, attendants, and domestic servants populate the painter's work with their often anguished presence.

Here, the bellboy seems sad and mistrustful. He poses facing the artist, seated, with his legs spread and his hands on his hips in a posture at odds with bourgeois decorum. His distant gaze conveys a deep despondency, most likely because of his social condition. The blood-red livery—a small hat, pants, and a jacket with gold buttons—hangs from his thin, distorted body and contrasts with the dark, blue-tinged background. Various shades of red mingle on the skin of the young man's lips, eyelids, cheeks, ears, and hands. Soutine was fascinated by the tragic symbolism of the color red—one that was inseparable from life and death. Found in many of his paintings, it is most striking in his depictions of beef carcasses. The sinuous brushstrokes, distorted face, and thickly painted surface give the entire composition of *Bellboy* an expressive, even dramatic power that is characteristic of Soutine's work.

Other important works
Self-Portrait, c. 1918. Princeton University Art Museum, Princeton, NJ.
Still Life with Rayfish, 1924. Museum of Modern Art, New York, NY.
Carcass of Beef, 1925. Minneapolis Institute of Art, Minneapolis, MN.

VIOLENT USE OF COLOR **p. 35** RED **p. 46**

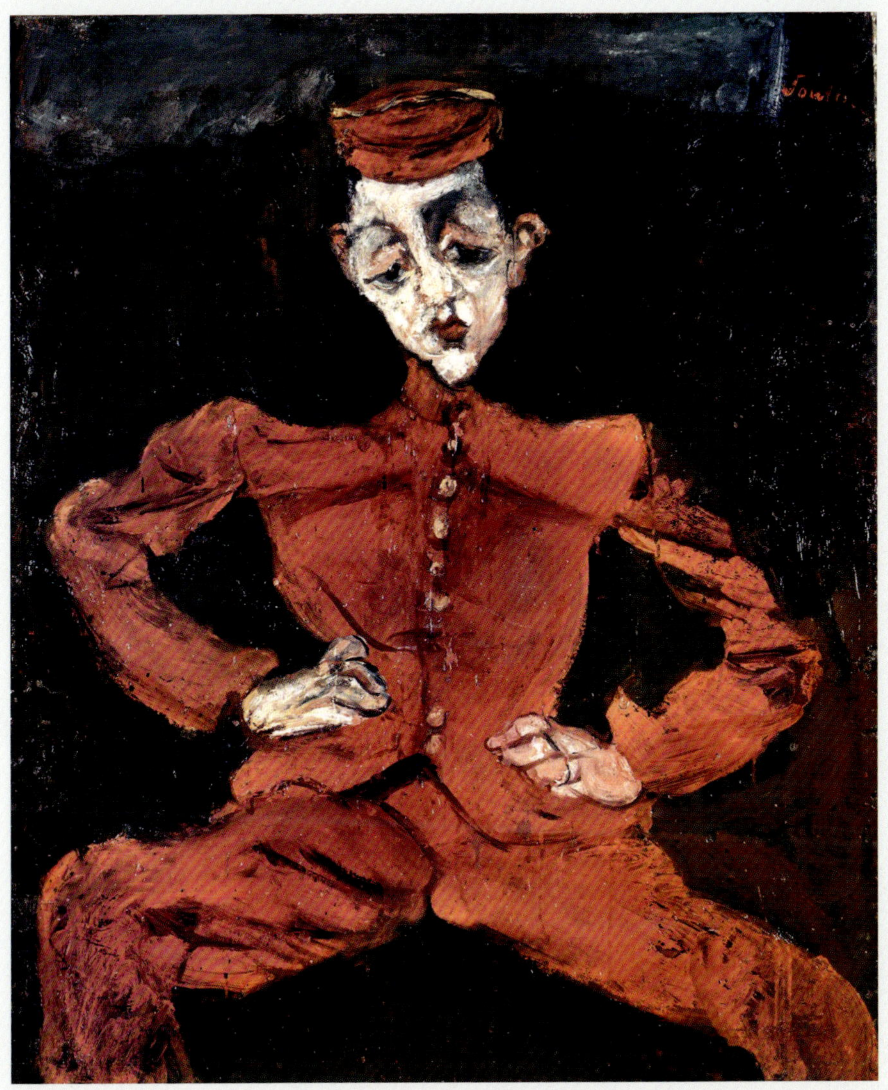

Several Circles

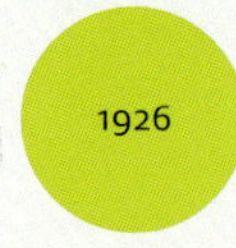

WASSILY KANDINSKY • OIL ON CANVAS • 4 FT. 7½ IN. × 4 FT. 7 IN. (140.7 × 140.3 CM) • SOLOMON R. GUGGENHEIM MUSEUM, NEW YORK, NY

WASSILY KANDINSKY (1866–1944)
Kandinsky is considered a pioneer of abstract art. A latecomer to painting, he explored the liberation of color and formal simplification, guided by a desire to express spirituality and utopia in his work. He wrote a number of texts in which color theory plays a central role. He brought together eight "elementary" colors in four highly symbolic contrasts: yellow-blue (representing proximity-distance), white-black (diffusion-concentration), red-green (activity-passivity), and orange-violet (body-mind).

Other important works
Color Study: Squares with Concentric Circles, 1913.
Lenbachhaus, Munich.
Composition 8, 1923.
Solomon R. Guggenheim Museum, New York, NY.
Yellow-Red-Blue, 1925.
Centre Pompidou, Paris.

In the 1920s, while he was a professor at the Bauhaus in Dessau, Germany, Wassily Kandinsky began exploring geometric forms of different colors arranged on dark grounds. In *Several Circles,* Kandinsky created a network of circles: some are opaque and overlapping, others translucent and blending together, and still others are haloed with another color. In his work *On the Spiritual in Art* (1911), he writes that color generates as much a physical effect on the viewer—"the eye is enchanted"—as it does a "vibration within [the] soul."

These various techniques establish a complex rhythm within the composition. The circle was Kandinsky's favorite motif: "Why does the circle fascinate me? It is (1) the most modest form, but asserts itself unconditionally, (2) a precise but inexhaustible variable, (3) simultaneously stable and unstable (4) simultaneously loud and soft (5) a single tension that carries countless tensions within it. The circle is the synthesis of the greatest oppositions. It combines the concentric and the excentric in a single form, and in balance. Of the three primary forms [triangle, square, circle], it points most clearly to the fourth dimension."

The composition, strengthened by the subtle interplay of "basic" colors (blue, yellow, red, green, black) and "demi-colors" (orange, pink, violet, brown), gives the whole work a cosmic power. For Kandinsky's painting does not break with the "real"; it invites a dual interpretation—figurative and abstract—that places great importance on the psychology of form and color.

CONTRASTS **p. 25** PRIMARY AND COMPLEMENTARY COLORS **p. 27** BLACK **p. 44** RED **p. 46** YELLOW **p. 47** BLUE **p. 48** GREEN **p. 49** ORANGE **p. 50** VIOLET **p. 51** BROWN **p. 52** PINK **p. 53**

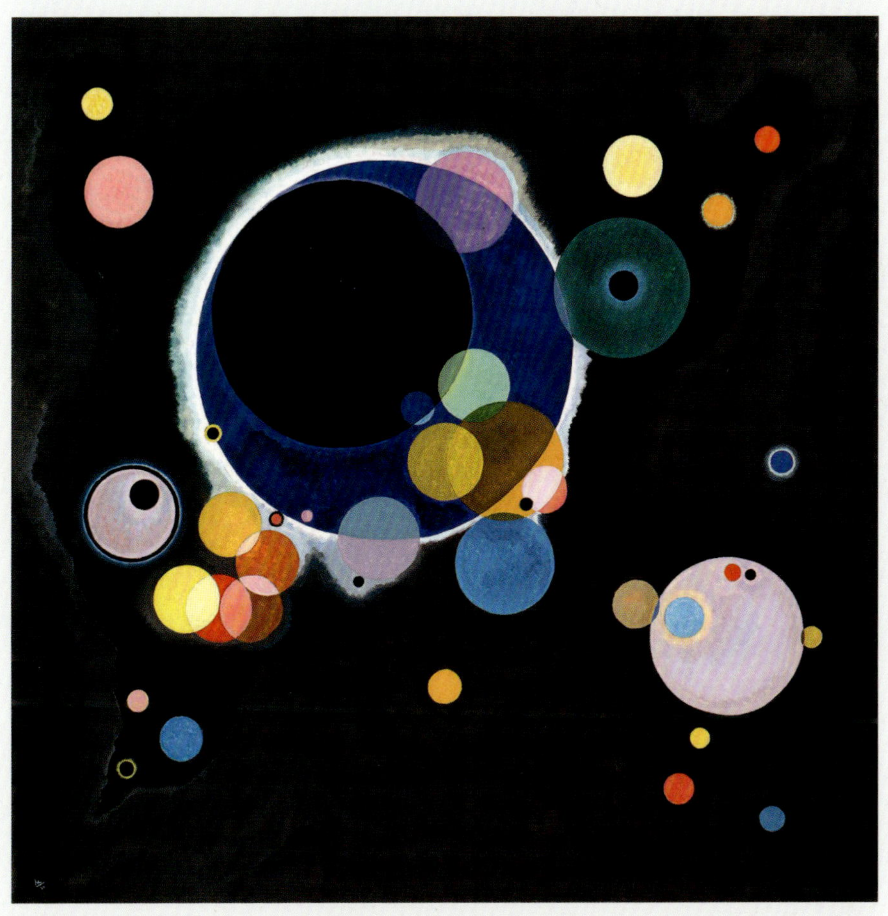

Black Abstraction

GEORGIA O'KEEFFE • OIL ON CANVAS • 2 FT. 6 IN. × 3 FT. 4 IN.
(76.2 × 102.2 CM) • THE METROPOLITAN MUSEUM OF ART, NEW YORK, NY

1927

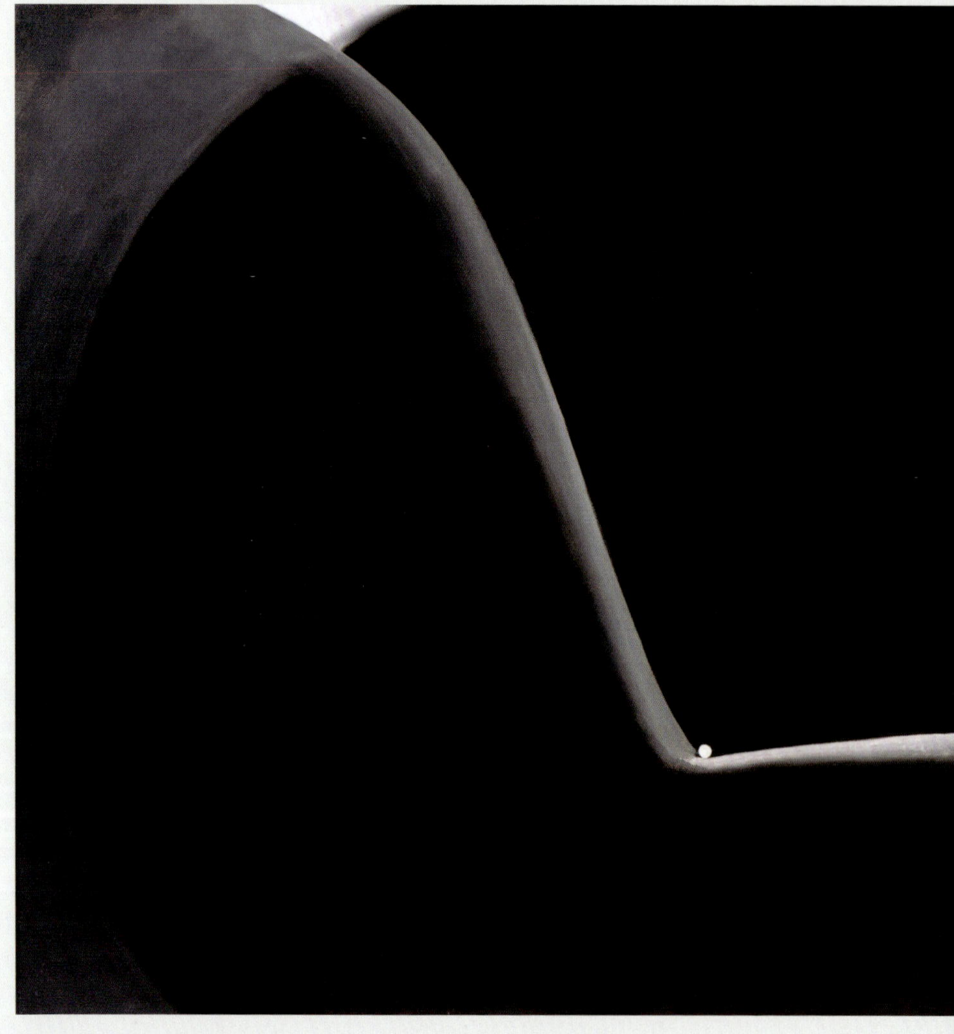

THE ARTIST'S STUDIO AND THE EXHIBITION SPACE **p. 40** BLACK **p. 44** WHITE **p. 45** GRAY **p. 54**

Other important works
Black Iris III, 1926. The Metropolitan Museum of Art, New York, NY.
Cow's Skull with Calico Roses, 1931. The Art Institute of Chicago, Chicago, IL.
Sky Above Clouds IV, 1965. The Art Institute of Chicago, Chicago, IL.

GEORGIA O'KEEFFE (1887–1986)

Georgia O'Keeffe was one of the most important American artists of the twentieth century. In 1915, in a series of charcoal drawings, she began inventing an abstract, organic language that she developed over the years alongside a figurative style. Her interest in scale (wide angle, close-ups, distance) generated a reflection rooted in perception, within which color—subtly shaded or applied in strident fields—played a crucial role.

In 1927, Georgia O'Keeffe created an astonishing painting in gray and black monochrome, except for a bright yellowish dot. The incomplete circle and its halos occupy most of the space. An undulating form, within which the bright pearl nestles, traverses the composition. O'Keeffe does not set abstraction against representation and, as often was the case, this painting was inspired by reality. With intentional restraint, it represents consciousness vacillating under the effects of anesthesia: "I had decided to be conscious as long as possible," wrote O'Keeffe in her 1976 autobiography. "The skylight began to whirl and slowly become smaller and smaller in a black space. I lifted my right arm overhead and dropped it. As the skylight became a small white dot in a black room, I lifted my left arm over my head. As it started to drop and the white dot became very small, I was gone."

A skilled colorist, O'Keeffe succeeded in creating a palette of grays and blacks almost as rich as that used in polychrome painting. This taste for achromatic monochrome, expressed several times throughout her work, evokes the world of photography (primarily black and white at the time) with which she was familiar through her marriage to the photographer Alfred Stieglitz (1864–1946) and her friendships with other photographers like Paul Strand (1890–1976) and Ansel Adams (1902–84).

Sculpture with Colour (Deep Blue and Red)

BARBARA HEPWORTH • PLASTER, STRING • 4½ × 6 × 4¼ IN. (11.5 × 15.2 × 10.7 CM) • BARBARA HEPWORTH MUSEUM AND SCULPTURE GARDEN, ST IVES (UK)

BARBARA HEPWORTH (1903–1975)

Barbara Hepworth was one of the greatest modern British sculptors. Early in her career, she freed herself from her academic training in favor of a powerful simplification of form that gradually abandoned figuration. In her sculptures, which could be geometric or organic, she also introduced "the hole," which enabled her to experiment with fullness and emptiness, interior and exterior, and light and shadow.

Other important works
Three Forms, 1935. Tate, London.
Sphere with Inner Form, 1965. Barbara Hepworth Museum and Sculpture Garden, St Ives.
Spring, 1966. Barbara Hepworth Museum and Sculpture Garden, St Ives.

Sculpture with Colour (Deep Blue and Red) belongs to a series of six pieces that Barbara Hepworth began in 1939, the first five made of plaster and the last of wood. It comprises two conoid sections with organic lines joined together. Red strings stretch between them, radiating outward to the opposite side from a single opening. The inner surface is painted ultramarine while the exterior is covered in white paint. The work rests on a base of white plaster and plywood.

At the time this piece was created, Hepworth had fled London to live on the southwest coast, near St Ives in Cornwall. Due to lack of space, time, and raw materials, she favored small and medium formats in plaster. This series was not Hepworth's first attempt at painted sculpture. Just before leaving the English capital, she had created another piece using painted plaster and red string, but with a different form.

The lines created by the string and the surfaces evoke mathematical tori and cyclides, which greatly interested Hepworth and her friend Naum Gabo (1897–1970). She was indebted to Piet Mondrian, whom she met and spent time with in the 1930s, for the use of primary colors associated with white. Polychromy brought the biomorphic structure to life and, according to Hepworth, made the connection with landscape: "The color in the concavities plunged me into the depth of water, caves, of shadows deeper than the carved concavities themselves. The strings were the tension I felt between myself and the sea, the wind, or the hills."

PRIMARY AND COMPLEMENTARY COLORS **p. 27** WHITE **p. 45** RED **p. 46** BLUE **p. 48**

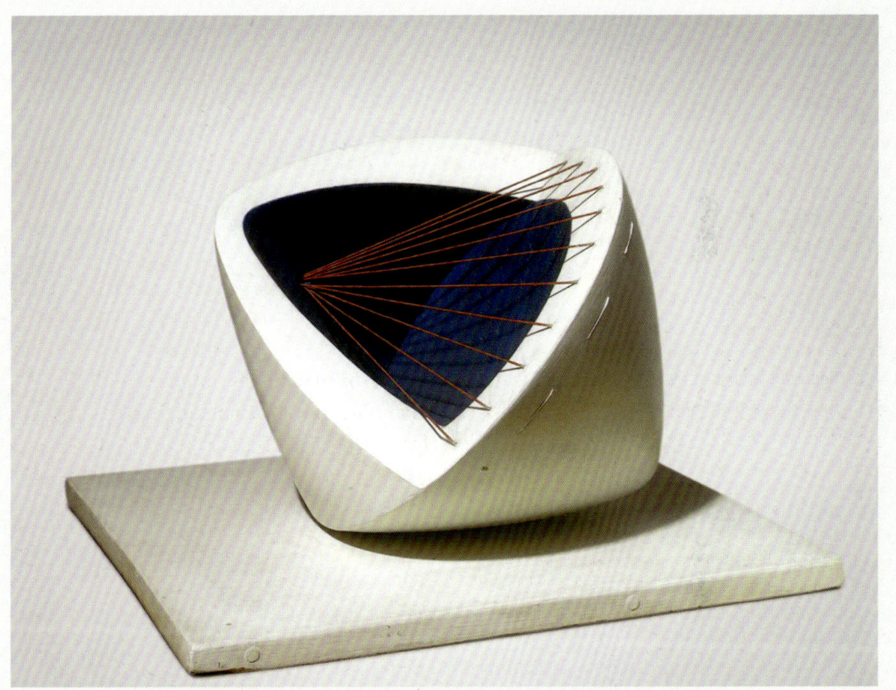

Self-Portrait as a Tehuana

FRIDA KAHLO • OIL ON MASONITE • 29¾ × 24 IN. (75.5 × 61 CM) •
THE JACQUES AND NATASHA GELMAN COLLECTION OF TWENTIETH CENTURY
MEXICAN ART, WEST PALM BEACH, FL

1943

In the 1940s, Frida Kahlo painted two self-portraits in
which she is depicted wearing a Tehuana headdress (from
Oaxaca state in Mexico), called a *resplandor* in Spanish.
In this first version, also titled *Diego on My Mind* in
reference to the small portrait of her husband, Diego
Rivera (1886–1957), adorning her forehead, the artist
represents her own face within the frame of cream, pink,
and light gray lace, tulle, and satin.

The voluminous fabric is reminiscent of a corolla. This
allusion to flowers is strengthened by the embroidered
motifs and even more directly by the floral tiara crowning
the young woman's head; it is probably made of
bougainvillea, arnica, and Mexican violets, the latter
being used in traditional medicine. Fine roots like blood
vessels escaping from the tiara intertwine with the white
threads sprouting from the *resplandor*. The background is
an ambiguous and indistinct earthy green color.

From the painting springs forth a kind of sap: a vital,
sexual energy, as evidenced by the image of the loved one
who occupies Kahlo's thoughts, but also an artistic and
spiritual energy generated by the combination of cultural
references and natural elements. The soft and fresh tones
endow the painting with an enduring sense of tenderness.
"The green miracle of the landscape of my body becomes
in you the whole of nature. . . . It's not love, or tenderness,
or affection, it's life itself."

WHITE **p.45** BLUE **p.48** GREEN **p.49** VIOLET **p.51** BROWN **p.52** PINK **p.53**

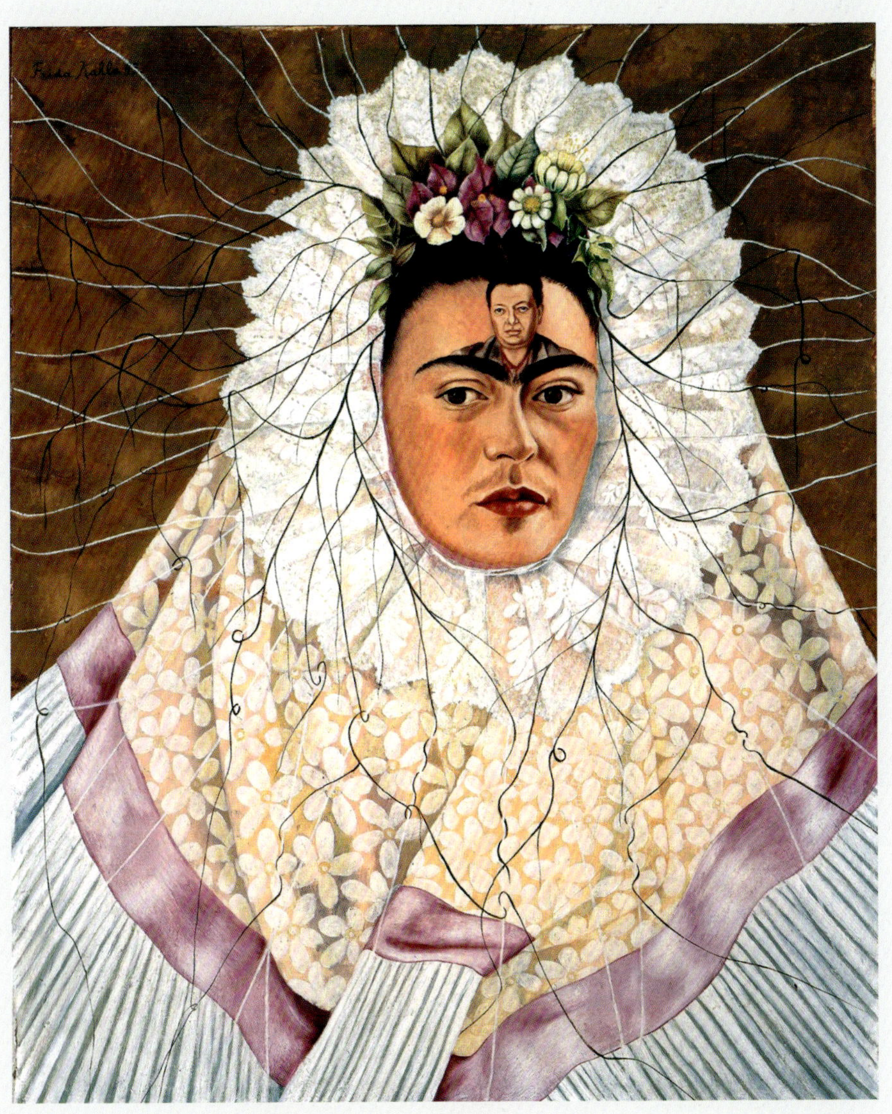

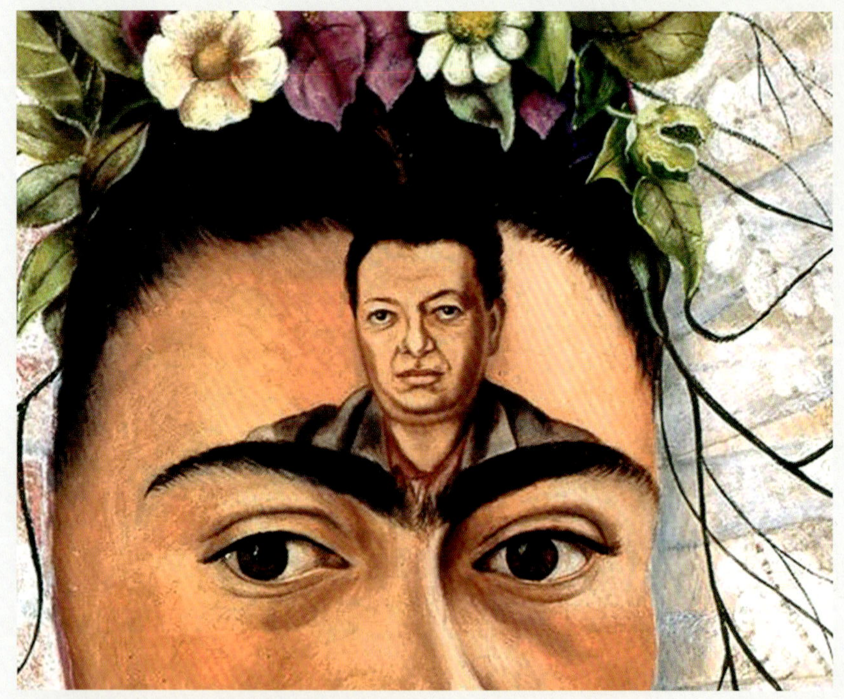

In the center of her forehead, like a tattoo, Frida Kahlo depicts her husband, the painter Diego Rivera. His portrait rests on the thick, black line of her eyebrows, which he liked to compare to a crow's wings.

FRIDA KAHLO (1907–1954)

Frida Kahlo, the daughter of a German-Jewish photographer father and a Mexican mother, devoted most of her work to portraiture and self-portraiture. Her often-autobiographical paintings combine complex influences from folk, Native American, and Mexican culture. Color played an important role in her work, and she was drawn to vivid hues (red, blue, green, pink) and ochers. Similarly, the facade of the house she shared with Diego Rivera in Mexico, and that eventually became a museum, is painted bright blue with red framework, and green windows and doors.

Other important works

The Two Fridas, 1939. Museo de Arte Moderno, Mexico City.
The Broken Column, 1944. Museo Dolores Olmedo, Mexico City.
The Wounded Deer, 1946. Private collection.

The *resplandor* that Frida Kahlo wears seems to come alive under her paintbrush. The rootlets, akin to long black hairs, escape from the flowered tiara and intertwine with the white threads unraveling from the woven lace. This network symbolizes Kahlo's rootedness in "Mexicanity" and the unfolding of an aesthetic nourished by popular traditions, among other things.

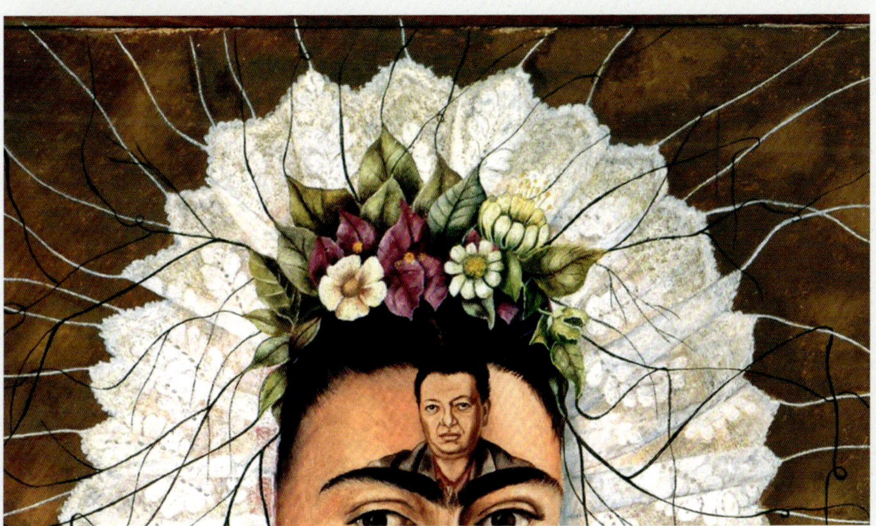

Vertical Constellation with Bomb

1943

ALEXANDER CALDER • PAINTED STEEL WIRE, PAINTED WOOD, WOOD •
30½ × 29¾ × 24 IN. (77.5 × 75.6 × 61 CM) • NATIONAL GALLERY OF ART, WASHINGTON, DC

**ALEXANDER CALDER
(1898–1976)**
Calder left an inventive and poetic body of work. From his miniature circus made of wire and salvaged materials to his moving sculptures, he revolutionized the history of sculpture. His interest in the environment surrounding a piece, evident in his monumental sculptures created after World War II and intended for display in public spaces, reveals a deep anchoring in "reality," even in his most abstract pieces.

Other important works
Calder's Circus, 1926–31.
Whitney Museum of American Art, New York, NY.
Romulus and Remus, 1928.
Solomon R. Guggenheim Museum, New York, NY.
Reims, Croix du Sud, 1969.
LaM, Lille.

In late 1930, after an eye-opening visit to Piet Mondrian's studio, Alexander Calder created his first kinetic sculptures, known as "mobiles," then his static sculptures, which he called "stabiles." The series *Constellations*, begun in 1943, belongs to this second category.

During World War II, there was a shortage of metal, Calder's preferred material for his three-dimensional pieces, so he began exploring wood shapes that he sculpted and assembled using stiff rods. Some of these forms—often organic although sometimes geometric—were painted in bold colors: black, white, red, bright blue, orange, or yellow. These stationary sculptures were intended for display on the ground or, like *Vertical Constellation with Bomb*, on a tabletop, or to be hung on walls.

The term "constellation," approved by his friend Marcel Duchamp (1887–1968), is a reminder of Calder's interest in astronomy. The series was derived from a set of sculptures titled *Universe*, which was created a decade earlier. The word also conveys the idea of a configuration of stars in space. While the ensemble is stationary, the repetition of certain forms at different scales and the use of an energetic palette suggest the idea of movement.

"How can art be realized?" asked Calder in 1932. "Out of volumes, motion, spaces bounded by the great space, the universe. Out of different masses, light, heavy, middling—indicated by variations of size or color— directional lines—vectors which represent speeds, velocities, accelerations, forces, etc. . . . Abstractions that are like nothing in life except in their manner of reacting."

PRIMARY AND COMPLEMENTARY COLORS **p. 27**

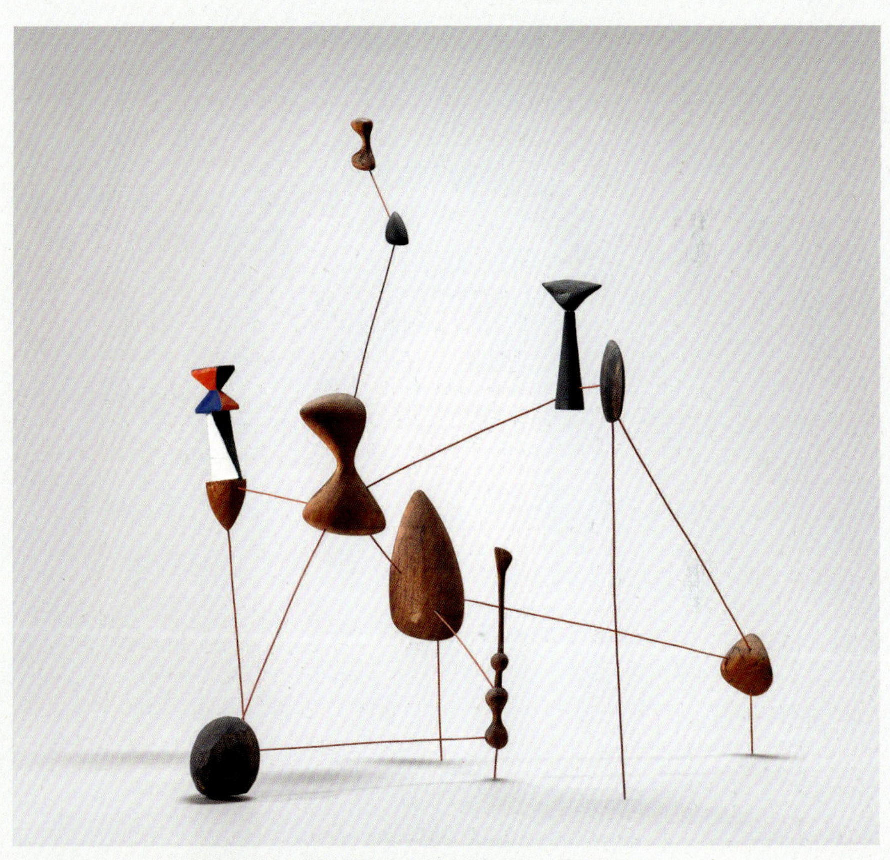

The Rosary Chapel

HENRI MATISSE • THE ROSARY CHAPEL, VENCE

1948
–
1951

In 1948, Henri Matisse, then residing at the Villa le Rêve, in Vence, created the architecture, interior furnishings, and liturgical objects for the Rosary Chapel. With the help of architect Auguste Perret (1874–1954) and master glassmaker Paul Bony (1911–82), the artist designed the building, stained glass, and ceramic decorative panels, as well as the stalls, holy water fonts, chasubles, candlesticks, ciboria, and other elements to create a total work of art—a testament and the climax of Matisse's explorations of color, synthesis, and decorative art.

Matisse favored simple lines and gave light a determining role. For the plant motifs in the stained glass—acanthus leaves and cactus shaped like a tree of life—he selected three bold colors—blue, green, and yellow—that symbolize, respectively, the Mediterranean sky, nature, and light, both from the sun and from God. The reflections created by filtering daylight animate the white walls as well as the white ceramic panels decorated with figurative line drawings similar to murals (Saint Dominic, the Madonna and Child surrounded by flowers, and the Stations of the Cross). Outside, glazed blue tiles crown the building while a tympanum (also depicting Saint Dominic and the Virgin Mary) and a tondo representing another Virgin and Child, both in ceramic, adorn the facades.

When the chapel was inaugurated in 1951, Matisse wrote to the bishop of Nice: "This work has taken me four years of exclusive and diligent work, and it is the result of my entire working life. Despite all its imperfections I consider it to be my masterpiece. . . . An effort which issues from a life consecrated to the search for truth." (*Matisse on Art*, 1978).

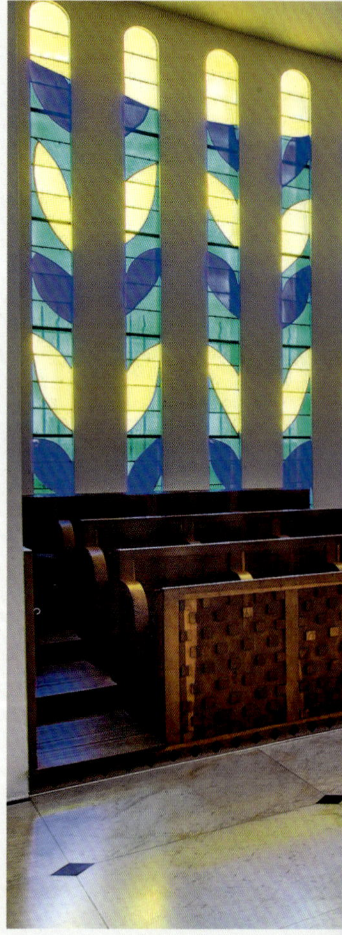

YELLOW **p. 47** BLUE **p. 48** GREEN **p. 49**

Other important works
Dance II, 1910. Hermitage Museum, Saint Petersburg.
Blue Nude II, 1952. Centre Pompidou, Paris.
The Sorrows of the King, 1952. Centre Pompidou, Paris.

HENRI MATISSE (1869–1954)

Color is central to Matisse's work, from his exuberant fauve period in the early twentieth century to his paper cut-outs in the 1940s, in which simplified form arose directly from color, and constituted a way for him to express his emotions: "My choice of color does not rest on any scientific theory; it is based on observation, on sensitivity, on felt experiences." (*Matisse on Art*, 1978).

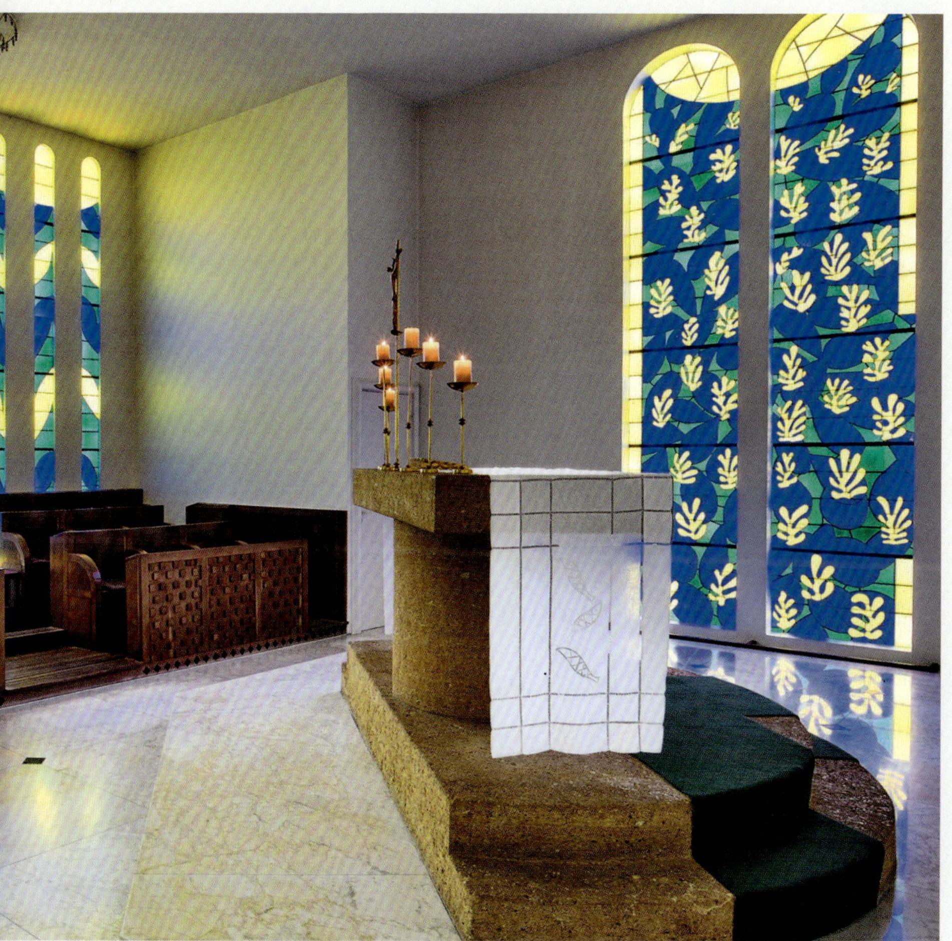

STAINED GLASS **p. 207**

White Center (Yellow, Pink and Lavender on Rose)

MARK ROTHKO • OIL ON CANVAS • 7 FT. 7 IN. × 5 FT. (230.6 × 152.7 CM) • PRIVATE COLLECTION

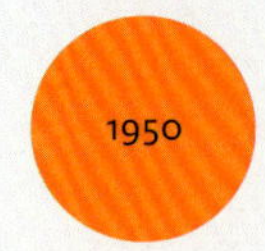

Other important works
No. 61 (Rust and Blue), 1953.
The Museum of Contemporary Art.
Los Angeles, CA.
Orange, Red, Yellow, 1961.
Private collection.
Untitled (Black on Grey), 1970.
Solomon R. Guggenheim Museum,
New York, NY.

When he painted *White Center* in 1950, Mark Rothko had been exploring for several years the possibilities of color in abstract compositions with simple forms. A single principle often predominated: the arrangement of colored squares or rectangles in the painting's vertical space.

Often, Rothko primed the canvas with a base coat of pigments mixed with rabbit skin glue to produce a matte finish. Using a commercial decorator's brush that gave blurred contours, he then painted rectangles in a different shade, in this case orange-yellows and pinks.

Rothko played with the optical qualities of colors, applying them with varying degrees of opacity or transparency, and creating illusions of distance or proximity on the surface of the canvas. The veils of paint gave each piece a unique luminosity. Although Rothko definitively abandoned figuration in these abstract works, he nevertheless viewed them as a way to translate something of the human experience: "I'm interested only in expressing basic human emotions—tragedy, ecstasy, doom, and so on—and the fact that lots of people break down and cry when confronted with my pictures shows that I *communicate* those basic human emotions" (quoted in Selden Rodman, *Conversations with Artists*, 1957).

PURE COLOR **p. 37** RED **p. 46** YELLOW **p. 47** ORANGE **p. 50** PINK **p. 53**

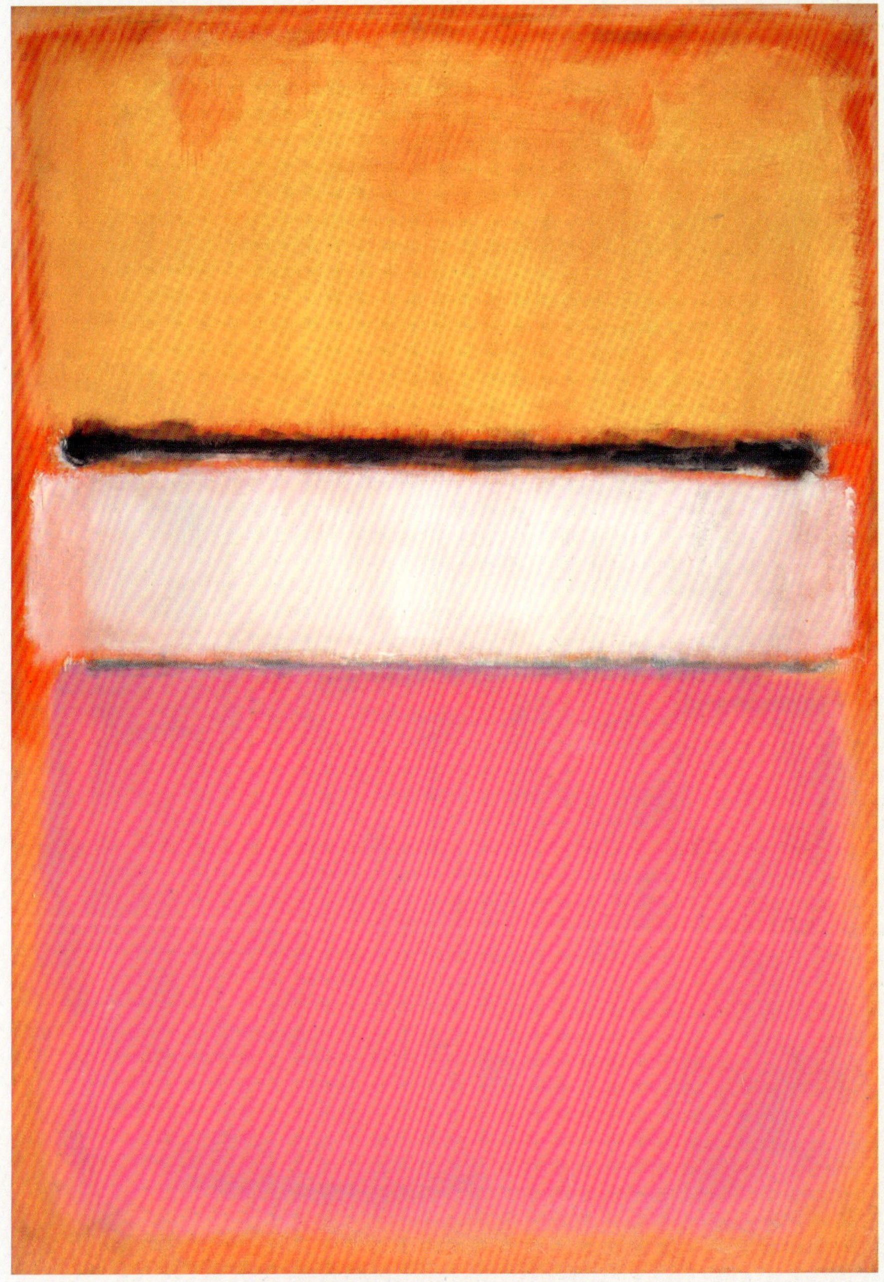

THE PAINTER'S TOOLS **p. 197** PRIMER, UNDERCOAT, AND VARNISH **p. 206**

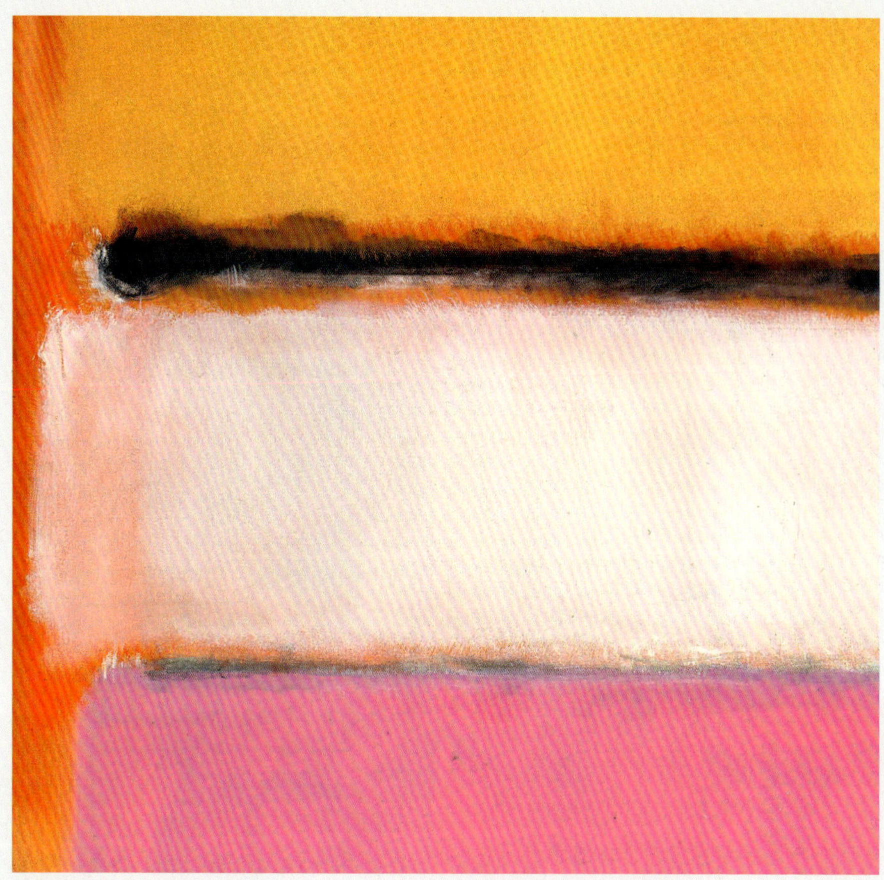

Rothko rarely applied colors in pure, flat fields. They intentionally vibrate with their neighbors, like black and white here, both applied on red, with one bordering on pink and the other orange-yellow. The blurry contours of each colored rectangle enhance this vibrational power.

MARK ROTHKO (1903–1970)
Originally from Russia, Rothko was, like other American artists of his generation, a figurative painter. Initially expressionist, he was later influenced by European surrealism before inventing a new formal and aesthetic approach in the 1940s that would earn him critical and commercial acclaim. He always painted two, three, or four rectangles of diaphanous color that seemed to vibrate with surprising vividness. Liberated from representation, Rothko established a direct relationship between painting and viewer, facilitated by large formats that demanded an immersive gaze.

Mark Rothko's painting invites contemplation. The way he applied successive layers of paint to the canvas resulted in incredibly rich colors. Here, a fairly diluted layer of yellow lets the orange ground show through in places.

Sky Cathedral

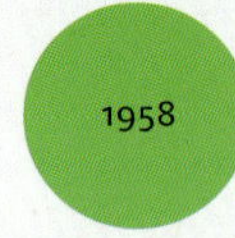

LOUISE NEVELSON • PAINTED WOOD • 11 FT. 3½ IN. × 10 FT. × 1 FT. 6 IN.
(343.9 × 305.4 × 45.7 CM) • MUSEUM OF MODERN ART, NEW YORK, NY

**LOUISE NEVELSON
(1899–1988)**
Nevelson was heavily influenced by cubism, especially the movement's approach to shadow and light, and the importance given to structure. During World War II, limited by rationing, she adopted wood as her preferred material. In the 1950s, in her monochrome, composite sculptures, she began reflecting on line, flatness, and surface at a time when painters like Barnett Newman (1905–1970), Mark Rothko (1903–1970), and Clyfford Still (1904–1980)—united under the label "abstract expressionism"—were undertaking similar reflections.

Sky Cathedral belongs to a cycle of wall sculptures, some of which reach monumental proportions, that Louise Nevelson began in the late 1950s. Made of wood salvaged from the streets of New York, they form complex, puzzle-like structures.

Boxes, cartons, and wine crates form cells into which chair rungs, dowels, and other turned-wood elements are affixed. Nevelson would then assemble these units together—sometimes she would even take elements from a previous work for use elsewhere.

A rhythm is created between void and solid, shadow and light, surface and depth, unified by monochrome paint—most often black but sometimes white, gold, or silver—that rendered the original function of the objects less evident. "I don't think I chose it for black," Nevelson told Diana MacKown in 1976 in a book of interviews. "I think it chose *me* for saying something. You see, it says more for me than anything else. In the academic world, they used to say black and white were no colors, but I'm twisting that to tell you that for me [black] is the total color. It means totality. It means: contains all."

The sculpture's title alludes to Nevelson's lifelong interest in spirituality. She viewed the work, whose very structure is full of contradictions, as a bridge between the realms of heaven and earth.

Other important works
Atmosphere and Environment X, 1969–70. Princeton University Art Museum, Princeton, NJ.
Dawn's Presence, 1972–75. Chrysler Museum of Art, Norfolk, VA.
Full Moon, 1980. Reynolda House, Winston-Salem, NC.

BLACK **p. 44**

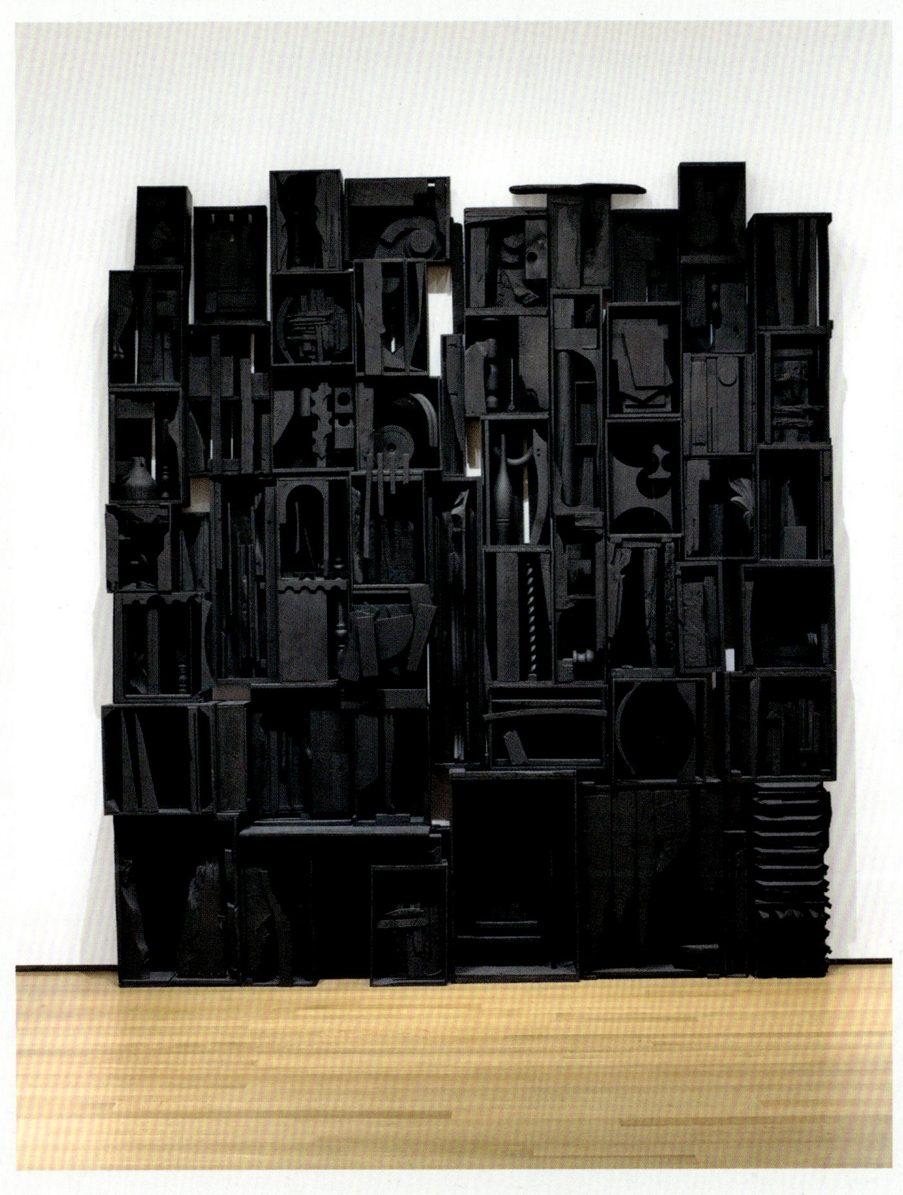

Concetto spaziale. Attese (T. 104)

1958

LUCIO FONTANA • POLYVINYL-ACETATE PAINT ON CANVAS •
4 FT. 1 IN. × 3 FT. 3½ IN. (125 × 100.5 CM) • CENTRE POMPIDOU, PARIS

**LUCIO FONTANA
(1899–1968)**
Space is the central theme in Fontana's work. Using various means like light, color, and incisions, he let the environment penetrate the work—painting, sculpture, or object—guided by a type of mysticism and the desire to free himself from materialism.

In 1958, while experimenting with perforating different supports (canvas and paper, then various materials like cellulose acetate and Plexiglas), Lucio Fontana created his first *tagli* (cuts), which he placed under the generic title *Concetto spaziale* (Spatial Concept): vertical or slightly slanted lacerations that disturb the monochrome surface of the painting, as though it has been slashed with a blade. The contrast between the uniformly painted canvas and the incision's dark slash conveyed a certain violence. The action underscored the three-dimensionality of the painting which, by opening to space, became a sculptural object. Fontana saw this radical, minimalist gesture as accessing the void and an evocation of the expanding universe. The subtitle, *Attese* (Waiting) refers to the artist's spiritual and contemplative quest. Here, pale pink polyvinyl-acetate paint, chosen for its covering qualities, lends a more carnal connotation to this double slash.

The *Concetti spaziali*, which occupied Fontana for a decade, until his death in 1968, were part of a wider inquiry into space that he undertook in 1946 in a series of manifestos: "The artists that call themselves 'spatial,'" explained Fontana to Raffaele De Grada in an unpublished interview in 1947, "want to break with tradition and are occupied with rendering a spatial vision. Just think: they even come to conceive art in a form that is so new as to make them think of being able to transmit it by means of television."

Other important works
Sphere, 1957. Museo Internazionale delle Ceramiche, Faenza.
Concetto spaziale. Attese, 1960. AKG Art Museum, Buffalo, NY.
Concetto spaziale. La fine di Dio (63-FD.17), 1963. Centre Pompidou, Paris.

MONOCHROMES **p. 36** PINK **p. 53**

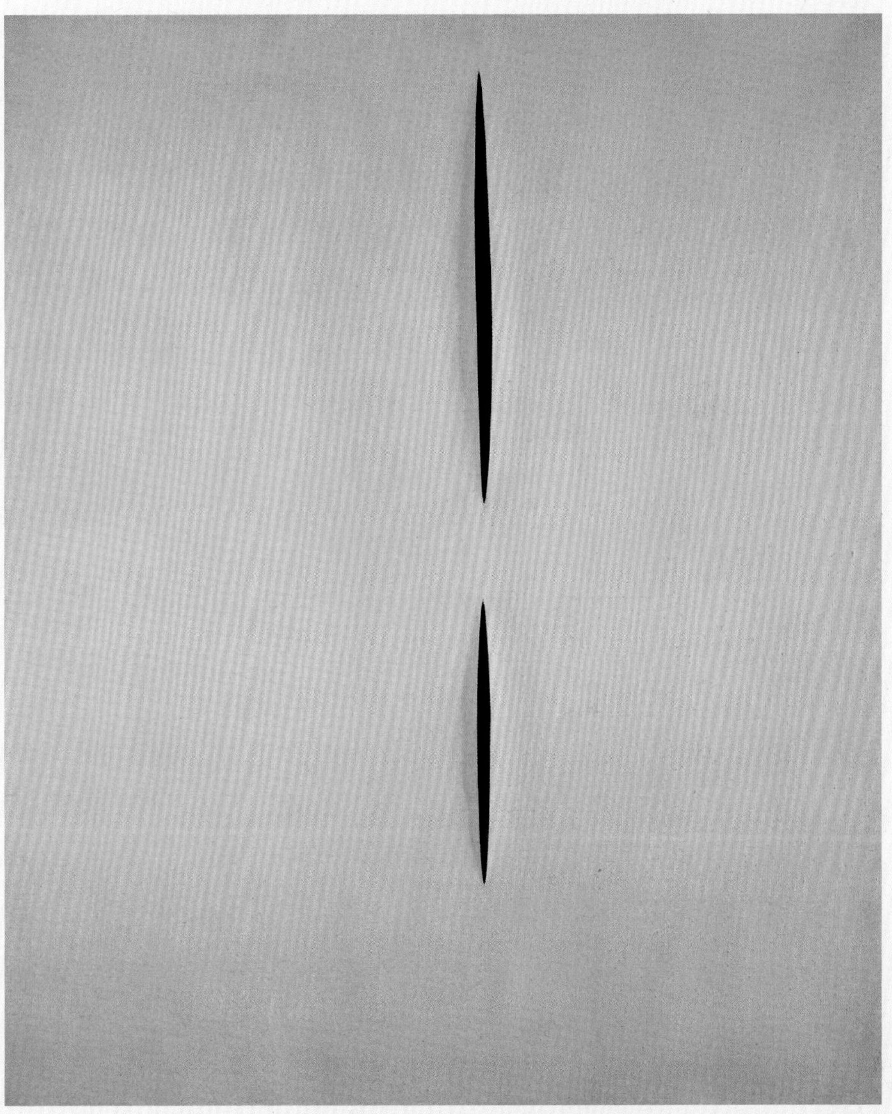

ACRYLIC AND VINYL PAINT **p. 205**

Blue Monochrome

YVES KLEIN • DRY PIGMENT IN POLYVINYL ACETATE ON COTTON OVER
PLYWOOD • 6 FT. 5 IN. × 4 FT. 7 IN. (195.1 × 140 CM) •
MUSEUM OF MODERN ART, NEW YORK, NY

1961

YVES KLEIN (1928–1962)
Klein began painting monochromes in various colors in 1949, before narrowing his focus to blue. In 1960, using an almost alchemical approach to painting, he enriched his palette with pink, associated with blood, and gold, associated with the transmutation of matter.

In 1960, at the French National Institute of Industrial Property, Yves Klein used a Soleau envelope (less expensive than a patent) to register the formula for the polymer used to bind the intense blue pigments he used in his monochromes—International Klein Blue (IKB) was officially created. By applying this formula to canvas using a roller, Klein gave this ultramarine blue a distinctive velvety texture. Over time, he applied the paint in increasingly thin, uniform layers. Here, he ever so slightly smoothed the corners of the painting to modify how the work is perceived against the background of the wall.

Klein created 194 blue monochrome paintings between the mid-1950s and his death in 1962. "Blue has no dimensions, it is beyond dimensions, whereas the other colors are not," he said at a lecture at the Sorbonne in 1959. "All colors arouse specific associative ideas, psychologically material or tangible, while blue suggests at most the sea and sky, and they, after all, are in actual, visible nature what is most abstract." This blue has the qualities of pure, spiritual space. Klein's artistic practice was guided by his involvement with judo, a sport traditionally rooted in the forces of nature (air, water, fire, earth) and one he excelled at—Klein was the first French person to obtain a fourth-degree black belt in the discipline. He was also highly influenced by the esoteric philosophy of the Rosicrucians. These sources of inspiration made him the most mystical of the New Realists.

Other important works
M 72. Monochrome jaune "violet," 1957.
Centre Pompidou, Paris.
Chéquier, 1959.
Centre Pompidou, Paris.
Le Rose du bleu (RE 22), 1960.
Private collection.

MONOCHROMES **p. 36** POP COLORS **p. 39** BLUE **p. 48**

BLUE PIGMENTS **p. 194** INDUSTRIAL MATERIALS **p. 209**

Shooting Painting

1961

NIKI DE SAINT PHALLE • PLASTER, PAINT, METAL, AND VARIOUS OBJECTS
ON PARTICLE BOARD • 5 FT. 9 IN. × 2 FT. 7½ IN. (175 × 80 CM) •
CENTRE POMPIDOU, PARIS

**NIKI DE SAINT PHALLE
(1930–2002)**
Niki de Saint Phalle made a name for herself with her painting-assemblage works and her shooting paintings. A member of the New Realists, she created "attack" art aimed at societal conventions and patriarchal norms. She would soon go on to create her first *Nanas*: colorful, sensual feminine figures that attacked good taste this time—and earned her full-blown fame.

Between 1961 and 1963, Niki de Saint Phalle created twelve "Shooting paintings" (known as *Tirs* in French). Using the same process each time, she first created what have been described as "prepared canvases": these were often a wood panel to which she attached found objects (shampoo bottles, fake weapons, containers, etc.), food, and plastic bags of colored paint, all of which she covered in white plaster to resemble a blank canvas.

Then during the performance, she shot a rifle at the painting, or invited other artists to do so, causing the bags to burst and paint to flow down the panel. With a sense for the dramatic, she often appeared dressed in white coveralls and black boots, skillfully wielding weapons like an Amazon warrior to draw attention to the sense of revolt and violence within.

The artist explained that through these actions, she was shooting at her own personal pain, as well as social injustice, institutionalism, war, and, of course, the history of art and the very idea of the painting: "I shot because I was fascinated to see the painting bleed and die. . . . White purity. Victim. Ready! Set! Fire! Red, yellow, blue—the painting is crying; the painting is dead. I have killed the painting. It is reborn." In this way, she parodied certain contemporary painting practices, especially American abstract expressionism and French lyrical abstraction.

Other important works
Stravinsky Fountain, 1983. Paris.
Nana on a Dolphin, 1998. National Museum of Women in the Arts, Washington, DC.
The Three Graces, 1999. National Museum of Women in the Arts, Washington, DC.

POP COLORS **p. 39** WHITE **p. 45**

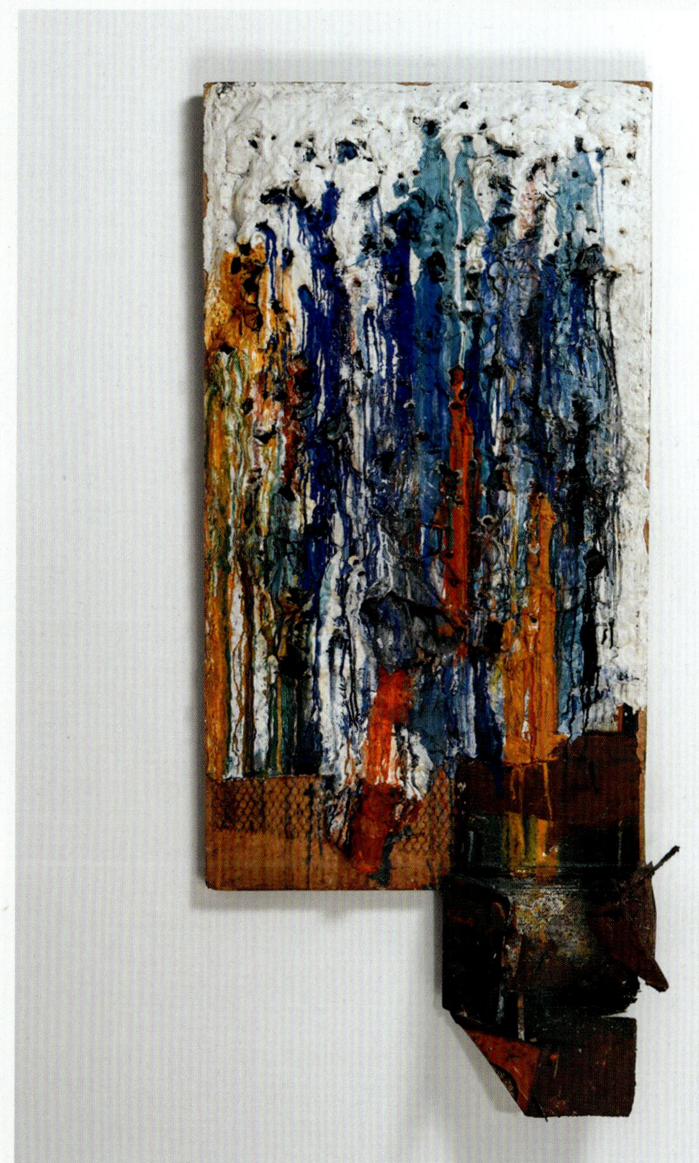

INDUSTRIAL MATERIALS **p. 209**

Gold Marilyn Monroe

ANDY WARHOL • SILKSCREEN INK AND ACRYLIC ON CANVAS •
6 FT. 11¼ IN. × 4 FT. 9 IN. (211.4 × 144.7 CM) •
MUSEUM OF MODERN ART, NEW YORK, NY

1962

ANDY WARHOL (1928–1987)
Ironic and multi-faceted, Andy Warhol was the postmodern artist par excellence. A painter, rock music producer, experimental filmmaker, and magazine editor, he surrounded himself with a set of semi-marginal figures. Poets, musicians, and models participated in the collective activities (parties but also work sessions) undertaken at the Silver Factory: a loft that the artist Billy Name (1940–2016) covered in aluminum sheets and silver spray paint, in a reference to space exploration, to the silver backing on older mirrors, and to the silver screen.

The year Marilyn Monroe (1926–1962) died, Andy Warhol created his first screen prints from a black-and-white promotional photograph of the actress taken nine years earlier by Gene Kornman (1897–1978) for the film *Niagara*, directed by Joseph Mankiewicz (1909–1993). He cropped the original image (Cambridge, MIT Libraries), then colorized it. Warhol first applied areas of color to the canvas: turquoise for her eyelids and collar, pink for her skin, red for her lips, and yellow for her hair. Then he screen printed the facial features. The rest is painted gold. This technique elevates the portrait of Hollywood's greatest star to an icon, in the Byzantine sense of the word, but one produced in the era of mass culture, with garish colors borrowed from advertising. Here, by reproducing and colorizing an image, Warhol—more fascinated than critical—brings to light the commodification of celebrities.

By using standardized, industrial means that enabled him to create many variations of the actress's face, Warhol proposed a radically different alternative to the heroic painter that abstract expressionism had resurrected a decade earlier, as well as to the concept of the artwork as an expression of originality. In *The Philosophy of Andy Warhol: from A to B and Back Again*, published in 1975, Warhol writes, "You see, I think every painting should be the same size and the same color so they're all interchangeable and nobody thinks they have a better painting or a worse painting."

Other important works
Campbell's Soup Cans, 1962.
Museum of Modern Art, New York, NY.
Marilyn Diptych, 1962. Tate, London.
Dollar Sign, 1981. Moco Museum,
Amsterdam.

POP COLORS **p. 39** RED **p. 46** YELLOW **p. 47** BLUE **p. 48** PINK **p. 53** GOLD **p. 56**

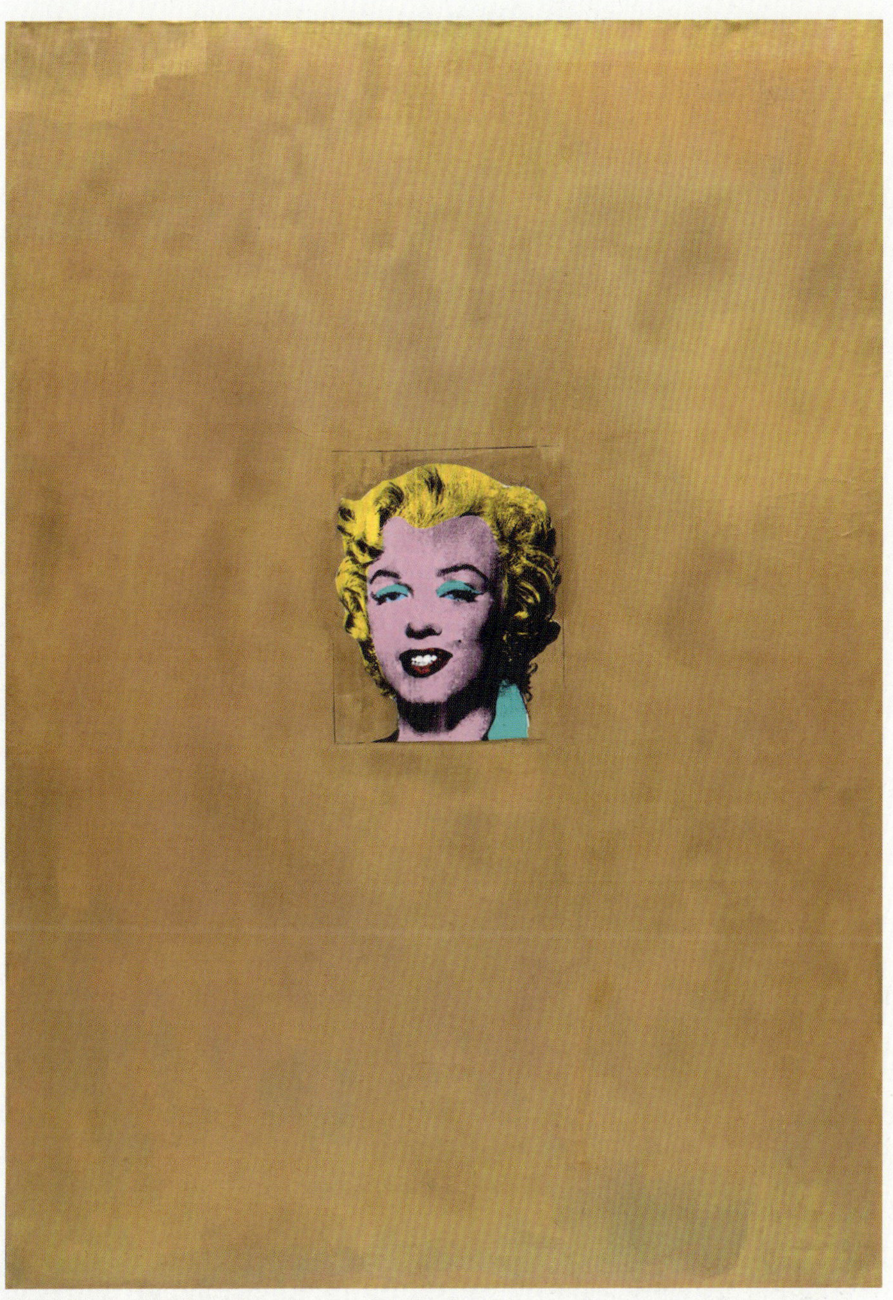

COLOR PRINTMAKING **p. 208**

Homage to the Square: Joy

1964

JOSEF ALBERS • OIL ON MASONITE • 30 × 30 IN. (76 × 76 CM) •
PRIVATE COLLECTION

In 1950, Josef Albers added a new twist to his research into color, which had been omnipresent in his work since the beginning, by undertaking a series titled *Homage to the Square*. He created more than two thousand of these homages, working on them almost daily until his death in 1976.

Each painting follows the same principle: three or four squares in different, opaque colors overlap, rising gradually toward the center. The challenge was to explore the relativity of color, what he called its deception, through combinations of colors and their interactions. Using a painter's knife and working from the smallest to the largest square, he applied color straight from the tube onto a Masonite panel covered with a layer of white gesso. Although each painting was composed in a similar manner, the colors used produce different movements in the eye of the viewer: some squares appear to move forward, others to move back or to shrink, and still others to vibrate with a singular light. In *Homage to the Square: Joy*, the yellow square creates a faintly veiled opening at the heart of the painting.

In 1952, Albers wrote, "We are able to hear a single tone. But we almost never (that is without special devices) see a single color unconnected and unrelated to other colors. Colors present themselves in continuous flux, constantly related to changing neighbors and changing conditions." Behind this homage to the square lies, in reality, a passionate homage to color.

Other important works
Homage to the Square: With Rays, 1959. The Metropolitan Museum of Art, New York, NY.
Homage to the Square: Stepped Foliage, 1963. National Gallery of Canada, Ottawa.
Manhattan, 1963/2019. MetLife Building, New York, NY.

PRIMARY AND COMPLEMENTARY COLORS **p. 27** YELLOW **p. 47** ORANGE **p. 50**

JOSEF ALBERS (1888–1976)

Albers was both a great educator and a pioneer of minimalism. Working at the Bauhaus, first as a teacher then as a professor, he went into exile in the United States in 1933 with his wife, Anni, also an artist and educator. Albers developed an awareness of color through the work of Vincent Van Gogh (1853–1890) and Edvard Munch (1863–1944). In his experiments with stained glass, furniture, typography, paper folding, and, of course, painting, he remained conscious of the subjective nature of perception.

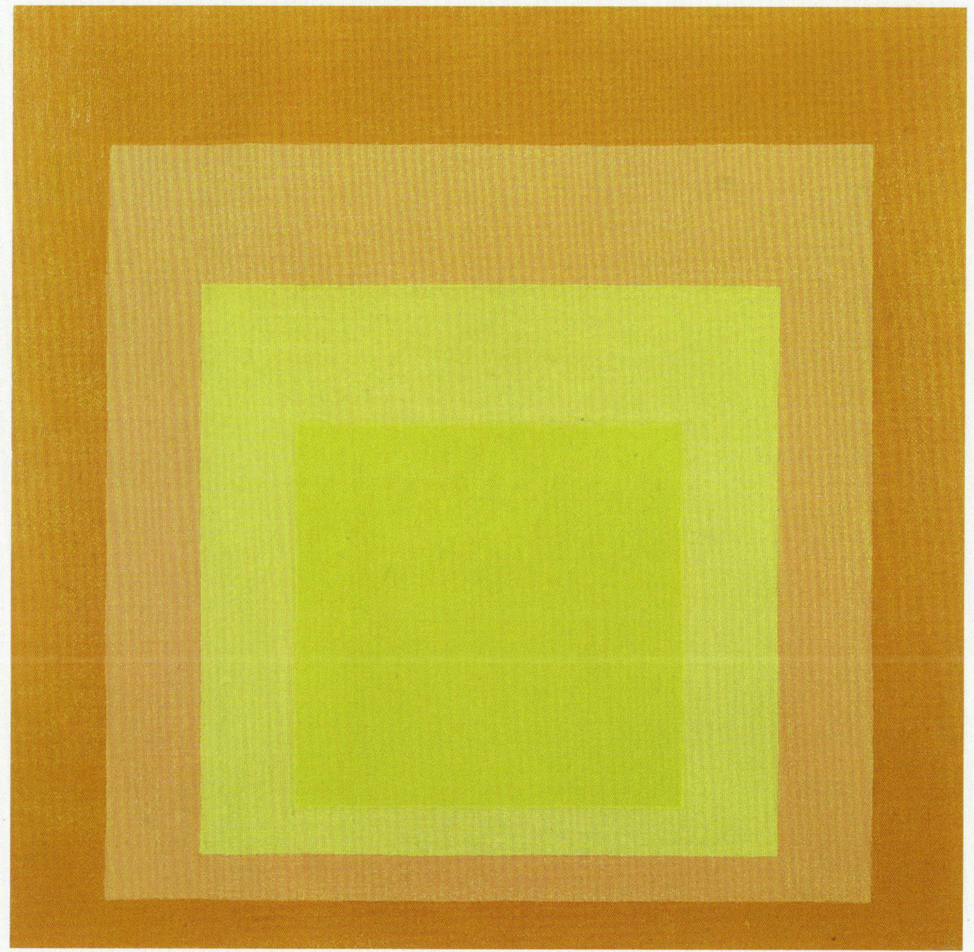

Flood

1967

HELEN FRANKENTHALER • ACRYLIC ON CANVAS • 10 FT. 4 IN. × 11 FT. 8½ IN.
(315.6 × 356.9 CM) • WHITNEY MUSEUM OF AMERICAN ART, NEW YORK, NY

HELEN FRANKENTHALER (1928–2011)

Helen Frankenthaler was a major contributor to the abstract expressionist movement. In the early 1950s, she developed a technique of soaking canvas—often in large formats—with areas of colored paint, in rejection of what she called the artist's "gesture." "I don't start with a color order but find the color as I go," she explained in *Artforum* magazine in October 1965. "I'd rather risk an ugly surprise than rely on things I know I can do." Later, she overlapped colors and created more distinct contrasts, and in the 1980s returned to the cubism that influenced her early work.

In Helen Frankenthaler's *Flood*, an influx of colors penetrates the canvas: ocher, blue, green, beige, mauve, beige-yellow, pink. This rhythm reveals much about the method Frankenthaler adopted in the early 1950s. The soak-stain technique paved a new path within abstract expressionism: color field painting, which had less heroic and virile connotations than the broader movement. Frankenthaler poured pigments diluted with turpentine on an unframed canvas placed on the floor. The volatile pigments soaked into the untreated textile like dye.

Along with most of the other abstract expressionists, Frankenthaler explored the flatness of the painting as a reaction against pictorial illusionism inherited from the Renaissance, and shared an obvious preference for color as a means of materializing this surface. But unlike some of her peers, she continued to reference the "real," primarily through nature. As she wrote to the curators at the Whitney Museum of Art, where the work has been held since 1968, "I think of my pictures as explosive landscapes, worlds and distances, held on a flat surface." The colors in *Flood* evoke the elements in one of these landscapes—earth, water, forest, hills, and an overcast sky.

Other important works
Mountains and Sea, 1952. National Gallery of Art, Washington, DC.
Small's Paradise, 1964. Smithsonian American Art Museum, Washington, DC.
Cameo, 1980. National Portrait Gallery, Canberra.

PURE COLOR **p. 37** YELLOW **p. 47** BLUE **p. 48** GREEN **p. 49** VIOLET **p. 51** PINK **p. 53**

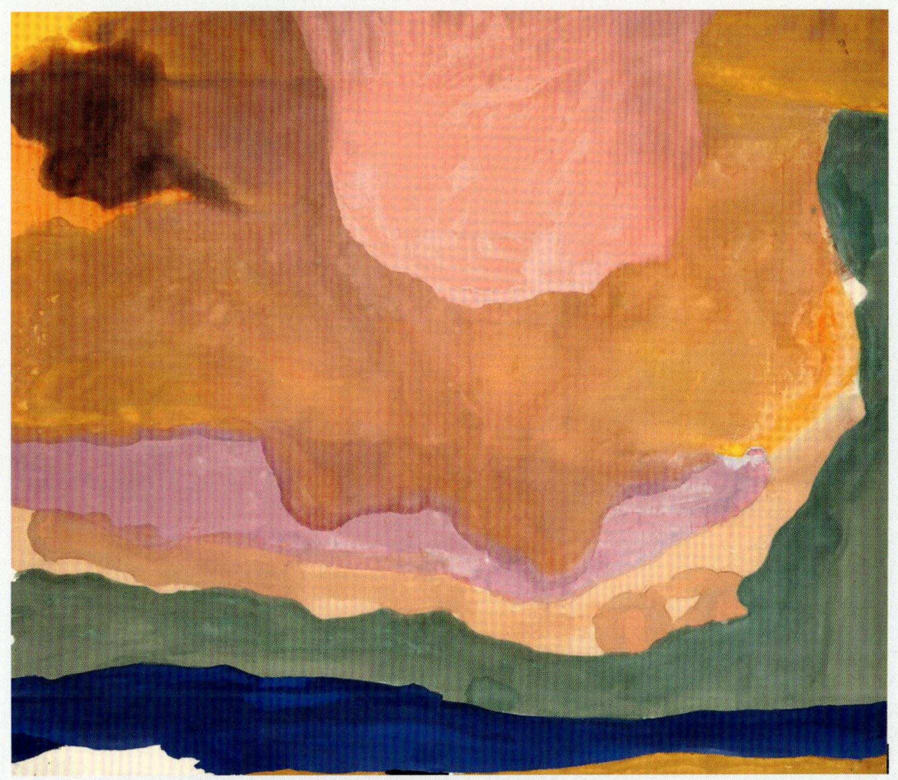

ACRYLIC AND VINYL PAINT **p. 205** PRIMER, UNDERCOAT, AND VARNISH **p. 206**

Coloration of the Grand Canal, Venice

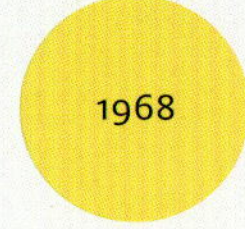

NICOLÁS GARCÍA URIBURU • PHOTOGRAPH • 30 × 10 IN. (76 × 50.5 CM) •
THE METROPOLITAN MUSEUM OF ART, NEW YORK, NY

**NICOLÁS GARCÍA URIBURU
(1937–2016)**
Uriburu was a pioneer of land art. Keen to liberate the work of art from its formal, iconographic, and aesthetic conventions, he performed large-scale actions in nature during which he dyed rivers and streams around the world green with fluorescein. Green, he emphasized, is also the color of hope.

On June 19, 1968, three days before the official opening of the 34th Venice Biennale, Nicolás García Uriburu, who was not part of the official program, boarded a gondola to create a unique monumental artwork. Guided by Memo, a gondolier, he poured 66 lb. (30 kg) of fluorescein—a non-polluting, non-toxic, and biodegradable dye—into the Grand Canal. This red powder turns fluorescent green when mixed with water. A two-mile (3-km) stretch of the canal took on this eyewatering hue. Venice, literally constructed on the lagoon, was the perfect setting for Uriburu to carry out this dramatic action, whose intention was to materialize the connections between nature and civilization, as well as their ecological implications. For hours after he released the colorant, the Venetian canals appeared to have fallen victim to some terrible pollution.

It was also a radical way to take painting out of the frame and to make it accessible to a wider audience. In a manifesto he wrote for the occasion, Uriburu states, "Art has no autonomous form any more. Art adopts nature's form: fluid, dynamic. Art has no more place outside of nature: (gallery, museum). It's place is inside of nature. It depends on the environment: the city, the waterways. . . . It surprises the public in its own vital space. . . . Art has life of its own: a beginning and an end. Art changes place, form, dimension. It varies according to meteorology, tides, currents."

Other important works
Coloration of the East River, 1970. New York, NY.
Coloration of the Seine, 1970. Paris.
Coloration of the Río de la Plata, 1970. Buenos Aires.

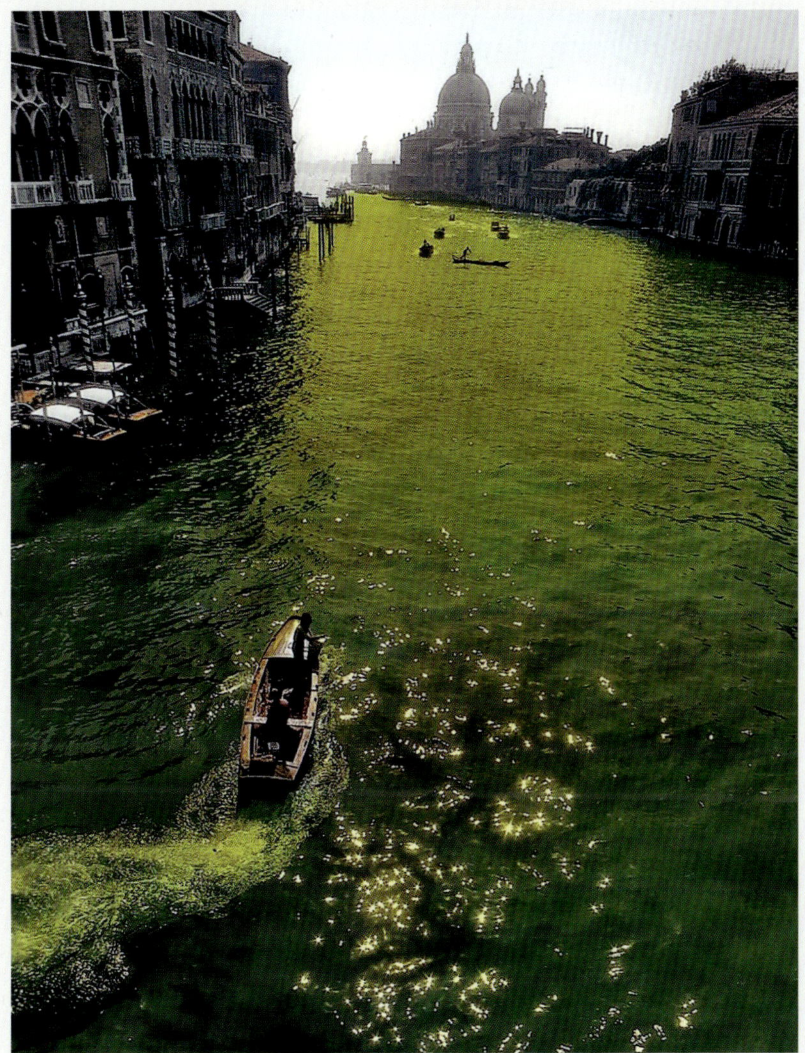

INDUSTRIAL MATERIALS **p. 209**

The Studio

PHILIP GUSTON • OIL ON CANVAS • 4 FT. × 3 FT. 6 IN. (121.9 × 106.7 CM) •
PROMISED GIFT OF MUSA GUSTON MAYER TO THE METROPOLITAN MUSEUM OF ART,
NEW YORK, NY

1969

PHILIP GUSTON (1913–1980)
Guston explored many artistic paths. Initially a draftsman who trained as a comics illustrator in his early career, he became a follower of social realism, and then an abstract painter, before abandoning abstraction to give free rein to amplified figuration.

In a studio, an artist wearing a hood that recalls the Ku Klux Klan paints a self-portrait while smoking a cigarette. This work was painted in the late 1960s, when Philip Guston, a leading figure in abstract expressionism, made an unexpected return to representational art: "I got sick and tired of all that purity," he explained in *ARTnews* in October 1970. "I wanted to tell stories."

The hooded figure became a recurring motif in his work. It was a reference to American history, but also a personal memory: he had witnessed Klan gatherings as a teenager in Los Angeles. A symbol of bigotry and evil, the hooded Klansman became a grotesque double for Guston. According to the art historian Craig Burnett, using the hood was a way for the painter to align himself with a history of figuration straddling social criticism and farce that had been practiced by artists from Goya to James Ensor (1860–1949), while escaping his own artistic torment. The motif appears alongside other ordinary, everyday objects that are present in painting after painting: a cigarette, a hand, a clock, and a naked light bulb.

The color red, mellowed by white to create a broad palette of pinks, is another decisive element in this studio scene, and one that appears in many other paintings that Guston created from the late 1960s onward. Often associated with green, blue, black, and orange in small areas of color, it became Guston's favorite hue. As cartoonish as the artist's lines, the color has a carnal, even meaty quality that reinforces the choice of figuration.

Other important works
Last Piece, 1958. Museum of Modern Art, New York, NY.
City Limits, 1969. Museum of Modern Art, New York, NY.
Painting, Smoking, Eating, 1973. Stedelijk Museum, Amsterdam.

BLACK **p. 44** WHITE **p. 45** RED **p. 46** BLUE **p. 48** GREEN **p. 49** PINK **p. 53**

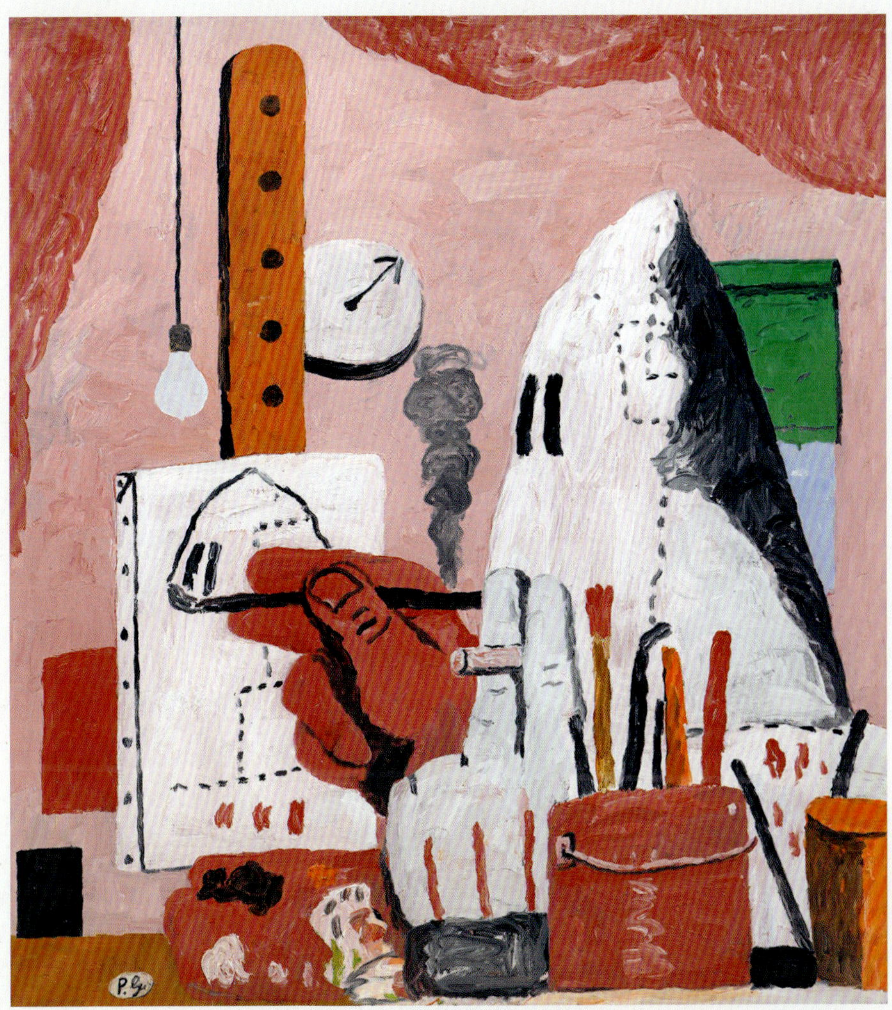

THE PAINTER'S TOOLS **p. 197**

Purple Atmosphere

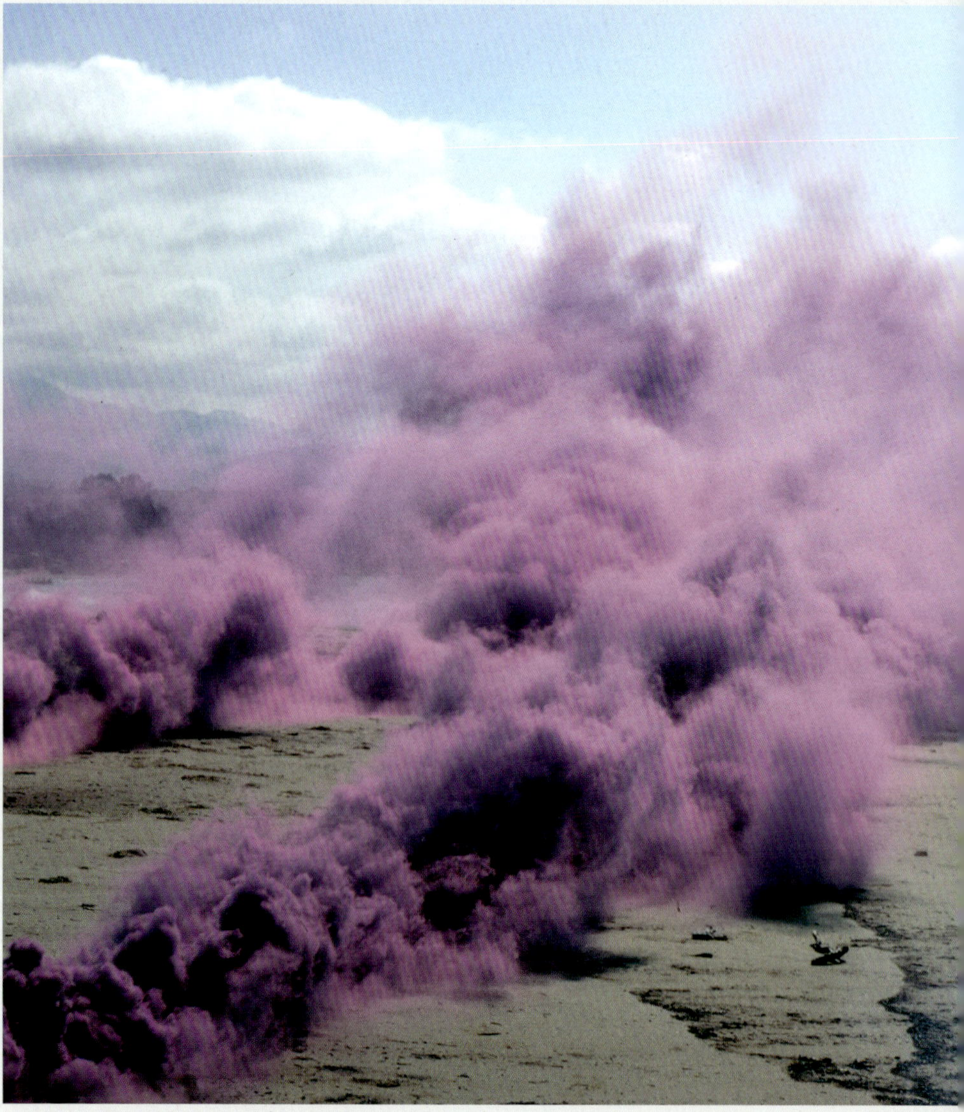

JUDY CHICAGO (BORN 1939)

Judy Chicago is a leading figure in American feminist art. In the late 1960s, she turned her attention to the condition of women and made her name with *The Dinner Party* (1974–79), an immense collaborative installation and a vibrant homage to great women in history.

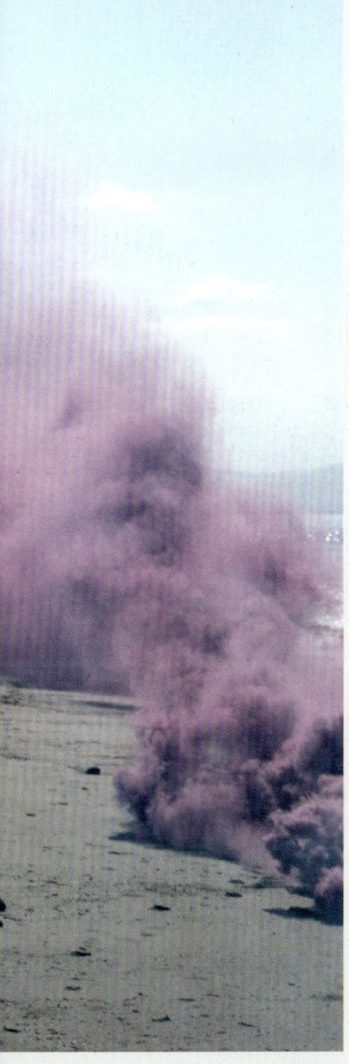

In the late 1960s, Judy Chicago—a young artist and recent graduate of the University of California—made an observation: the local art scene was dominated by men. Between 1968 and 1974, in response to this domination, she developed a series of thirty landscape performances, her primary goal being to "feminize the atmosphere." In some, she focused on traditionally female activities like kindling the hearth or worshipping certain goddess figures, using fireworks to create colorful emanations that permeated urban, desert, or seaside landscapes with soft plumes of smoke. But this softness, this sensuality, as art critic Géraldine Gourbe notes in *Judy Chicago: To Sustain the Vision* (2020), also acquires an insurrectional dimension and a revolutionary power.

These actions are also remarkable for their fleeting, elusive character, opening a new path within land art. "My work represents a significant challenge to that of many of my male peers whose work involves bulldozers and other heavy equipment and leaves a permanent scar on the land," Chicago told *Dazed* magazine in 2020. "In contrast, I use environment-friendly smokes that create moments of intense beauty but leave no permanent marks."

In 1969, violet fireworks set off on a Santa Barbara beach formed an ephemeral sculpture and momentarily redefined the landscape with their billowing smoke. The colored air rapidly dissipated into the dramatic backdrop of the Pacific Ocean. Chicago's quest to liberate art is driven by an exploration of color: here, she chose violet, but she also used orange, red, and green in this series of performances—bright, intense colors that contrast with minimalist orthodoxy, inclined to neutral shades.

→ INDUSTRIAL MATERIALS **p. 209**

Odalisque (Hey, Hey Frankenthaler)

LYNDA BENGLIS • POURED PIGMENTED LATEX • 3 FT. 4 IN. × 2 FT. 10½ IN. (101 × 87.63 CM) • DALLAS MUSEUM OF ART, DALLAS, TX

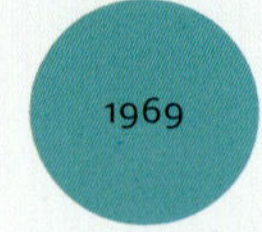

LYNDA BENGLIS (BORN 1941)

Conscious of materiality and its forms, Lynda Benglis defied modernism's purity in the 1960s with her *Wax Paintings*, *Fallen Paintings*, and then, in the 1970s, her *Expansions*. She also worked with video, photography, and media such as advertisements, invitations, and posters to emphasize power relations, prejudice, and the excesses of consumerism.

Other important works
Contraband, 1969. Whitney Museum of American Art, New York, NY.
Quartered Meteor, 1969–75. Tate, London.
Amazing Grace, 1980. Private collection.

In 1969, Lynda Benglis went to the Helen Frankenthaler (1928–2011) retrospective at the Whitney Museum of American Art in New York. Frankenthaler was known for her soak-stain technique that consisted of pouring diluted pigments on canvases spread on the floor. In reaction to these paintings, Benglis experimented with pouring colored latex on the floor. The resulting works obliterated the traditional conventions of the painting intended to be hung on a wall, which Frankenthaler's generation of abstract expressionists were still practicing, and of the sculpture-in-the-round on its stand. In creating this giant pour in pure, vibrating colors—red, yellow, blue, and green—that spread over the floor space, Benglis modified the viewer's relationship to the work.

The word "odalisque," popular in nineteenth-century French orientalist painting, is a nod to the archetype of the reclining, eroticized female figure, as well as to the new artistic practices carried out horizontally, on the ground, by Frankenthaler and Benglis herself.

Irony is an important element in Benglis's work, and she gave these pieces the generic title of *Fallen Paintings*, whose double meaning alludes to the myth of the woman corrupted by vice (the fallen woman) and to the death of easel painting. Benglis's poured latex works, which invade the aseptic museum or gallery space with a living energy and a touch of vulgarity, are also a response to the austere minimalism that reigned in the contemporary art scene.

PURE COLOR **p. 37** RED **p. 46** YELLOW **p. 47** BLUE **p. 48** GREEN **p. 49**

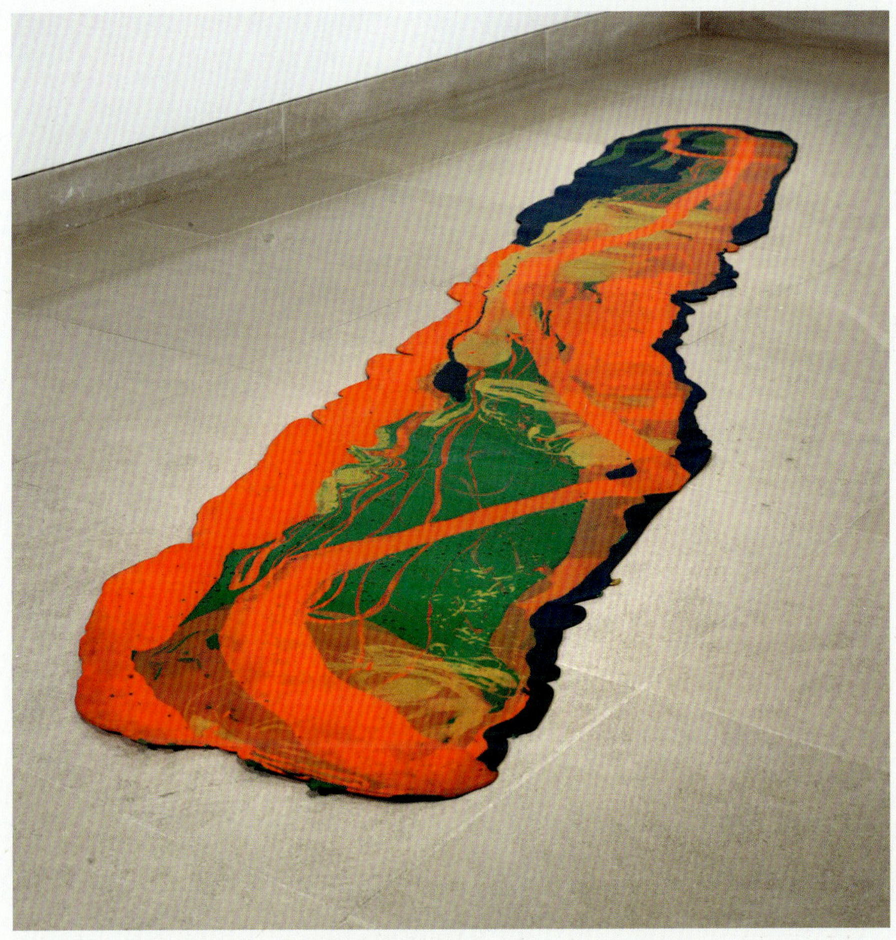

My Parents

DAVID HOCKNEY • OIL ON CANVAS • 6 × 6 FT. (182.9 × 182.9 CM) •
TATE MODERN, LONDON

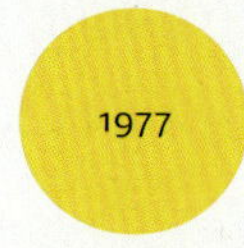

**DAVID HOCKNEY
(BORN 1937)**
In the early 1960s—a time when abstraction dominated the artistic scene—David Hockney began an ongoing reaffirmation of the importance of the subject in painting. He works in the traditional genres of portraiture, landscape, still life, and interiors, and his work often reveals autobiographical inspirations and a passionate love of color.

Other important works
A Bigger Splash, 1967.
Tate, London.
Mr and Mrs Clark and Percy,
1970–71. Tate, London.
*Portrait of an Artist
(Pool with Two Figures)*, 1972.
Private collection.

In the 1970s, David Hockney tried several times to paint his parents' portraits, but he never achieved a satisfactory result. In the end, he created this arrangement that perfectly translates the singularity of each parent's personality.

In a simple, structured setting, Hockney represents his mother, Laura, seated facing him, her lips in a half smile. His father, Kenneth, also seated, is absorbed in Aaron Scharf's (1922–1993) *Art and Photography*, published in 1968. A shelf in the background holds a translation of Marcel Proust's (1871–1922) *In Search of Lost Time* (1913–27), as well as a tome on the work of the painter Jean Siméon Chardin (1699–1779), known for his interior scenes. A reflection of a reproduction of *The Baptism of Christ* (1448–50, National Gallery, London) by Piero Della Francesca (c. 1415–1492) is visible in the mirror—perhaps a reference to Hockney's parents' Christian faith—and his own *Invented Man Revealing Still Life* (1975, The Nelson-Atkins Museum of Art, Kansas City, MO). These erudite allusions echo the work's very composition—a legacy of the long tradition of portraiture.

Hockney's extensive explorations into color—an important aspect of his oeuvre—here resulted in a palette that is unusual for this long codified genre. Dominated by bright, luminous colors—aqua, almond, mauve, yellow, shocking pink, and red—it is nonetheless softened by several more subdued colors: beige with straw highlights, brown, and very dark blue. Combining innovation and tradition once again, the painter borrows from Johannes Vermeer (1632–1675) the intense use of ultramarine blue for reflections and shadows in the hair and on the skin, and in the father's suit and shoes.

POP COLORS **p. 39** YELLOW **p. 47** BLUE **p. 48** GREEN **p. 49** VIOLET **p. 51** BROWN **p. 52** PINK **p. 53**

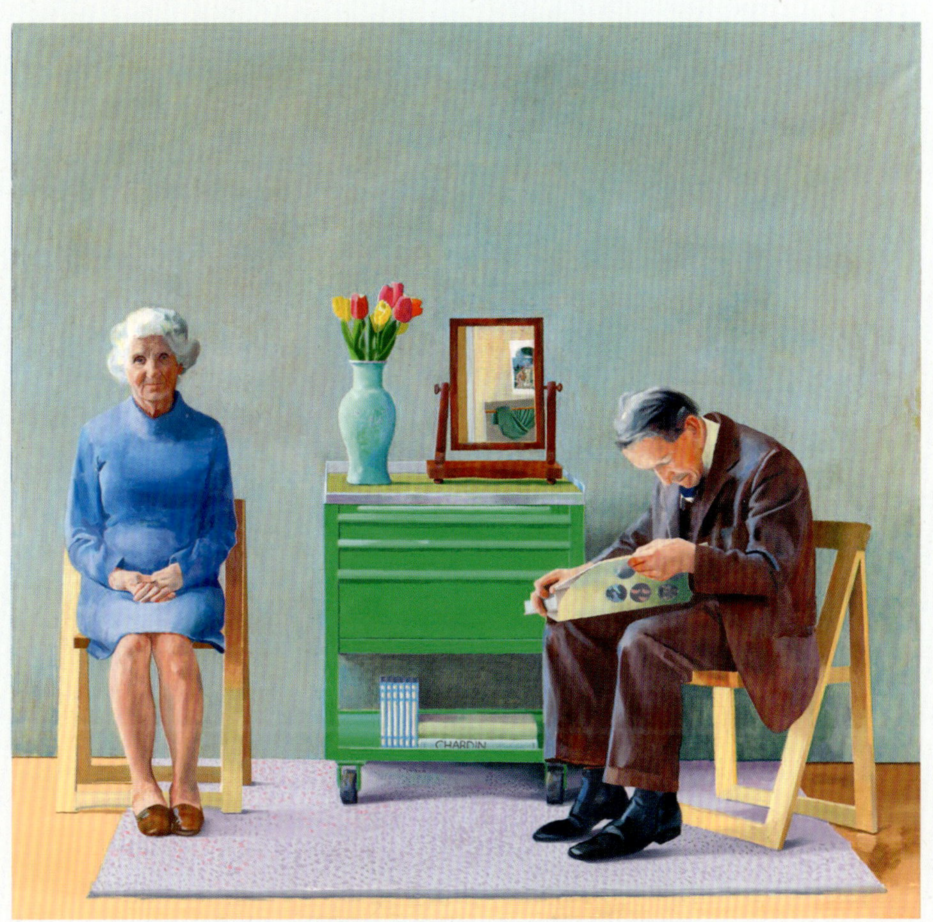

BLUE PIGMENTS **p. 194**

Six Colorful Inside Jobs

JOHN BALDESSARI • VIDEO • 32:53 MIN. • MUMOK, VIENNA

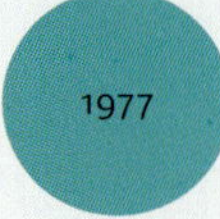
1977

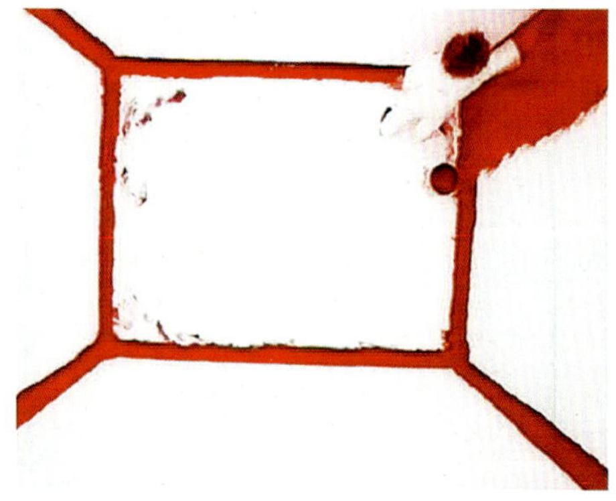

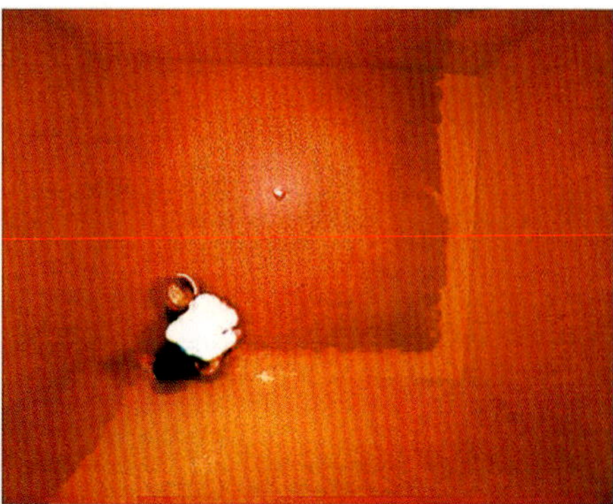

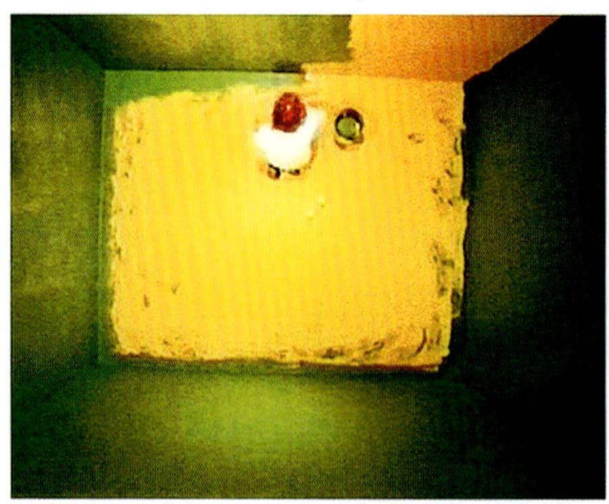

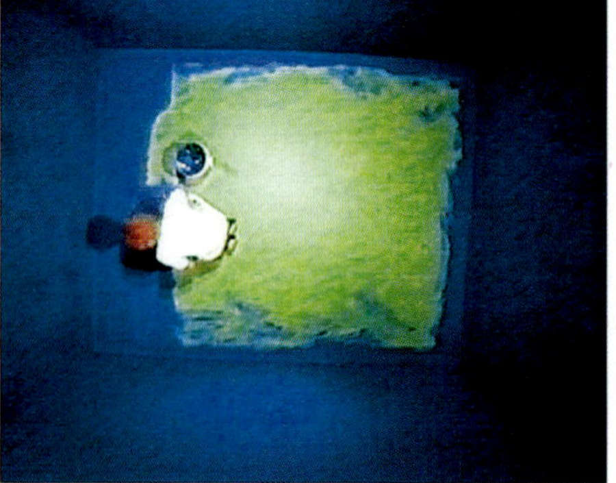

JOHN BALDESSARI (1931–2020)

Baldessari was a major figure in US West Coast conceptual art. Photography and video allowed him to playfully and humorously explore mass culture, and the relationships between language and image. He often used bold colors as a way to introduce a disruptive element into the work and lead the viewer to wonder, "What am I looking at?"

PRIMARY AND COMPLEMENTARY COLORS **p. 27** RED **p. 46** YELLOW **p. 47** BLUE **p. 48** GREEN **p. 49** ORANGE **p. 50** VIOLET **p. 51**

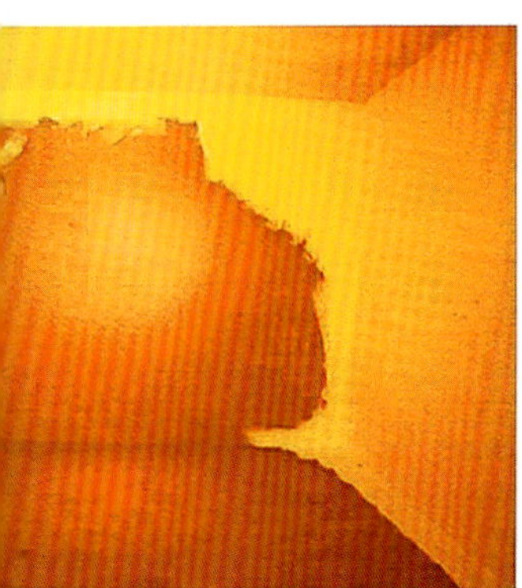

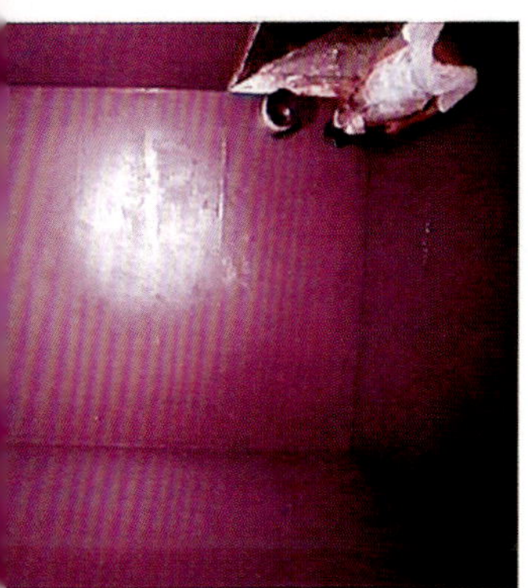

With *Six Colorful Inside Jobs*, John Baldessari asks a question that runs through his entire body of work: what is art? Here, he questions the difference between artist and house painter. When he was young, he was tasked by his father with maintaining rental properties. To pass the time, he painted the walls, telling himself by turns that he was painting a wall or making a painting: "It would just be a conceptual exercise," he explains in a recording for the Museum of Modern Art in New York. "The physical activity was the same, I was just calling it differently each time. So I began to think about what separated one from the other. Why was one different?"

In this video, Baldessari films from above a man repainting a room, as though seen in surveillance footage. The white room becomes red on Monday, then orange on Tuesday, yellow on Wednesday, green on Thursday, blue on Friday, and finally violet on Saturday—in other words, the three primary colors and their complementary secondary colors. Six colors for six working days; "the seventh day," laughs the artist, "one would rest, you know, in the Biblical sense." The expression "inside job" in the title is a pun, referring to a crime committed by someone within a company or organization. Baldessari films a repetitive, daily action that seems to have little in common with artistic practice. By choosing conventional, standardized colors, he strips them of any symbolic meaning.

Other important works
Wrong, 1967. Los Angeles County Museum of Art, Los Angeles, CA.
What Is Painting, 1968. Museum of Modern Art, New York, NY.
Throwing Three Balls in the Air to Get a Straight Line (Best of Thirty-Six Attempts), 1973. Princeton University Art Museum, Princeton, NJ.

→ THE PAINTER'S TOOLS **p. 197**

Shade

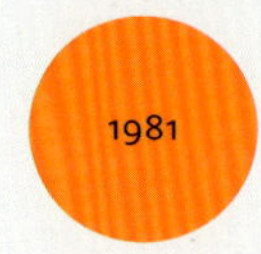

BRIDGET RILEY • OIL ON CANVAS • 5 FT. 6 IN. × 4 FT. 8 IN. (168 × 143 CM) • KUNSTHAUS ZÜRICH, ZURICH

BRIDGET RILEY (BORN 1931)

Initially introduced to Georges Seurat's color theories before being influenced by Victor Vasarely (1906–1997), Bridget Riley focused her attentions on abstraction in 1961, in paintings executed exclusively in black and white. It was only in the late 1960s that she added gray, then color. Using contrasts and straight or curved lines, she created powerful optical effects that destabilize the gaze through vibratory or centrifugal movements.

Other important works
Movement in Squares, 1961. Arts Council Collection, London.
Cataract 3, 1967. British Council, London.
Nataraja, 1993. Tate, London.

After traveling to Egypt in the winter of 1979–80, Bridget Riley undertook a new series of works in bright oil paint, rather than her usual acrylics, because it offered more pigment saturation. The series was called *Egyptian Palette*. Riley wanted to communicate the brightness of color that she had observed in works she discovered at the Egyptian Museum in Cairo and in tombs in the Valley of the Kings. In a lecture for the Royal Institute of British Architects in 1984, later published as "A Visit to Egypt and the Decoration for the Royal Liverpool Hospital," she recalled how deeply she had been influenced by these colors: "These basic colours were used for everything. For painting the inside and outside of their buildings, for their boats and vehicles, for their furniture and pottery, for their clothes and beads. In each and every usage these colours appeared different but at the same time they united the appearance of the entire culture. Perhaps even more important, the precise shades of these colours had evolved under a brilliant North African light and consequently they seemed to embody this light and even to reflect it back from the walls of the underground chambers which no daylight ever reached."

Riley carried out several paintings in blue, turquoise, red, yellow, and black, to which she sometimes added white, as in *Shade*. A series of thin colored bands appear in seemingly random order. The contrasts provoke a vibration, a movement in the viewer's eye, and convey the brightness of the Middle East. Unlike other paintings in the same series, such as the luminous *Achæan* (1981, Tate, London), here she uses less turquoise and obtains a more balanced effect, as though the painting had been mellowed by the shade mentioned in the title of the work.

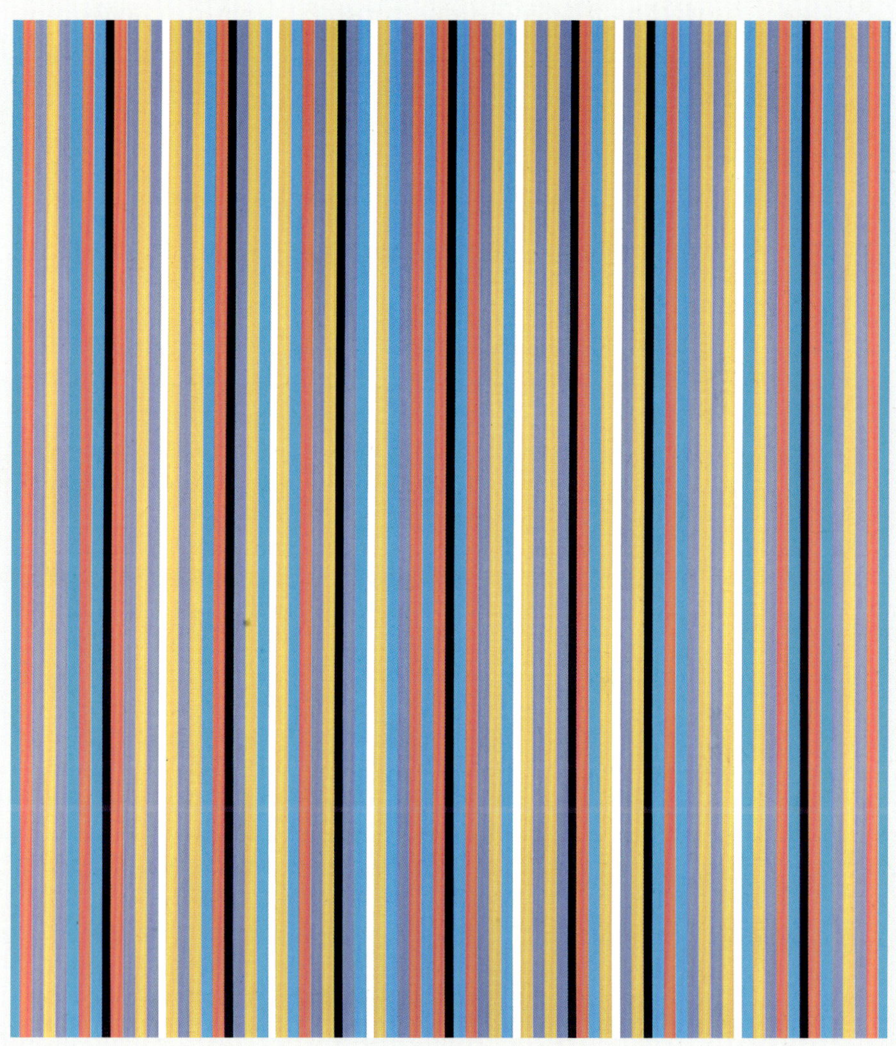

Painting 324 × 362 cm, 1986 (Polyptych I)

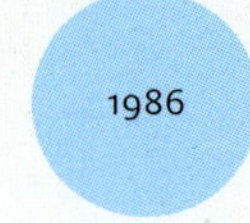

PIERRE SOULAGES • OIL ON CANVAS • FOUR OVERLAPPING PANELS,
EACH 2 FT. 8 IN. × 11 FT. 11 IN. (81 × 362 CM) • MUSÉE SOULAGES, RODEZ

**PIERRE SOULAGES
(1919–2022)**
Soulages earned acclaim in the late 1940s for his abstract, gestural work. But it was his *Outrenoir* ("beyond black") and its infinite possibilities that occupied him for more than forty years, in painting, drawing, printmaking, and even stained glass, as in the Abbey Church of Sainte-Foy in Conques, France (1987–94).

Between 1985 and 1987, Pierre Soulages created a series of nine, nearly square multi-panel paintings of the same dimensions, each comprising four overlapping rectangular canvases. Depending on whether they are viewed from the front or from the side, these paintings either reveal powerful lines of force or subtle paint work.

In this series, Soulages alternates between horizontal or vertical lines and diagonal lines, and between smooth and striated areas. Black, which might be thought of as uniform and without nuance, becomes a luminous space that produces effects of light. Until 1979, the painter used black with other hues—brown, white, or blue—before eliminating them to create what he would later call his *Outrenoir* ("beyond black" or "ultra-black"). In these works, he experimented with the thickness and texture of pigments applied to the canvas, and used relief to introduce light into optical perception, beyond the color black. This is what interested Soulages, and nothing else—not representation, image, or language.

For his one hundredth birthday in 2019, he recalled his discovery of the "*outrenoir*" during a conversation with Arnaud Laporte on France Culture radio: "I was painting and the color black had invaded the canvas. I seemed to be at a hopeless dead-end. . . . This new thing was going so far inside me that I carried on like this until I was exhausted. I went to sleep. And two hours later, when I went back to see what I had done, instead of feeling depressed about what I was doing, I realized that something had happened. I realized that I wasn't working with black, but with light reflected by the conditions of a black surface."

MONOCHROMES **p. 36** BLACK **p. 44**

Other important works

Gouache and Ink in Paper 65 × 50 cm, 1957, 1957. Private collection.
Painting 202 × 453 cm, 29 June 1979, 1979. Centre Pompidou, Paris.
Painting 222 × 314 cm, 24 February 2008, 2008. Pierre Soulages collection, Paris.

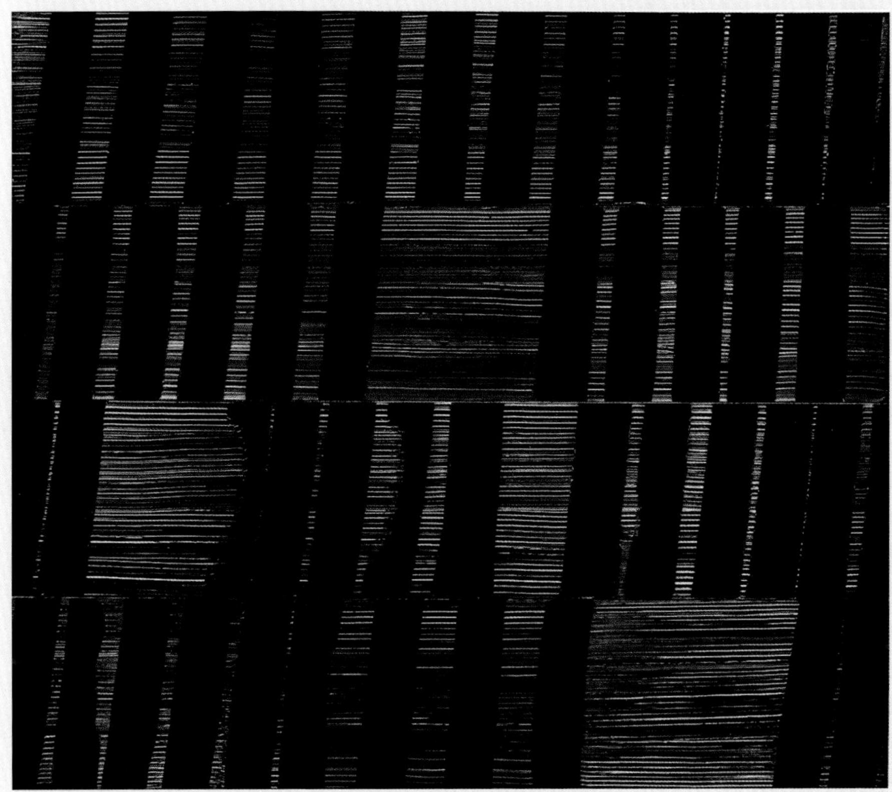

BLACK AND BROWN PIGMENTS **p. 196**

Untitled (to Don Judd, Colorist) 1–5

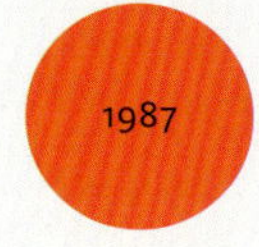

DAN FLAVIN • FLUORESCENT TUBES AND METAL • 4 × 4 FT. (122 × 122 CM) •
NATIONAL GALLERIES OF SCOTLAND, EDINBURGH, AND TATE MODERN, LONDON

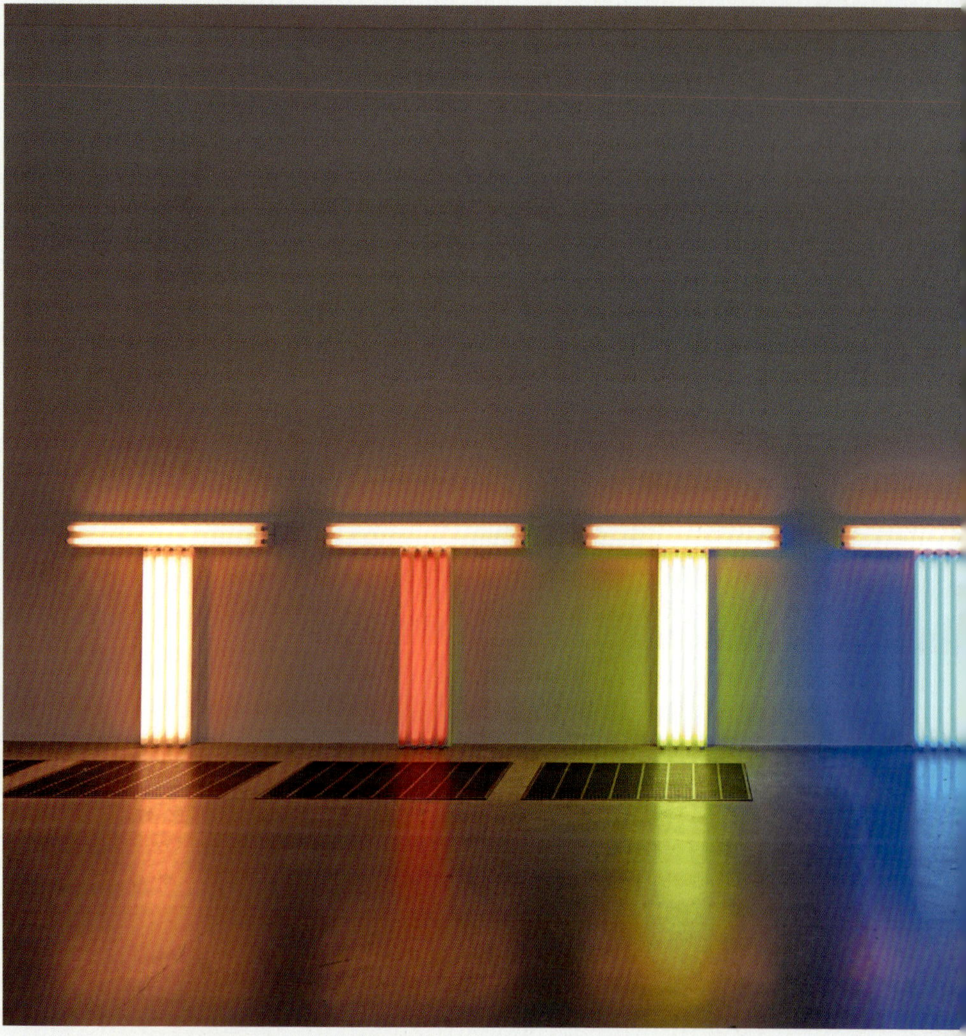

RED **p. 46** YELLOW **p. 47** BLUE **p. 48** GREEN **p. 49** PINK **p. 53**

Untitled (to Don Judd, Colorist) 1–5 is a tribute to the minimalist artist Donald Judd (1928–1994) and his use of color. Flavin met Judd in the early 1960s and the two of them developed a strong friendship. Judd made structures with industrial materials like sheet metal, Plexiglas, and plywood, which he colored using industrial methods.

In this large-format work, Flavin used fluorescent tubes to create five T-shaped forms in pink, red, yellow, green, and blue—all the colors commercially available at the time. The palette is accentuated by the use of three tubes of each hue and by the luminescent quality of the electrical device itself, which projects a colored aura on the wall and ground, and in so doing acts on the space surrounding the work. Flavin used a mass-produced material whose colors, dimensions, and wattage were standardized.

The titles of Flavin's works often pay tribute to an artist, as is the case here, a philosopher, or a collector who he appreciated. This combination anchors his conceptual work in daily life and confers unusual physicality, even while adhering to a minimalist perspective. However, Flavin points to a very spontaneous approach in his work: "It is what it is," he explained in *Art International* in 1987. "There is no overwhelming spirituality you are supposed to come into contact with. . . . It's in a sense a 'get-in-get-out' situation. And it is very easy to understand. One might not think of light as a matter of fact, but I do. And it is, as I said, as plain and open and direct an art as you will ever find."

DAN FLAVIN (1933–1996)

In 1963, Flavin began creating artworks with a single primary material: the fluorescent tube. Working within the constraints of an ordinary, manufactured product, he created installations that transform the exhibition space with the color and light they project.

INDUSTRIAL MATERIALS **p. 209**

Wall Drawing #610

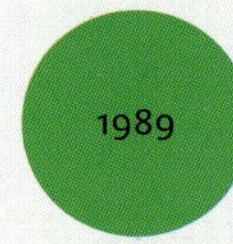

SOL LEWITT • COLOR INK WASH • VARIABLE DIMENSIONS •
YALE UNIVERSITY ART GALLERY, NEW HAVEN, CT

In 1968, Sol LeWitt began a vast series of wall drawings—twelve hundred in all—that he would pursue until his death in 2007. Much like Renaissance frescoes, these monumental, site-specific drawings were generally carried out by LeWitt's assistants and were destined to be destroyed when the exhibition ended. The ideas behind these conceptual works were more important than their production: assistants, like performers, were encouraged to follow the artist's instructions to the letter. LeWitt made preparatory sketches with pencil and paper, and included rough indications for color when it appeared. "I used the elements of these simple forms—square, cube, line, and color—to produce logical systems," he explained in *BOMB* magazine in 2003. "Most of these systems were finite; that is, they were complete using all possible variations."

Originally created for the Joan Miró Foundation in Barcelona, *Wall Drawing #610* is part of a group of wall drawings executed in colored ink wash that was begun in the early 1980s, and which introduced isometric forms. Here, the staircase is rendered with little regard for illusionist perspective: the base and left-hand edge, parallel with the edge of the wall, create an impression of two-dimensional flatness. LeWitt was very familiar with the world of printing and he obtained bright colors through a similar process of layering ink: to create the orange area, a layer of red, two layers of yellow, and a final layer of red were applied to the wall.

RED **p. 46** YELLOW **p. 47** ORANGE **p. 50**

SOL LEWITT (1928–2007)

Formerly a graphic designer, Sol LeWitt began reflecting early in his career on how to go beyond painting, which he felt had collapsed with abstract expressionism. In the early 1960s, he worked outside of the frame, on the wall and the floor, then exhausted formulas and systems he repeated in series, like the *Wall Drawings*, becoming a leading figure in conceptual art.

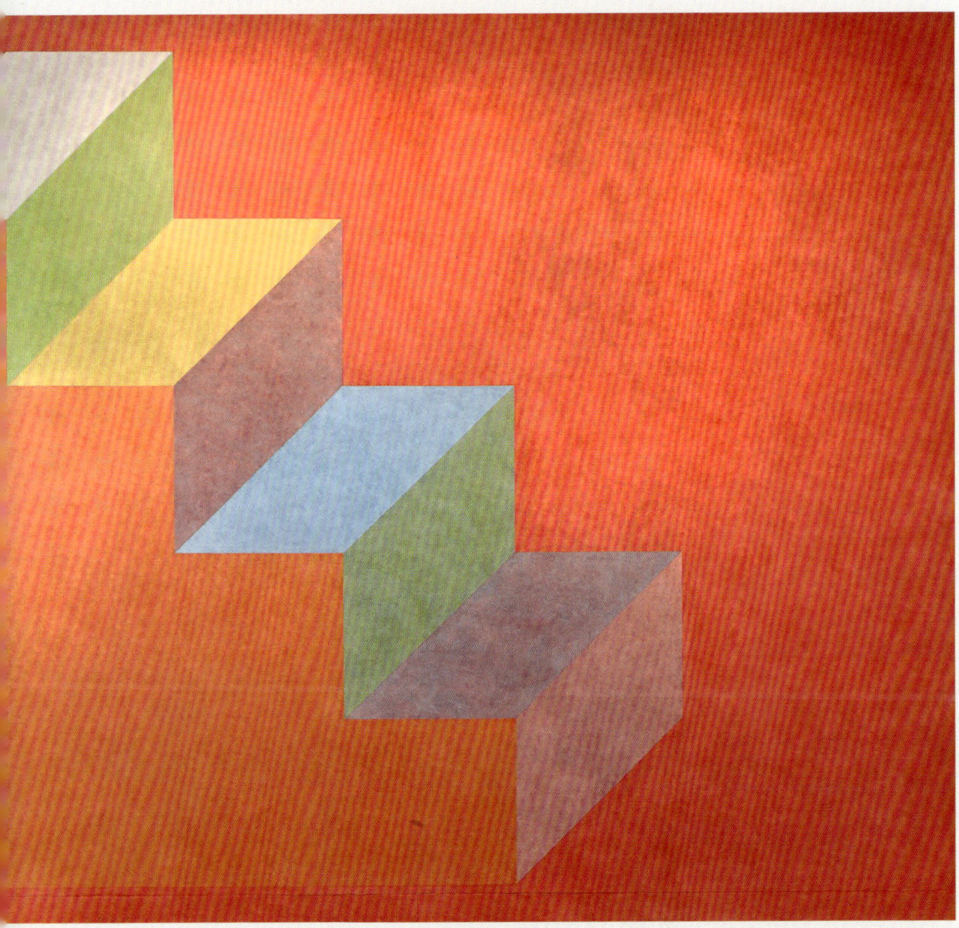

Other important works

Color Bands, 2000. Smithsonian American Art Museum, Washington, DC.
Splotch #3, 2000. Private collection.
Wall Drawing #1136, 2004. Tate St Ives, Cornwall.

FRESCO **p. 201**

The Gates

CHRISTO AND JEANNE-CLAUDE • VINYL AND NYLON FABRIC GATES •
DISPLAYED FEBRUARY 12–28, 2005, IN CENTRAL PARK, NEW YORK, NY

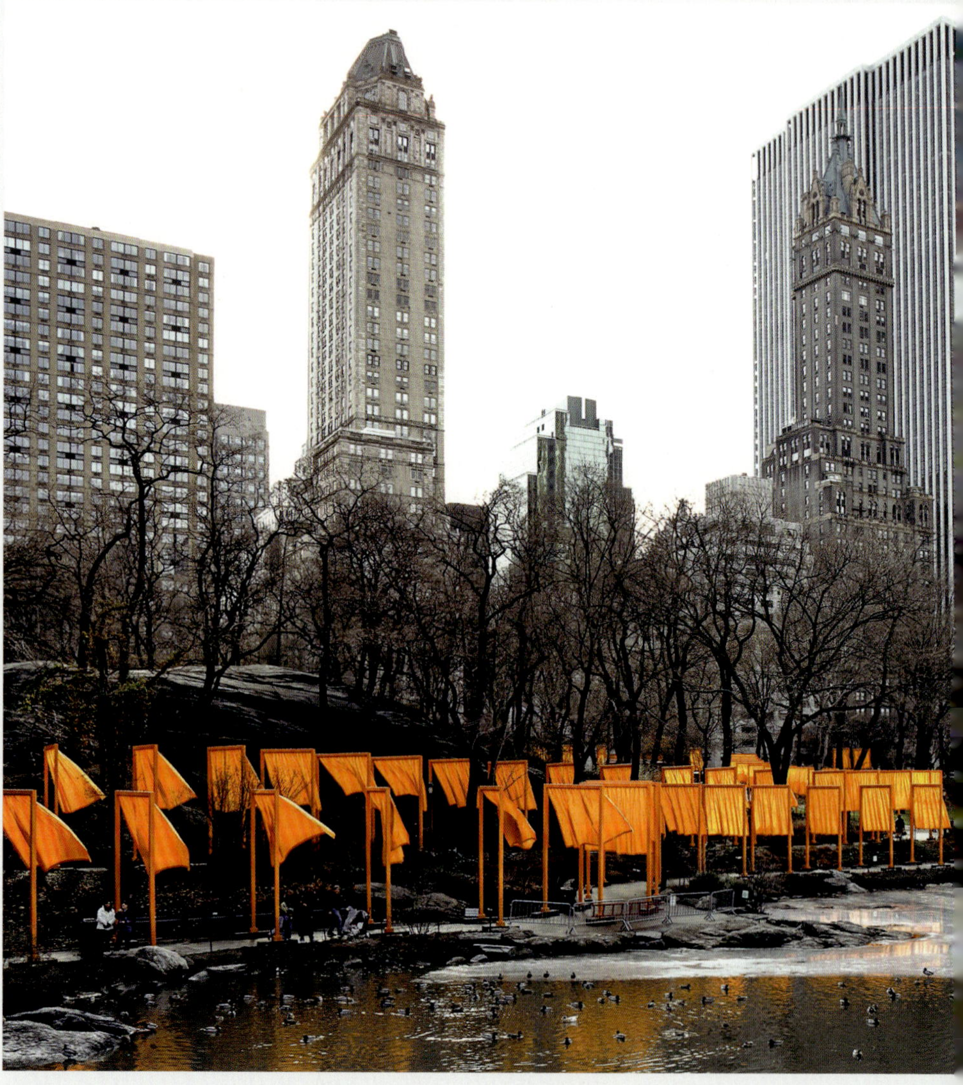

ORANGE **p.50**

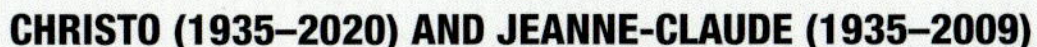

CHRISTO (1935–2020) AND JEANNE-CLAUDE (1935–2009)
Beginning in the 1960s, the couple developed a monumental body
of work in the same vein as land art. They carried out "wrappings":
temporary installations involving iconic buildings such as the
Reichstag in Berlin (1995) and natural sites. The use of white or
brightly colored fabric introduced color into landscapes on an
architectural scale.

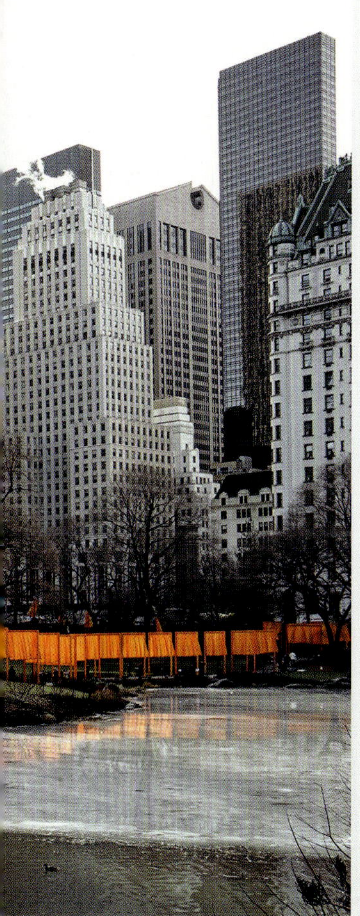

In February 2005, the artist-couple Christo and Jeanne-Claude presented a monumental temporary exhibition in Central Park, New York. Comprising 7,503 saffron-colored, 16-foot (5-meter) gates positioned on paved surfaces and blooming with nylon panels of the same color, the work formed a 23-mile (37-km) path through the heart of the park. The work was visible through bare-branched trees from buildings near the site, including from the roof of The Metropolitan Museum of Art. The installation was designed to be experienced up close, to be literally traversed, but also observed from afar: it was both experience and image.

The sinuous walkways and continuous movement of the fabric, as well as the play of light and shadow that it produced brought the installation to life, an impression strengthened by the warm color chosen by Christo and Jeanne-Claude; it vibrated in the gray winter light and contrasted with the grid pattern of New York's streets. "[W]e chose saffron," explained Jeanne-Claude in the review *L'En-je lacanien* in 2005, "because it is a color that changes a lot depending on the intensity of the light. In February, the sun is very low on the horizon, and this produces huge variations from golden yellow to deep red. When the sun passes behind the fabric, it will be golden, while the parts that are in shadow will turn much redder. It is quite simply an aesthetic color that we like very much."

The Gates also alludes to the Japanese tradition of *torii* gates placed at the entrance to Shinto shrines. A stroll through Central Park took on a spiritual dimension, inspired by the installation itself and strengthened by this sacred touchstone.

INDUSTRIAL MATERIALS **p. 209**

Femme

2007

LOUISE BOURGEOIS • GOUACHE ON PAPER • 23½ × 18 IN. (59.7 × 45.7 CM) •
NATIONAL GALLERIES OF SCOTLAND, EDINBURGH, AND TATE MODERN, LONDON

**LOUISE BOURGEOIS
(1911–2010)**
Louise Bourgeois's own life was her main source of inspiration. She made many allusions to her childhood, which was marked by her father's adultery and her mother's heroism, the latter often embodied in the figure of the spider. Red is given a strong presence, sometimes contrasted with black—the color of suicide and mourning, according to Bourgeois—or blue, which she considered a protective color.

In 2007, Louise Bourgeois painted an entirely red female figure using a few simple, deceptively naive strokes. Nude and viewed frontally, the woman has very long hair that hides her arms; she has no facial features. Bourgeois projected drops of water, like tears, on the sheet of paper so that the gouache, diluted much like watercolor, took on a liquid appearance. The monochrome use of red evokes the blood flowing through this female body, as well as the menstrual cycle, human warmth, and—associated with nudity—sexuality.

Red is omnipresent in the work of Louise Bourgeois, and she considered it to be a symbol of power and intensity, of strong and negative emotions—ambiguous meanings that have clung to red since ancient times. More precisely, in an interview with Cecilia Bloomberg in 1998, the artist, almost intoning, declared, "Red is the color of pain. Red is the color of violence. Red is the color of danger. Red is the color of shame. Red is the color of jealousy. Red is the color of reproach. Red is the color of grudges. Red is the color of blame" (quoted in Frances Morris, *Louise Bourgeois*, 2007).

The female body and its related themes are also recurring elements in her polymorphic work: directly or indirectly, she addressed themes of maternity, birth, childbirth, breastfeeding, and kinship in drawings like this one, as well as in sculptures, installations, prints, and embroidery.

Other important works
Cumul I, 1969. Centre Pompidou, Paris.
Maman, 2002. Tate, London.
Father and Son, 2005. Olympic Sculpture Park, Seattle.

RED **p. 46**

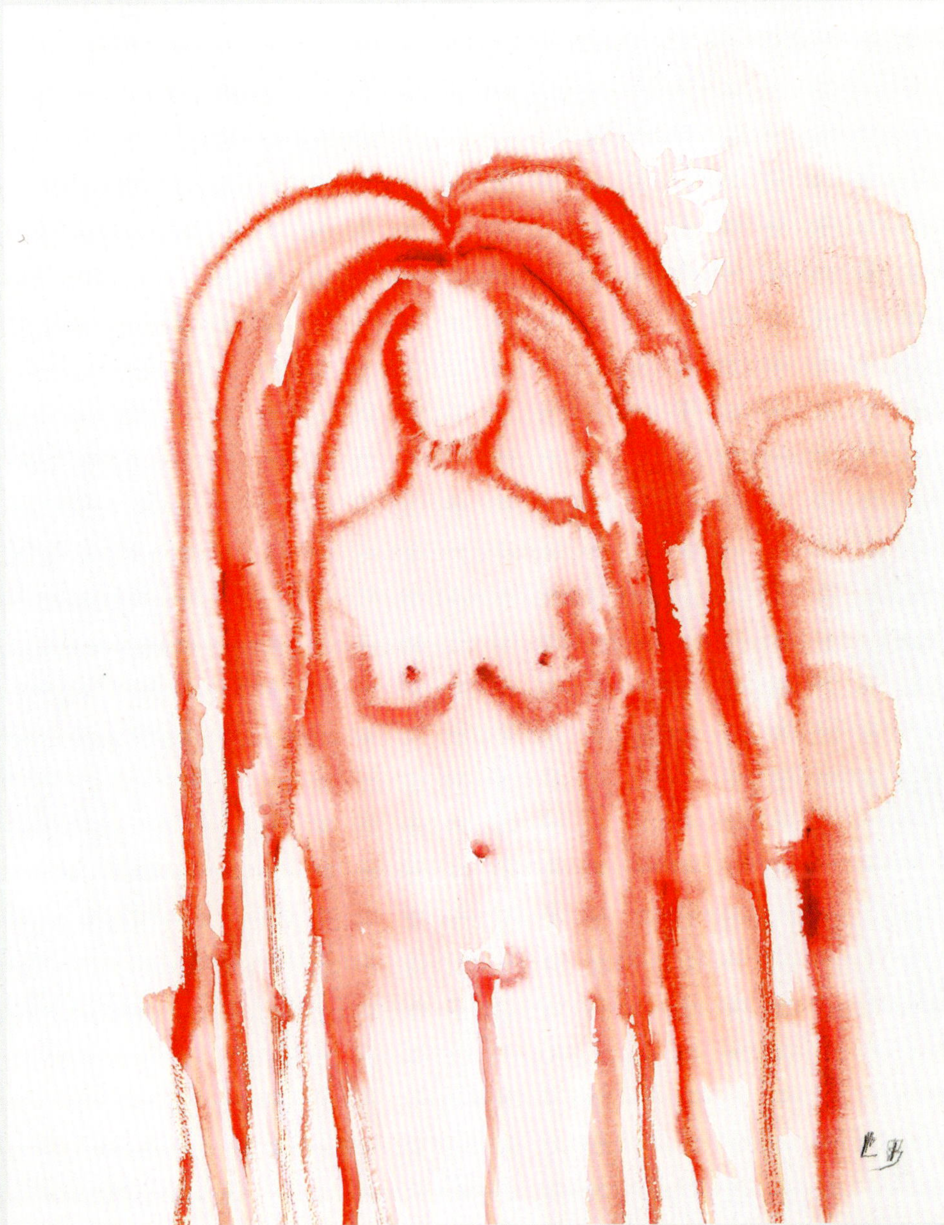

WATERCOLOR AND GOUACHE **p. 202**

Au-delà

SHEILA HICKS • COTTON, LINEN, SYNTHETIC FIBER, LEATHER •
VARIABLE DIMENSIONS • MUSÉE D'ART MODERNE DE PARIS, PARIS

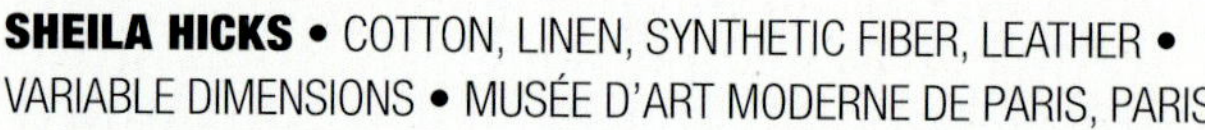

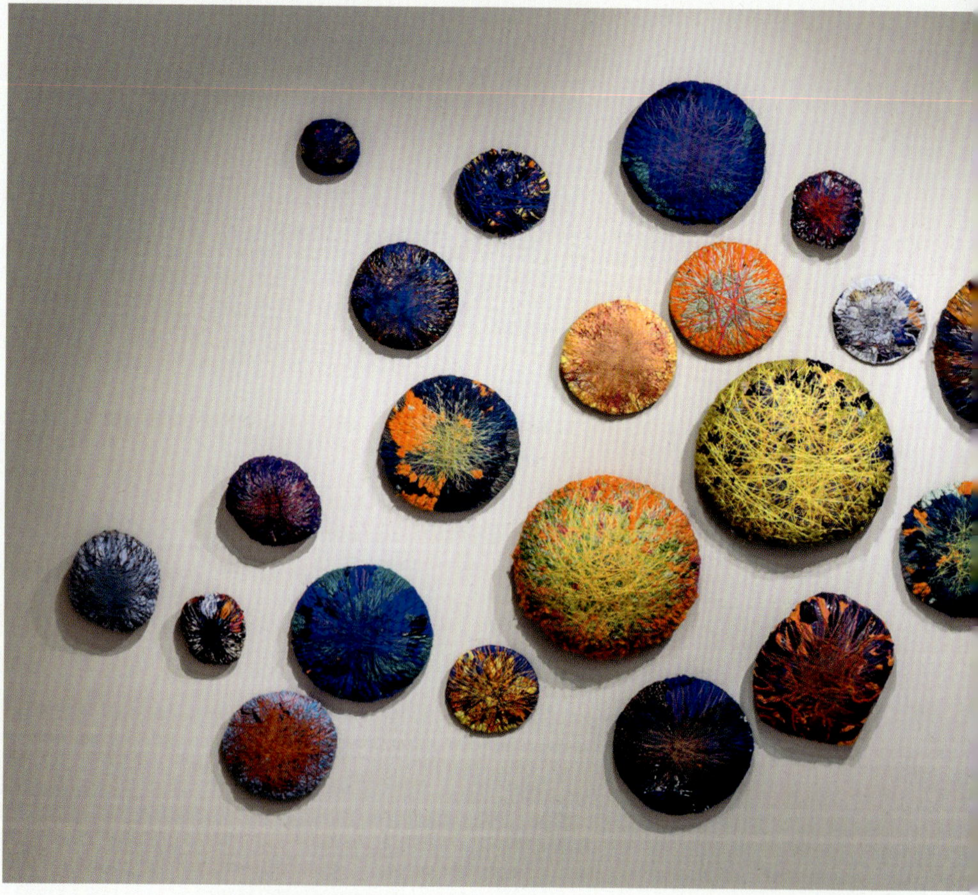

RED **p. 46** YELLOW **p. 47** BLUE **p. 48** GREEN **p. 49** ORANGE **p. 50**

SHEILA HICKS (BORN 1934)

As a student at Yale University, Sheila Hicks studied with Josef Albers, one of the greatest colorists of the twentieth century, who introduced her to his wife, Anni, a leading textile artist. Hicks became passionate about weaving and studied South American techniques. Her practice combines art and craft, and she takes a collective approach in her studio on the Quai des Grands-Augustins in Paris, created in 1964 and still active today.

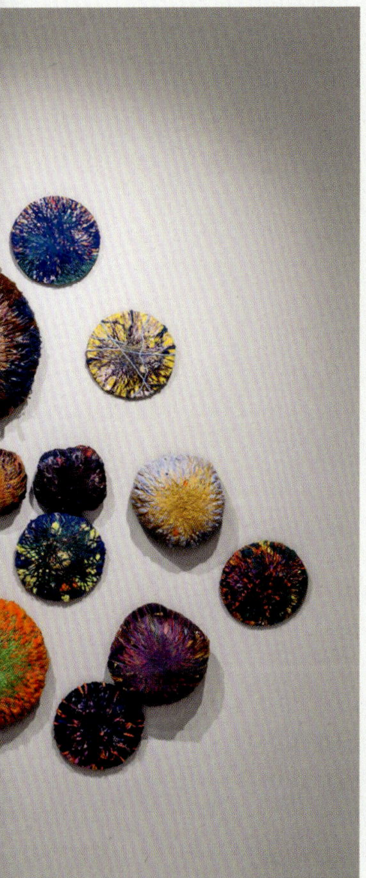

In 2017, Sheila Hicks created a textile installation for the Museum of Modern Art in Paris. She chose to enter into dialog with Lucio Fontana's luminous sculpture *Neon Structure for the Ninth Milan Triennial* (1951/2012), located in the museum's reception area. To the planetary trajectories traced in space by the Italian artist, she responded with a collection of satellite-like bodies. Thirty-one textured, multicolored textile pebbles of various sizes—with diameters ranging from 12 to 37 inches (30 to 95 cm)—contrast with the cold, linear quality of Fontana's smooth, white neon tubes.

This constellation vibrates with rich contrasts, the fruit of Hicks's extensive work selecting colors for the threads. Bright blues stand alongside watery greens, soft oranges cut through pale blues, intense purples pepper yellow golds, shades of turquoise overlap fluorescent oranges in a dense, threaded material akin to giant balls of yarn.

"The colors are the keys," explained Hicks in 2004 in an oral history interview for the Archives of American Art (Smithsonian Institution, Washington, DC). "My palette is influenced by light, geography. . . . Number one, [I choose] colors—and then the textures and the shapes, but mostly the color and the texture. In fact, every idea— every idea I have starts with texture and color, and they are inextricable. I do not see color without texture and I do not see texture without color. My dreams are an explosion of color."

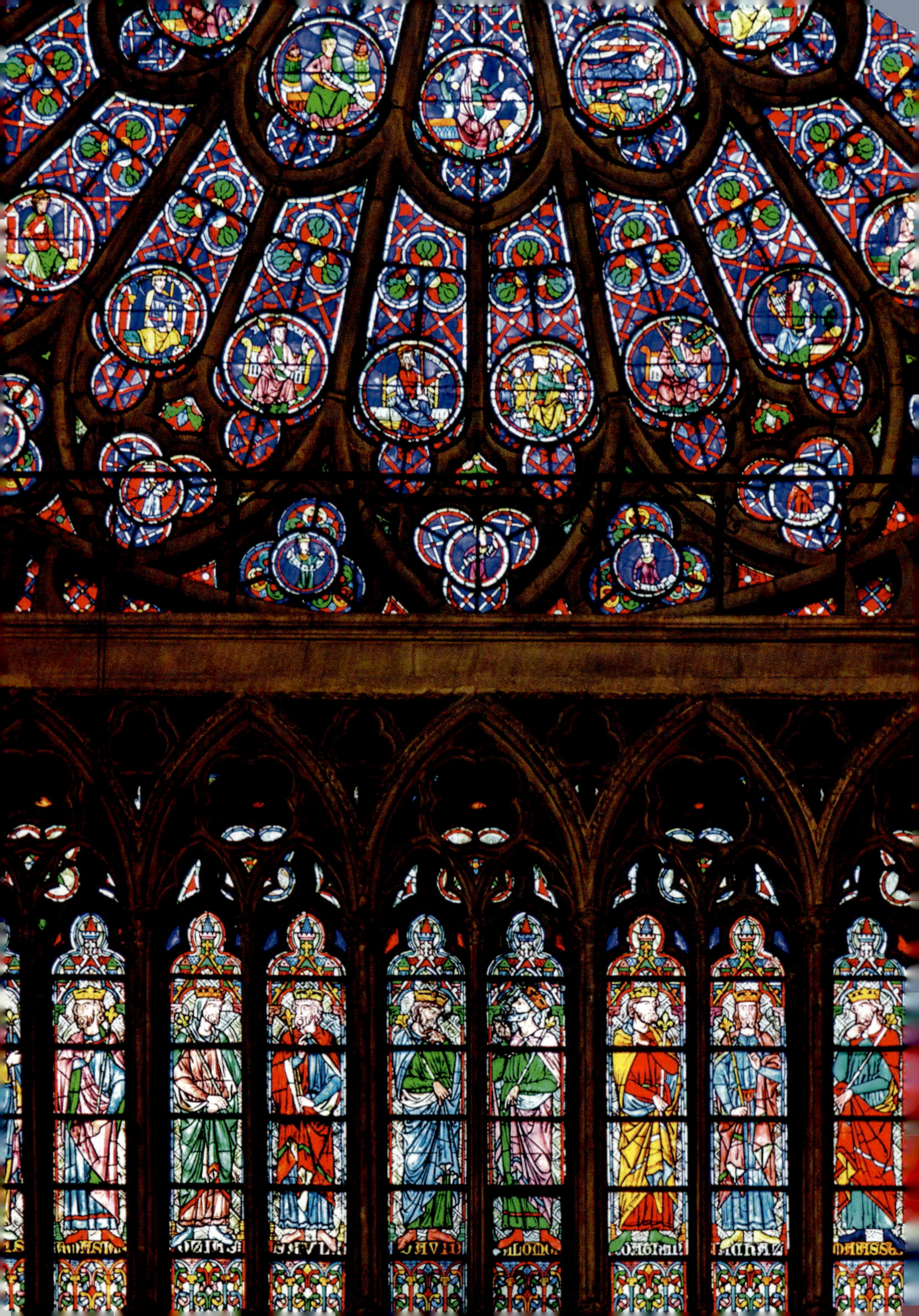

Materials and Techniques

Natural and Synthetic Pigments

Since prehistoric times, humans have extracted pigments and created paint and dyes from the natural resources at their disposal. Three color families dominated this period: ochers, from yellow to brown to red; black; and white. Clay soils containing iron or manganese oxides were ground and sometimes carbonized, then diluted in water. In the Neolithic period, bone white, made from the ashes of animal bone or horn, was also used. Bone black was made by firing animal bones in the absence of oxygen to produce charcoal. The same process was used to make charcoal from wood.

During antiquity and the Middle Ages, the color palette expanded as new minerals were used; some, like orpiment—a sulfide of arsenic resembling gold—were toxic. Gradually, color found new applications, notably for painting on wood panels, plant fibers, and parchment, which required binders. To this end, fish glue was used to make azurite (blue), oleoresins to make copper resinate pigments (green), and egg yolk to make chrysocolla (turquoise blue).

The first synthetic pigment, known by the Romans as Egyptian blue, dates from antiquity. Since the nineteenth century, synthetic pigments have multiplied, supplanting their natural counterparts and paving the way for new shades.

MAIN CHARACTERISTICS

Even today, natural binders are used in the composition of certain paints: acacia sap (gum arabic) in watercolors, beeswax in polish, and linseed, nut, or safflower oil in oil paint.

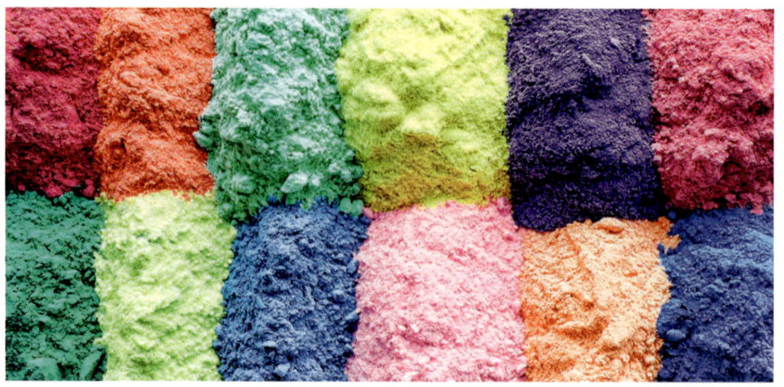

Colored powders used for the Holi festival in India.

White Pigments

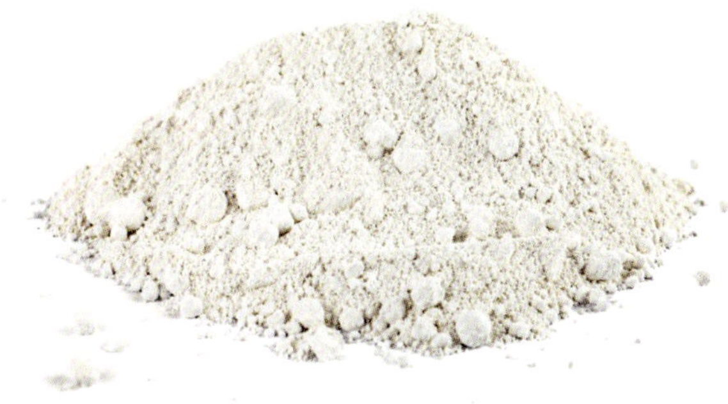

White pigment.

The first white pigments were lime whites obtained by grinding limestone—a soft, sedimentary rock composed primarily of calcium carbonate formed by the accumulation of the calciferous skeletons of marine phytoplankton.

Gradually, other ways of making white pigments emerged. Lead white (or ceruse), used from antiquity to the nineteenth century, was prepared using a highly toxic mixture of lead carbonate, vinegar fumes (acetic acid), and carbon dioxide: after three months, the gray lead changed to a pure white. Until the nineteenth century, both artists and industry used lead white, but because of its poisonous nature, it was eventually replaced by zinc white (or Chinese white), made of pure zinc oxide. But this white had poor covering qualities, and in the early twentieth century, it was replaced by titanium white, which is made by immersing titanium dioxide in sulfuric acid to obtain a precipitate through hydrolysis that is then heated. The result is an opaque, neutral pigment that when mixed with other colors has a significant lightening effect.

MAIN CHARACTERISTICS

White pigments are described according to the geographic origins of the limestone used: Bologna chalk or Champagne chalk, for example. From the High Renaissance onward, lime white was used to make gesso, the primer utilized by artists for panel painting.

PREHISTORIC CAVE ART **p. 12** POLYCHROMY IN ANCIENT EGYPT **p. 13** WHITE **p. 45** MUKUDJ MASK **p. 110**

Yellow Pigments

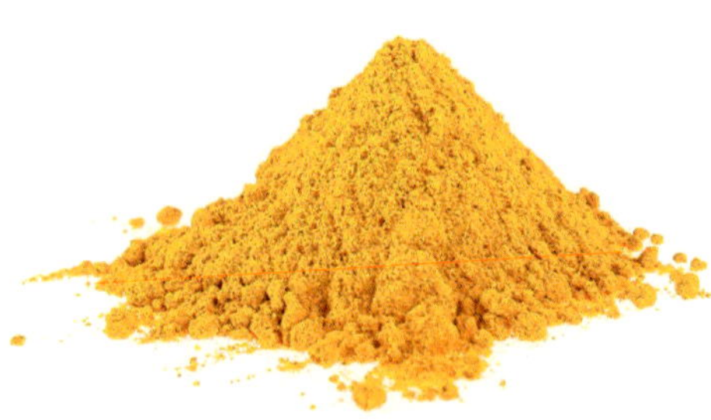
Safflower pigment.

MAIN CHARACTERISTICS
Orpiment contains sulfide of arsenic, which makes it toxic. Despite this, the pigment was very popular in ancient Egypt—where it was even used in cosmetics—in Rome, and during the Middle Ages, especially for use in illuminated manuscripts.

The first yellow pigments, used in prehistoric times, were derived from clay soils containing iron or manganese oxides that were ground and sometimes charred, then diluted in water.

Other yellow pigments like orpiment—an orangey-yellow mineral approximating gold—appeared during antiquity. In China, it was called "feminine yellow," while the more orange-colored realgar (or ruby of arsenic), also containing sulfide of arsenic, was called "masculine yellow." In Europe, realgar was gradually abandoned in favor of minium, to produce orange shades, or saffron, to achieve pure yellows. Saffron pigments, made from the stigmas of crocus flowers infused in egg white, had two disadvantages: eighty flowers were needed to produce one gram of stigmas and the pigment was not lightfast. The rather bright Naples yellow was used by painters in the late Renaissance.

According to legend, the pigment came from the lava of Vesuvius, hence its name. In reality, it was made with lead oxide heated with an antimony compound.

In the late eighteenth century, crocoite—a rare ore—was discovered in Russia. Consisting of lead chromate, it produced bright but unstable artificial yellows that often turned green. A century later, these yellows faded in popularity in favor of long-lasting, opaque pigments made with cadmium—a rare metal commercialized in the 1840s that was immensely popular with the impressionists.

Red and Purple Pigments

In addition to the iron or manganese oxides used to produce ocher reds in prehistoric times, brighter pigments were introduced by the ancients. Minium, for example, composed of toxic lead oxide, delivered a flaming red. Tyrian purple—which the Phoenicians made using a long and complex, malodorous process involving the secretions of the Mediterranean gastropods *Murex brandaris* and *Thais haemastoma*—was used to produce reds tinged with violet or blue that were revered by those with power in Republican Rome.

In the Middle Ages, carmine (or lacquer red), a lacquer-pigment used in illuminated manuscripts, was imported to Europe. It was made using resins from the cochineal insect, which were dried, then ground and washed; the more affordable kermes red was made using a similar process with another insect. Carmine had one major flaw: it was not lightfast. Painters preferred to use vermilion: a beautiful, artificial red pigment produced by the noxious combination of mercury and sulfur (two key alchemical ingredients), or the aforementioned minium, more reddish-brown in color. Madder and especially alizarin crimson, derived from madder root cultivated in Europe from the thirteenth century onward, was used in the composition for oil-based glazes.

Finally, in the early twentieth century, cadmium, which was used in certain yellows and reds, was combined with selenium to create a non-toxic red that could replace vermilion.

MAIN CHARACTERISTICS
Red pigments were among the first to be mastered, giving rise to stable, intense dyes and paints early on in human history.

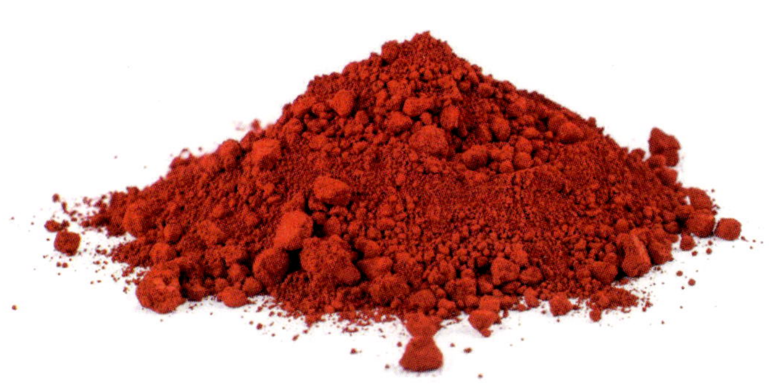

Carmine pigment.

PREHISTORIC CAVE ART **p. 12** INDIA'S HOLI FESTIVAL **p. 15** RED **p. 46** STAINED GLASS IN THE BASILICA OF SAINT-DENIS **p. 68**

Blue Pigments

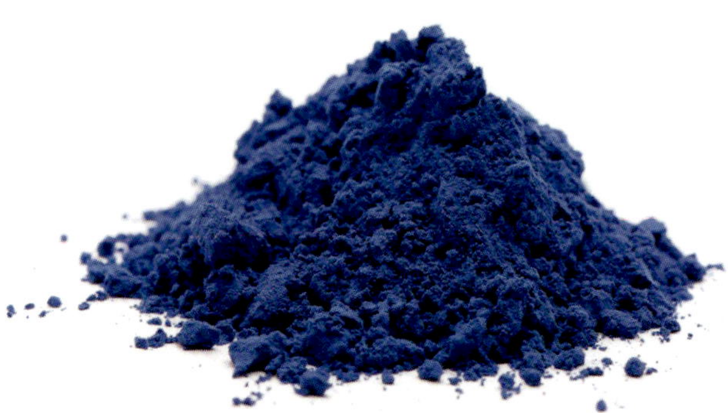

Indigo blue pigment.

Naturally occurring blue pigments are rare, which is why the ancient Egyptians invented the first synthetic pigment. The Romans called it "Egyptian blue" and its complex composition remained a secret until the nineteenth century. This glassy, alkaline glaze gave the objects it adorned—amulets, statues, beads—a hue ranging from green to blue.

Azurite, a bright blue mineral found in Europe, was widely used by painters. When crushed and washed, it produced shades from light to dark blue, depending on the fineness of grind. Another mineral, chrysocolla, also produced hues ranging from turquoise to pale green depending on the fineness of grind, and was most often used with water-based painting techniques like tempera or watercolor.

Reputed as being more expensive than gold, lapis lazuli (which gives the color ultramarine) never replaced azurite precisely because of its high cost. This metamorphic stone, historically imported from Afghanistan, had to be cleansed of its impurities, ground, then mixed with pitch, mastic, turpentine, and linseed oil or wax and heated to form a paste before being plunged in an alkaline bath: the result was a deep, purple-tinged blue coveted by medieval illuminators and Renaissance painters. In the nineteenth century, lapis lazuli was replaced by a less expensive synthetic pigment.

MAIN CHARACTERISTICS

Indigo, derived from the leaves of the indigo plant, has been used since antiquity. It flooded the European market in the sixteenth century, following the "discovery" of America. Its large-scale production, fueled by colonization and slave labor, put an end to the cultivation of woad—the only plant indigenous to Europe capable of making blue pigment. Indigo was used particularly in fresco painting.

Green Pigments

Few green pigments exist in nature. Deposits of clay soil containing celadonite or glauconite were exploited by prehistoric humans, but for centuries, copper-bearing minerals, often toxic and unstable, were artists' only sources of green. These major flaws influenced the color's symbolic meaning, which is ambiguous, to say the least—green represents change, destiny, chance, and rebirth, but also envy and poison.

When ground and washed, malachite—a secondary copper mineral—produced beautiful greens for medieval illuminators, and Renaissance and classical painters. Used since antiquity, the more dangerous and unstable verdigris, which reacted with the sulfur in other pigments and turned brown, was nonetheless appreciated for the bright color it produced. Verdigris, which appears naturally on oxidized copper, could be obtained by suspending a copper plate over a vinegar bath. Several layers were needed to obtain an opaque color.

In the late eighteenth century, efforts were made to create brighter greens. An emerald green more toxic than its predecessors was developed using a combination of verdigris and arsenic. Commonly used in wallpaper, the substance released lethal gas that caused many deaths, until public outcry forced government regulation and it fell out of use.

MAIN CHARACTERISTICS
In the nineteenth century, to the delight of artists, research into chemistry led to the development of synthetic pigments like green chrome oxide, more opaque than emerald green, and cobalt green, which has less tinting power but is very stable.

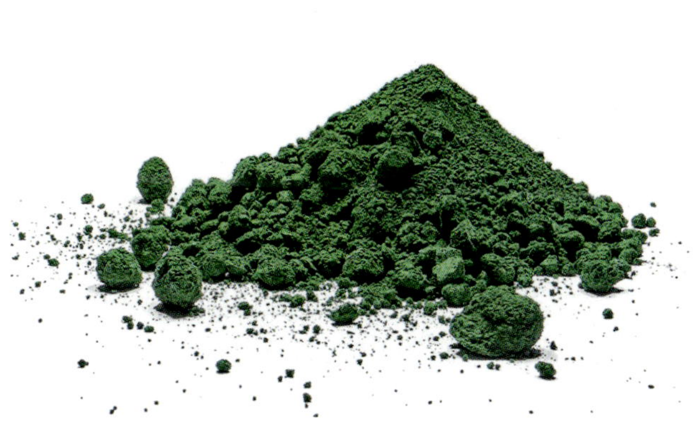

Chromium oxide pigment.

Black and Brown Pigments

Charcoal pigment.

Black and brown pigments were among the first to be used by prehistoric humans, who preferred to use plant- or animal-based sources. Charcoal and bone black (or ivory black) were made by charring wood or bone in the absence of oxygen.

Bone black has been popular with artists since antiquity. The finer it is ground, the denser the blue-tinged color becomes. There are many applications for bone black, which can be mixed with water, oil, or gum arabic (sap from the acacia tree).

Ancient Egyptians also used a deep smoke black made from the charred residues (soot) of oil, resin, or tallow lamps, and candles. Similar to bone black, smoke black is compatible with many binders, making it a versatile color.

During the Renaissance and increasingly so in the nineteenth century, especially in England, painters used a singular pigment: Mummy Brown, made from ground Egyptian mummified remains and originally used for medicinal purposes. It was used with an oil binder to create glazes and shadows.

MAIN CHARACTERISTICS

Charcoal can be made from any wood, although color manufacturers prefer grapevine or willow branches. It is used untreated for drawing, or ground to a powder and mixed with a binder to make a paint. Peach black, a variation of charcoal made from calcinated peach pits, is used to make watercolors.

PREHISTORIC CAVE ART **p. 12** POLYCHROMY IN ANCIENT EGYPT **p. 13** BLACK **p. 44**
PAINTING 324 × 362 CM, 1986 (POLYPTYCH I) **p. 176**

The Painter's Tools

The vast, rich history of painters' tools and practices could fill a book of its own. Prehistoric artists invented instruments to facilitate the application of pigmented material and develop specific visual effects. Archeologists have observed several techniques in prehistoric painted caves (Chauvet-Pont-d'Arc, c. 36,000 BP; Lascaux, c. 19,000 BP): blowing pigments onto walls with a hollow bone; the use of brushes and sticks of charcoal; painting and shading with fingers; hand prints; and etching with flint implements or sharpened bones.

In antiquity, as new pigments were mastered and innovative practices emerged, some of these techniques were perfected, others abandoned, and still others created. The ancient Egyptians had sophisticated tools: reed pens embellished with horse or human hair, and wood or ivory palettes with small paint wells. The Romans also used horsehair to make paintbrushes, as well as seaweed and sea sponges.

Paintbrushes improved and diversified during the Middle Ages and the Renaissance: hog bristle and ox-ear hair held paint, polecat hair was stiff, horsehair and squirrel fur were popular for watercolor painting, goat hair was ideal for applying varnish, etc. Brushes could be round, pointed, or fan-shaped. Like the painter's knife, the flat brush with a metal ferrule, invented in the nineteenth century, encouraged thicker and more gestural brushstrokes.

In the mid-twentieth century, painters embarked upon an altogether new and direct relationship with paint as material, abandoning traditional studio techniques: pigments were dripped from brushes or pots, projected or applied with fingers or entire bodies, used with industrial tools, and more.

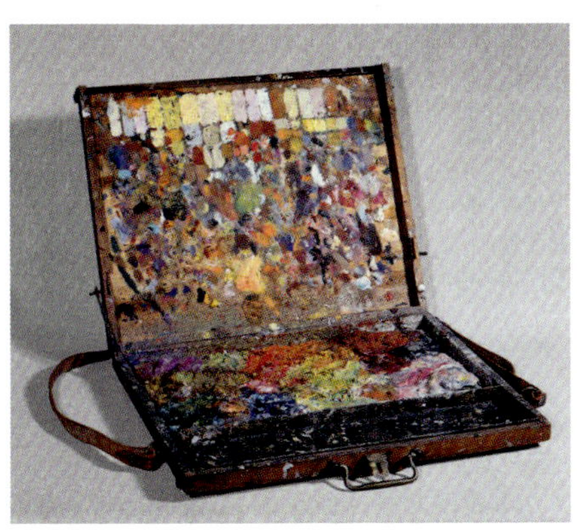

Pierre Bonnard's palette, nineteenth century. Petit Palais (Musée des Beaux-Arts de la Ville de Paris), Paris.

PREHISTORIC CAVE ART **p. 12** POLYCHROMY IN ANCIENT EGYPT **p. 13**

Polychrome Sculpture in the West

Greek and Roman sculpture was originally polychromatic. Statues and figures in marble and limestone, as well as wood, were embellished with often dazzling pigments (iron oxides, azurite, madder, green earth, smoke black, lead white, etc.) that polishing further enhanced. Additional elements (tinted glass paste, silver, gold, enamel, etc.) were added to metal statues to enliven surfaces. Chryselephantine statues, which appeared in Greece in 600 BCE, combined ivory and gold on a wood structure—an extravagant technique reserved for statues of gods.

Religious polychromatic statuary was equally important in the Middle Ages. Porous wood or stone surfaces were covered with a white or subtly tinted primer, and a light undercoat (calcium carbonate, lead white) was applied to enhance colors. Besides white (lead white) and black (charcoal and bone black), red (vermilion, madder) was omnipresent and used with yellow (ocher), blue (azurite, and less often lapis lazuli), and green (verdigris).

Although some sculptors continued to work in polychromy, the style gradually fell out of use in favor of the classical ideal. It was not until the nineteenth and twentieth centuries that color made a comeback in sculpture, in the work of artists like Honoré Daumier (1808–1879) and Charles Ray (born 1953).

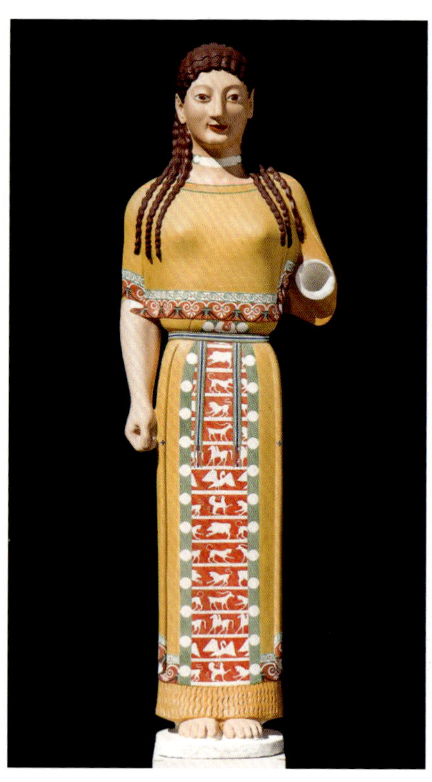

Colored reconstruction of a Greek statue from the Acropolis of Athens.

MAIN CHARACTERISTICS

In ancient Greek and Rome, polychromy—a highly codified practice—made it easier to identify the figures depicted, contributed an emotionally engaging realism, and gave works a symbolic radiance befitting the gods they honored.

Working with Gold

Since ancient times, artists have appreciated gold for its glow and its ability to reflect light, but also for its sophistication and stability, as unlike some other metals, it does not tarnish. Gold is found on Egyptian sarcophagi, in Greek statuary, and in Roman mosaics, and is omnipresent in Byzantine icons and in Western medieval illuminated manuscripts.

In these manuscripts and in easel painting, gold was used in two ways: as gold leaf or shell gold. Gold leaf involves applying fine sheets of the precious metal to a prepared surface (parchment or wood, for example). The gilded surface can be etched or stamped, or even worked in relief, to create decorative motifs.

Shell gold is made by combining gold powder and gum arabic (acacia sap) to form a water-soluble mixture that is applied using a paintbrush similar to watercolor paints. Due to the high cost of gold and the metal's symbolic value, it has long been reserved for specific applications associated with power and the divine. For the same economic reasons, substitutes for gold were invented, such as orpiment (made of highly toxic sulfur of arsenic) and "purpurine," developed by the painter Cennino Cennini (c. 1360–c. 1440), who revealed the recipe in his *Treatise on Painting* (late 15th–early 16th century).

IN DETAIL
In the twentieth century, the artist Gustav Klimt integrated gold into his compositions after visiting the Basilica of San Vitale in Ravenna, famous for its gilded mosaics. In his portrait of Adele Bloch-Bauer (1907), he combined painting with areas of gold leaf, particularly for the model's dress and coat, and the armchair on which she leans.

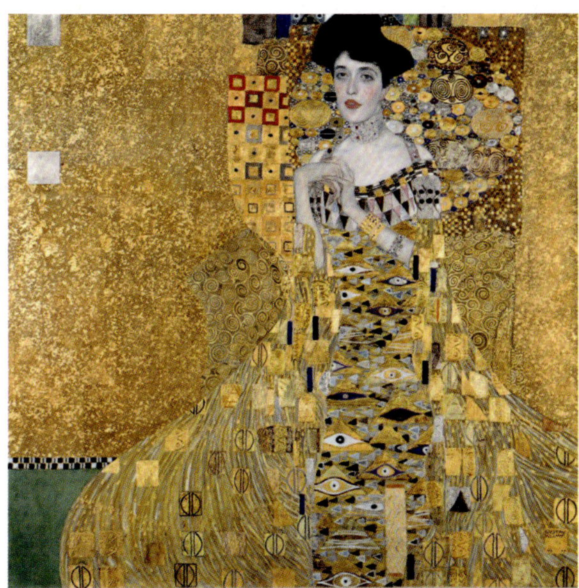

Gustav Klimt, *Portrait of Adele Bloch-Bauer I*, 1907. Oil, gold, and silver on canvas. Neue Galerie, New York, NY.

GOLD **p. 56** *PORTRAIT OF ADELE BLOCH-BAUER I* **p. 114**

Tempera

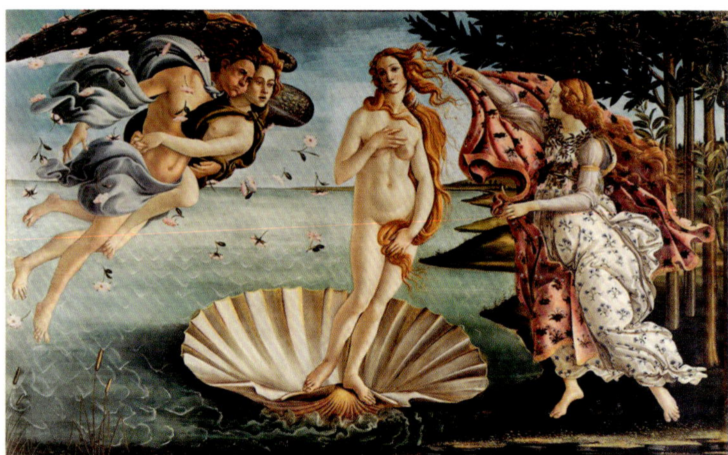

Sandro Botticelli, *The Birth of Venus*, 1484–85. Tempera on canvas. Uffizi Gallery, Florence.

Tempera (or distemper) was popular with artists up to the Renaissance, when it was superseded by oil paint. It was particularly popular for painting walls and wood panels.

To use tempera, the painter would first apply several layers of gesso (a primer made of plaster and animal glue) to the support (usually wood) to obtain a smooth surface, and then apply an undercoat. Then, powdered pigment was mixed with equal parts emulsified egg (to act as a binder) and water. The egg could be replaced by another binder such as casein (milk protein), gum arabic (acacia sap), or an animal glue.

Tempera dries quickly and had to be used rapidly. Each color was applied with small, precise strokes or cross-hatching using a fine brush. Tempera creates luminous, rich, opaque colors. It is finished with oil or resin varnish applied to the completed work.

Tempera reached its apogee in the late Middle Ages and early Renaissance in Italy, with Sienese painters particularly famed for their mastery of the medium.

IN DETAIL

Sandro Botticelli (1445–1510) used tempera to paint *The Birth of Venus*, now considered one of the most celebrated paintings of the Italian Renaissance. On a layer of blue-white gesso primer, he applied radiant pigments—some, like the green used for plants and the blue of the sea, have oxidized over time and lost their intensity. Botticelli infused the composition with singular light by adding touches of gold to the hair, fabrics, angels' wings, and landscapes.

DIVINE COLOR **p. 17**

Fresco

The technique known as *buon fresco* or "true" fresco involves applying pigments diluted in water in layers directly to a wall coated with fresh plaster before it has dried. The calcium hydrate contained in the coating becomes calcium carbonate on contact with the atmosphere. The plaster crystalizes and locks in the pigments, forming a very resistant colored surface.

Fresco requires great skill. A full-scale drawing (known as a cartoon) is transferred to the wall. The painter must be able to estimate the *giornata*: the amount of work possible in one day, before the plaster dries. He must therefore work quickly but also accurately; fresco does not allow overpainting, so if an error is made, the area must be scraped clean before a fresh coat of plaster is applied. Failing that, it must be worked dry (*secco*).

Frescoes are rarely executed exclusively with the *buon fresco* technique, because many pigments cannot be applied to a wet surface. Due to all these constraints, some artists prefer to use the dry method (*fresco secco*), mixing pigments in limewater to imitate the more demanding technique. However, *fresco secco* is more fragile and deteriorates over time because the pigmented surface is not as hard as *buon fresco*.

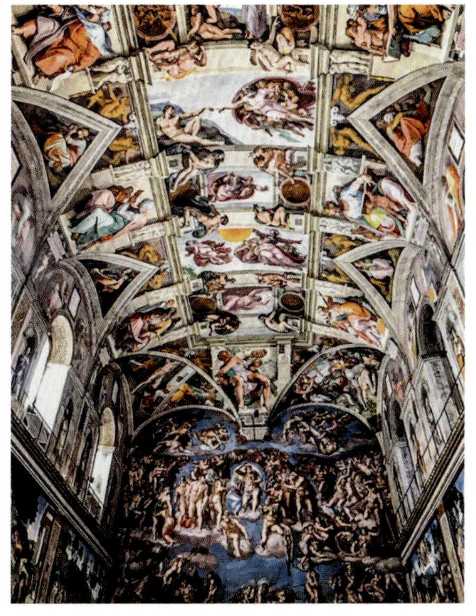

Michelangelo, Sistine Chapel ceiling, 1508–12. Fresco. Vatican Museums, Vatican City.

IN DETAIL

Michelangelo used the *buon fresco* technique, popular with Italian artists in the late Middle Ages and High Renaissance, to paint the ceiling of the Sistine Chapel. He accepted the commission from Pope Jules II even though he considered himself more of a sculptor than a painter. The master artist created a range of bright, iridescent colors (orange, light green, mauve, etc.) that rendered the motifs highly visible and contributed to the work's success.

POLYCHROMY IN ANCIENT EGYPT **p. 13** TRICLINIUM OF THE VILLA OF LIVIA **p. 66** *WALL DRAWING #610* **p. 180**

Watercolor and Gouache

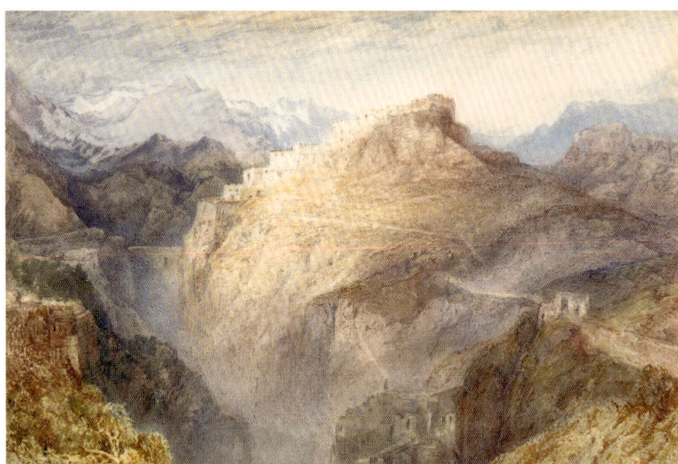

Joseph Mallord William Turner, *The Fort of L'Esseillon, Val de Maurienne, France*, 1835–36. Watercolor on paper. The Metropolitan Museum of Art, New York, NY.

Like tempera and fresco, watercolor and gouache are water-based painting techniques. They both contain a binder, most often gum arabic (acacia sap), although gum tragacanth might also be used, to ensure that pigments adhere to the support.

Watercolor is carried out primarily on paper, which, because of it lightness and low adherence, produces textural effects. It is difficult to correct mistakes with watercolor, but it encourages great spontaneity, which is particularly conducive to painting outdoors. It is more or less translucent depending on dilution strength and produces delicate colors. But watercolor is fragile, and sensitive to light and ambient humidity.

Gouache is a form of watercolor with a more matte, more opaque finish that results from lower dilution and a higher proportion of gum arabic, to which is added an ingredient such as lime, egg white, or glycerin. Gouache is used on fine supports—in the Middle Ages this was primarily parchment—and paper.

MAIN CHARACTERISTICS

In late-eighteenth-century England, watercolor was no longer used for preparatory studies only and became an art in its own right. Its inherent qualities—fast drying and easy to transport— quickly earned it a following, and William Blake (1757–1827) and Joseph Mallord William Turner forged the technique's reputation.

Oil Paint

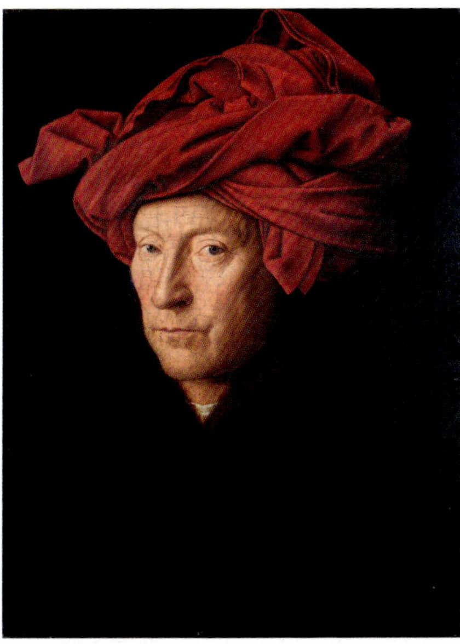

Jan Van Eyck, *Portrait of a Man (Self-Portrait?)*, 1433. Oil on oak. National Gallery, London.

Until the early fifteenth century, painters primarily used two techniques that produced highly opaque colors: tempera (a mixture of pigments, water, and glue or egg yolk) and fresco (pigments mixed with water and applied to wet or dry plaster).

In the fifteenth century, artists discovered a new use for oil, which until then had mainly been used as a varnish: they created a paint by combining refined oil with pigments and a thinner (water and egg, and later turpentine oil). This formula produced extraordinarily delicate color effects that were fluid and pearly, and also allowed incredible precision in the depiction of materials and surfaces: bright, buttery, matte, satiny, silky, rough, soft, metallic, etc. The palette now included infinite shades, and color could be worked using the glazing technique by applying successive layers of pigments mixed with a larger quantity of binder.

However, one constraint emerged: it took a long time for each layer of paint to dry. In addition to this, the pigments or varnish applied to the completed work might oxidize over time and change the way colors appeared.

From the Renaissance, oil painting, which could be used on wood or canvas, became the easel painter's preferred technique. In the mid-twentieth century, the invention of synthetic resin paints (acrylic or vinyl) did not put an end to oil painting; the technique still has many fans who appreciate its intense colors.

MAIN CHARACTERISTICS
The Flemish painter Jan Van Eyck was one of the first artists to perfect the oil painting technique. He began with light colors then, as he added pigments and thinner to his mixture, coaxed out dark tones and shadows. The transparency of oil brings light into the heart of the composition.

THE INVENTION OF OIL PAINT **p. 18** THE COLOR RENAISSANCE **p. 19** *MADONNA OF CHANCELLOR ROLIN* **p. 70**

Paint in Tubes

Until the eighteenth century, artists made their colors themselves using pigments purchased from apothecaries. They ground these pigments and combined them with a binder (vegetable oil, wax or resin, egg, water, urine, fish glue, etc.), selected according to personal formulas and intended use. Each binder gave a specific intensity and brightness to color and implied a specific method of application and precise drying time. These mixtures could not be stored and were intended to be used quickly.

In the early nineteenth century, the first ready-to-use paints were commercialized, packaged in small pig's bladder sacs, but these, too, needed to be used rapidly. It was not until the 1840s that a collapsible metal tube, first sealed with a clamp and later a screwcap, was patented. The tube made artists' work easier, but perhaps more importantly it encouraged them to leave the studio to paint outdoors. From then on, they were no longer content to make preparatory sketches outside: they took to the road with their easels and brushes. Subsequent generations of artists left the studio, fascinated by the possibilities of plein air painting.

Throughout the nineteenth century, a gradual industrialization of painting coincided with the development of synthetic pigments, produced from the combination of several chemical ingredients, which offered a greater variety of colors.

MAIN CHARACTERISTICS
Among the first artists to adopt the new plein air genre were the painters of the Barbizon school, who spent entire days wandering the trails in the Forest of Fontainebleau outside of Paris to work outdoors, on the spot.

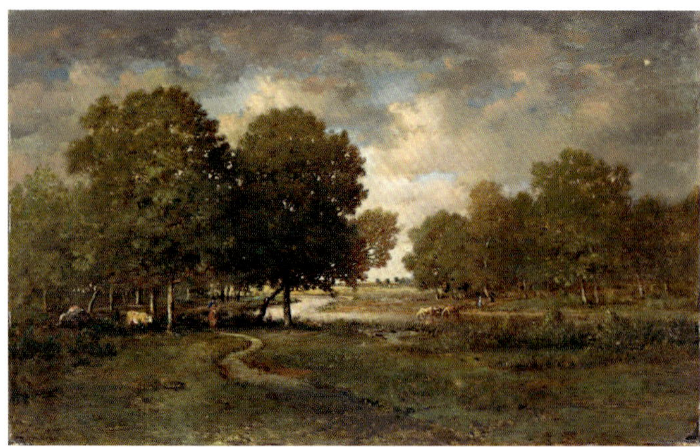

Théodore Rousseau, *A River in a Meadow*, c. 1840. Oil on wood. The Metropolitan Museum of Art, New York, NY.

IMPRESSIONISM AND PLEIN AIR PAINTING **p. 32** *IMPRESSION, SUNRISE* **p. 100**
FIELD WITH IRISES NEAR ARLES **p. 102**

Acrylic and Vinyl Paint

Synthetic paints appeared on the market in the 1950s. Intended for industrial use, they were primarily acrylic and, to a lesser extent, vinyl.

Acrylic paint contains a synthetic resin derived from acrylic acid that is used as a binder and can be diluted in water. It has many advantages: it is resistant, fast-drying, inexpensive, compatible with many supports (canvas, wood, metal, plastic, clay, concrete, cement, etc.), free of toxic solvents, can be used as a wash (highly diluted in water) or impasto, and is highly adhesive. Soon, manufacturers were presenting artists with new, often brilliant colors, some of them fluorescent, others phosphorescent, and still others metallic. Acrylic can be combined with additives (gel, sand, or powdered marble, for example) that produce highly varied textural effects.

The freedom that these new resources represented in comparison with oil paint was also evident in the proliferation of tools available to artists to work with acrylic or vinyl paint: there were the traditional brush and knife, of course, but also the roller or house painter's brush, industrial airbrush or spray gun, sponge, and rag.

MAIN CHARACTERISTICS
Some abstract expressionists, among the first generation to have access to synthetic paints, invented alternative methods of applying paint to canvas: they squirted or dripped it, like Jackson Pollock, or let it spread across the canvas, like Helen Frankenthaler.

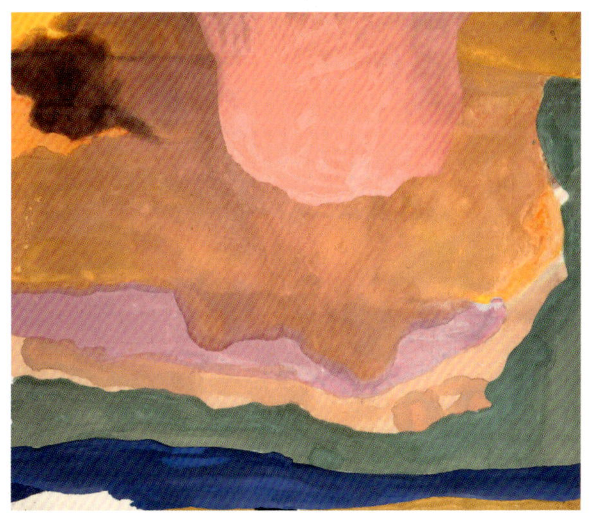

Helen Frankenthaler, *Flood*, 1967. Acrylic on canvas. Whitney Museum of American Art, New York, NY.

CONCETTO SPAZIALE. ATTESE (T. 104) **p. 150** *FLOOD* **p. 160**

Primer, Undercoat, and Varnish

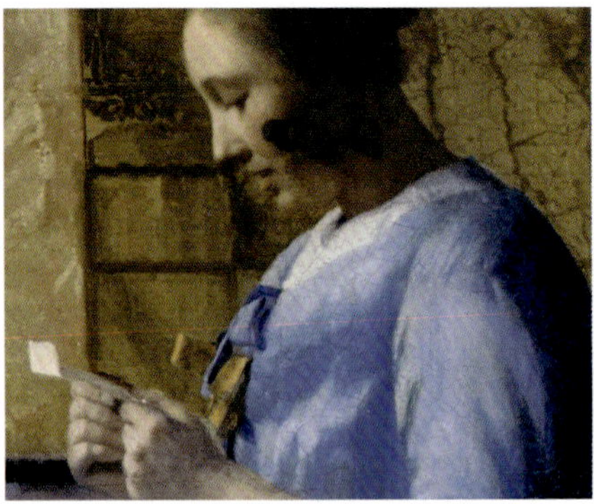

Johannes Vermeer, *Woman in Blue Reading a Letter*, 1662–65. Oil on canvas. Rijksmuseum, Amsterdam.

MAIN CHARACTERISTICS
Varnishes have aesthetic value because they impart a glossy or matte finish to the pictorial surface. They have the disadvantage of crackling or oxidizing over time, and so must be removeable in order to be cleaned off and replaced.

For centuries, the application of a primer, then an undercoat (or base layer), and a varnish have been fundamental steps in the execution of a painting.

Primer is used to smooth the surface of a wood panel or canvas before painting a tempera or oil-based composition. With wood, artists often use gesso—a white plaster made of a mineral (powdered lime or gypsum) mixed with animal glue. When working with canvas, they apply a gelatinous coat of sizing (rabbit skin glue) followed by thin layers of calcium carbonate and of lead white. In the case of *buon fresco*, the fresh plaster applied to the wall acts like a primer. However, for fresco executed on dry walls (*fresco secco*), painters recommend preparing the wall with different glue- or oil-based formulas. It is essential to let the primer dry sufficiently, sometimes up to several weeks, before beginning to paint.

The undercoat or base layer strongly influences the way colors appear. If the undercoat is white, like the one used by Jan Van Eyck, for example, pigments will appear brighter; in Van Eyck's case, he followed this with a layer of oil paint in a light, warm tone. If the base layer is red-brown or umber and diluted, as it often was in the late Renaissance and seventeenth century, it will deepen colors. A gray base layer, used in some paintings by Titian, offers a kind of neutrality.

Completed tempera is often covered with a protective oil-based varnish. The same is true for oil paintings. This varnish is composed of a natural, slightly tinted resin (mastic, amber, etc.) combined with a solvent (turpentine, for example) and an adjuvant (such as beeswax) or, in more recent times, a synthetic resin (acrylic resin).

MADONNA OF CHANCELLOR ROLIN **p. 70** *SYMPHONY IN FLESH COLOUR AND PINK: PORTRAIT OF MRS. FRANCES LEYLAND* **p. 96** *WHITE CENTER* **p. 144** *FLOOD* **p. 160**

Stained Glass

Stained glass is composed of colored or stained-glass panels assembled in a lead framework, and is used for decoration. It developed in the Middle Ages and became a highly valued form of artistic expression. Window glass is produced when silica (sand) and potassium (ashes, for example) or lye fuse at a temperature between 2200°F and 2700°F (1200°C and 1500°C). Metal oxide pigments are added during the fusion process to color the glass.

For a traditional panel, the design begins with a template. Once the glass is blown and flattened, or poured and rolled flat, it is cut with a red-hot iron rod, a diamond-tipped cutter, or a wheel cutter, and assembled according to the final pattern. The master glassmaker then paints figurative or ornamental motifs on the cut glass in grisaille, using a vitreous paint made of metal oxides diluted in distilled water and mixed with gum arabic (acacia sap) as well as a flux of finely ground glass. The grisaille glass is then fired a second time, at 1100°F (600°C), to set the pigments. The pieces of glass are set in the iron framework, which is soldered at each intersection; sometimes putty is applied to make the glass waterproof.

Abandoned in the sixteenth century, stained glass made a comeback in the nineteenth century owing to the neo-Gothic movement, and the revalorization of craft practices in artistic circles such as the pre-Raphaelites, the Arts and Crafts movement, and the Nabis. In the twentieth century, painters like Sophie Taeuber-Arp, Henri Matisse, and Pierre Soulages modernized stained glass.

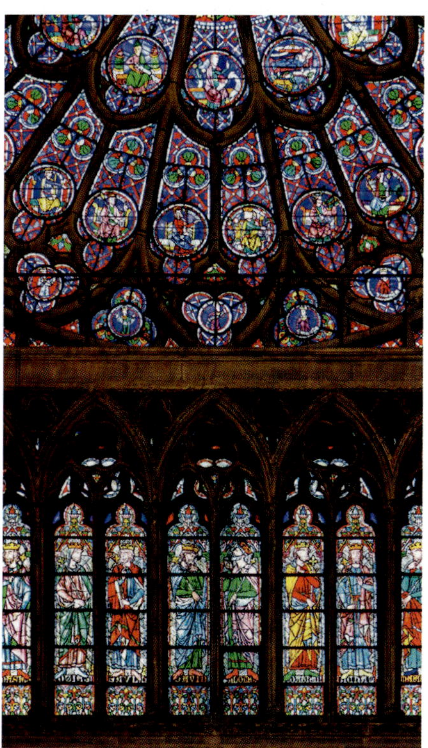

MAIN CHARACTERISTICS
Stained glass flourished in the Middle Ages. Light colors in the Romanesque period gave way to a smaller, but very intense palette in the Gothic period, which included dark blue, bright red, purple, as well as intense yellow and paler green.

Stained glass in Notre-Dame Cathedral in Paris, thirteenth century.

DIVINE COLOR **p. 17** STAINED GLASS IN THE BASILICA OF SAINT-DENIS **p. 68** THE ROSARY CHAPEL **p. 142**

Color Printmaking

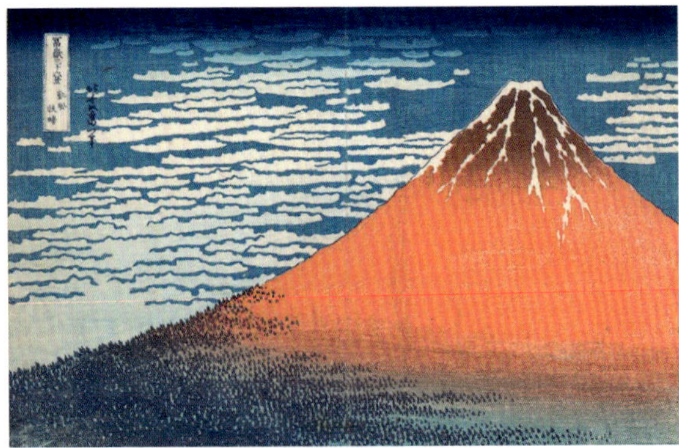

Hokusai, *South Wind, Clear Sky*, also known as *Red Fuji*, c. 1830–32. The Metropolitan Museum of Art, New York, NY.

Color printmaking developed in Europe from the fifteenth century onward. Regardless of the technique used—wood engraving (or xylography), aquatint, and later lithography and silk-screen printing—the process demands meticulous preparation and often close collaboration between engraver and printer. Each color necessitates a different matrix or carrier surface (plate), which means the sheet of paper has to pass through the printing press as many times as there are matrices. Registration marks are used to position the matrix and ensure that colors are applied correctly.

In the West, color printmaking was initially intended for illustrated books, and was then used to produce individual prints. As in painting, pigments were combined with a binder, in this case linseed or nut oil, to make tinted printing ink. Aquatint gave an impression of flat color in etchings, and tonal variations were created by using successive acid baths that bit into the metal plate.

In the nineteenth century, color lithography was used to make many copies, although it required a matrix for each color, like wood printing. The technique was used to produce inexpensive popular images (such as Épinal prints in France), which were distributed around the world in the late nineteenth and early twentieth centuries.

Silk-screen printing—an industrial technique that delighted pop artists—involves transferring a stenciled design to a mesh screen and does not require a press. The result is often bright fields of color, as opposed to shading.

MAIN CHARACTERISTICS

In Japan, the *nishiki-e* technique adopted by wood engravers follows the same process as Western printmaking. In the nineteenth century, the golden age of Japanese printmaking, it was not uncommon for a print to contain twenty-some colors, requiring as many matrices and passes through the press.

CONTRASTS **p. 25** IN PRAISE OF SHADOWS IN JAPAN **p. 30** *THUNDER GOD* **p. 90** *GOLD MARILYN MONROE* **p. 156**

Industrial Materials

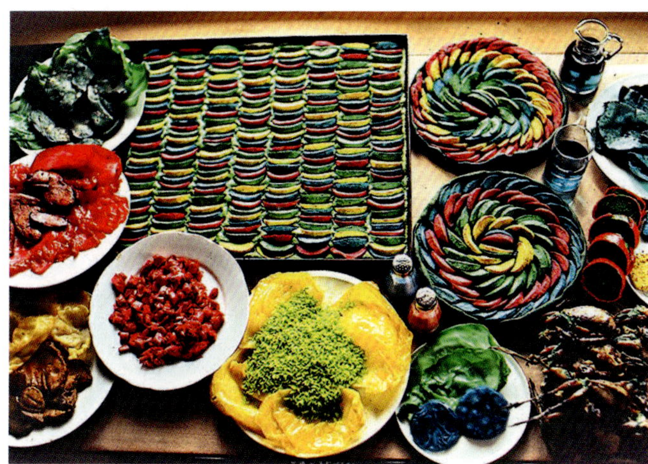

Antoni Miralda and Dorothée Selz, *Eat Art Dinner*, 1971.

In the 1910s, the incorporation of everyday objects into artworks challenged not only the discourse on art and its nature, but also the very materiality of the works themselves. The prime example was the smooth, immaculate, manufactured white of the porcelain urinal used by Marcel Duchamp in his ready-made *Fountain* (1917)—an altogether novel apparition in the art world.

From the 1960s, artists increasingly began to find new uses for industrial materials like resins, latex, vinyl, neon and fluorescent lights, medical and food colorants, fireworks, and nylon in their artistic practices. Most often these new applications favored standardized colors, with properties that responded to commercial and manufacturing demands, such as resistance, brightness, shine, or even fluorescence or phosphorescence.

IN DETAIL

In June 1971, in Dusseldorf, the artists Antoni Miralda (born 1942) and Dorothée Selz (born 1946) served an experimental dinner with a whiff of pop art in the restaurant of Daniel Spoerri's Eat Art gallery: a banquet "served in four colors." Food and drink dyed with bright colors were served to guests. This performance piece demystified art by making it edible—fit to be digested by the viewer.

For these artists, industrial borrowings were a means of rethinking the status of the work and the artist's place in society by challenging the traditional framework of painting or sculpture, by modifying the relationship to the exhibition space, and by dismantling the idea of the heroic figure of the brilliant, inspired creator.

Hue, Saturation, and Brightness

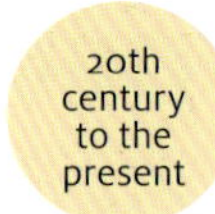

An HSB cylinder (hue, saturation, brightness).

In psychophysiology, three parameters are used to measure and describe color: hue, saturation, and brightness (HSB). The HSB model is codified in three dimensions in the form of a cylinder.

Hue corresponds to our perception of color. In the HSB color model, hue is measured in degrees on a circular scale from 0 to 360, inspired by Isaac Newton's color wheel.

Saturation refers to a color's purity or vividness, depending on the quantity of gray that it contains, and is expressed as a percentage. The HSB model represents saturation as the radius of a circular section of the cylinder.

Finally, brightness refers to a surface's luminosity, necessary to the perception of color; it ranges from white (100 percent reflection) to black (0 percent reflection) via gray. In the HSB model, brightness is represented by a vertical axis running through the cylinder.

MAIN CHARACTERISTICS
The HSB model for measuring and describing color is widely used in the fields of computer graphics and graphic design.

BLACK **p. 44** WHITE **p. 45** GRAY **p. 54** THE RAINBOW **p. 59**

Visual Color and Material Color

20th century to the present

There are two primary approaches to understanding color and the ways of mixing it: visual color (the colors of the visible spectrum) and material color (pigment).

Visual colors are those observed as light passes through a prism. Each color corresponds to a wavelength range on the electromagnetic spectrum situated, for the human eye, between 390 and 780 nanometers (nm). Violet is located between about 390 and 455nm, blue between around 455 and 492nm, green between about 492 and 577nm, yellow between about 577 and 597nm, orange between about 597 and 622nm, and red between about 622 and 780nm. Mixing the prism's primary colors—red, green, and blue—produces white light: in this case, known as additive mixing, all wavelengths reach the human eye.

When material color is mixed, each addition removes a set of wavelengths, like a filter; this process is called subtractive mixing. So when short blue wavelengths are combined with long yellow wavelengths, what remains are medium-length green wavelengths. The combination of primary material colors (cyan, magenta, yellow) produces a dark gray that is close to black.

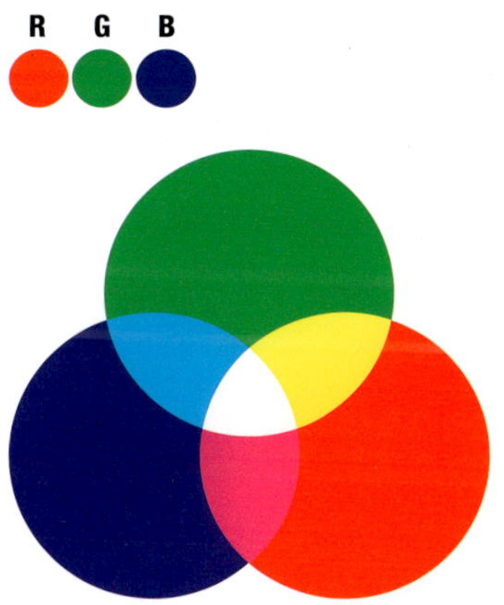

MAIN CHARACTERISTICS
Visual color expressed in RGB code (red, green, blue) is used notably in color display devices such as computers and televisions, while material color, and especially subtractive mixing, is used in four-color process printing.

Models for additive mixing (red, green, blue) and subtractive mixing (cyan, magenta, yellow) of colors. In the four-color printing process, black ink is used in addition to the subtractive primaries: the "K" stands for "key" and represents the black plate.

The World in Black and White

What we commonly refer to as black-and-white photography (i.e., photography without color) is a convention that appeared after the medium was invented in the 1820s by Nicéphore Niépce (1765–1833). The first photographic processes (daguerreotype, albumin print, calotype) produced images in shades of bister, ranging from brown to pale yellow.

In the late nineteenth century, the technically innovative silver gelatin print produced black-and-white photographs that were reminiscent of engravings and prints. From then on, an infinite palette of grays translated chromatic values from the "real" world in shades from dark to light. As photographers mastered the different parameters involved in taking shots (film speed, exposure time, aperture) and making prints, and began making modifications directly on the negative, they were able to play with the intensity of contrasts, the depth of blacks, and the softness of grays in their images.

MAIN CHARACTERISTICS

In the spring of 1961, the American photographer Robert Frank (1924–2019) explained the importance of black and white in his work, in an interview published in the review *Aperture*: "Black and white are the colors of photography. To me, they symbolize the alternatives of hope and despair to which mankind is forever subjected. Most of my photographs are of people; they are seen simply, as through the eyes of the man in the street. . . . But realism is not enough—there has to be vision, and the two together can make a good photograph. It is difficult to describe this thin line where matter ends and mind begins."

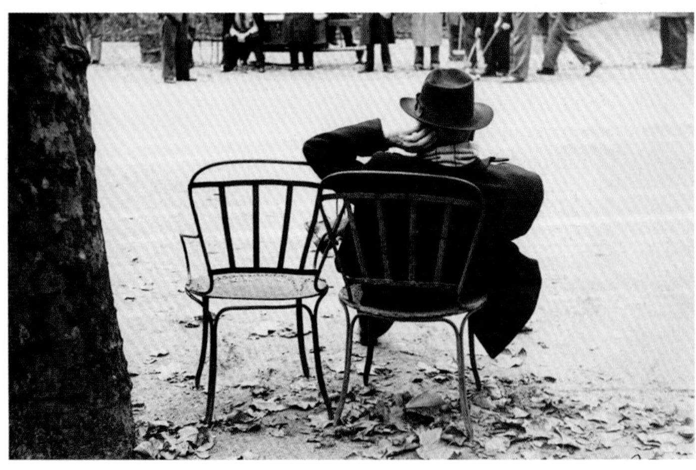

Robert Frank,
Public Gardens, 1951.
Musée Carnavalet,
Paris.

The World in Color

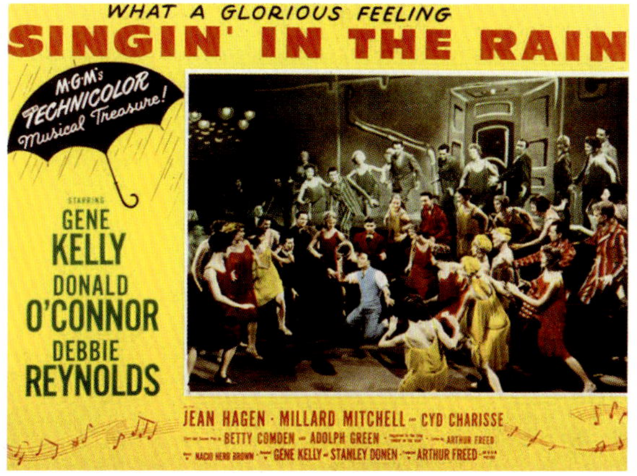

Singin' in the Rain film poster, 1951.

MAIN CHARACTERISTICS
While the earliest examples of film colorization, which involved hand-applying ink to film, date to the first decade of the 1900s, it was in the following decade that color movies were developed by the Technicolor Motion Picture Corporation, although they did not immediately attract the interest of film producers.

After several decades of experimentation, the first color photography process to be released outside of limited circles was the autochrome, invented by the Lumière brothers and commercialized in 1907. The process used a glass plate, to which microscopic red-, green-, and blue-tinted grains of potato starch had been affixed with a sticky varnish and coated with a panchromatic emulsion, to produce a single positive transparency. The autochrome was popular for its fresh, acidulous, and pastel colors until the 1930s, when it was superseded by simpler-to-use color films like Kodachrome and Agfacolor. The choice between black and white or color now came down to aesthetic preference, and some photographers outright rejected one or the other.

The film industry finally adopted color in the 1930s. Technicolor was the most popular process used by studios in the

Golden Age of Hollywood, appreciated for its saturated, enchanting colors that were perfect for conveying the American dream. They were magnified in movies by Victor Fleming (*The Wizard of Oz*, 1939), Vincente Minnelli (*An American in Paris*, 1951), Stanley Donen and Gene Kelly (*Singing in the Rain*, 1951), and Alfred Hitchcock (*Rear Window*, 1954).

However, the process required three films (one for each primary color), which made it expensive, and Technicolor became obsolete in the late 1950s; it was replaced by the Eastmancolor single-film process. Nonetheless, the term "Technicolor" lives on in popular speech as a byword for vivid, abundant color.

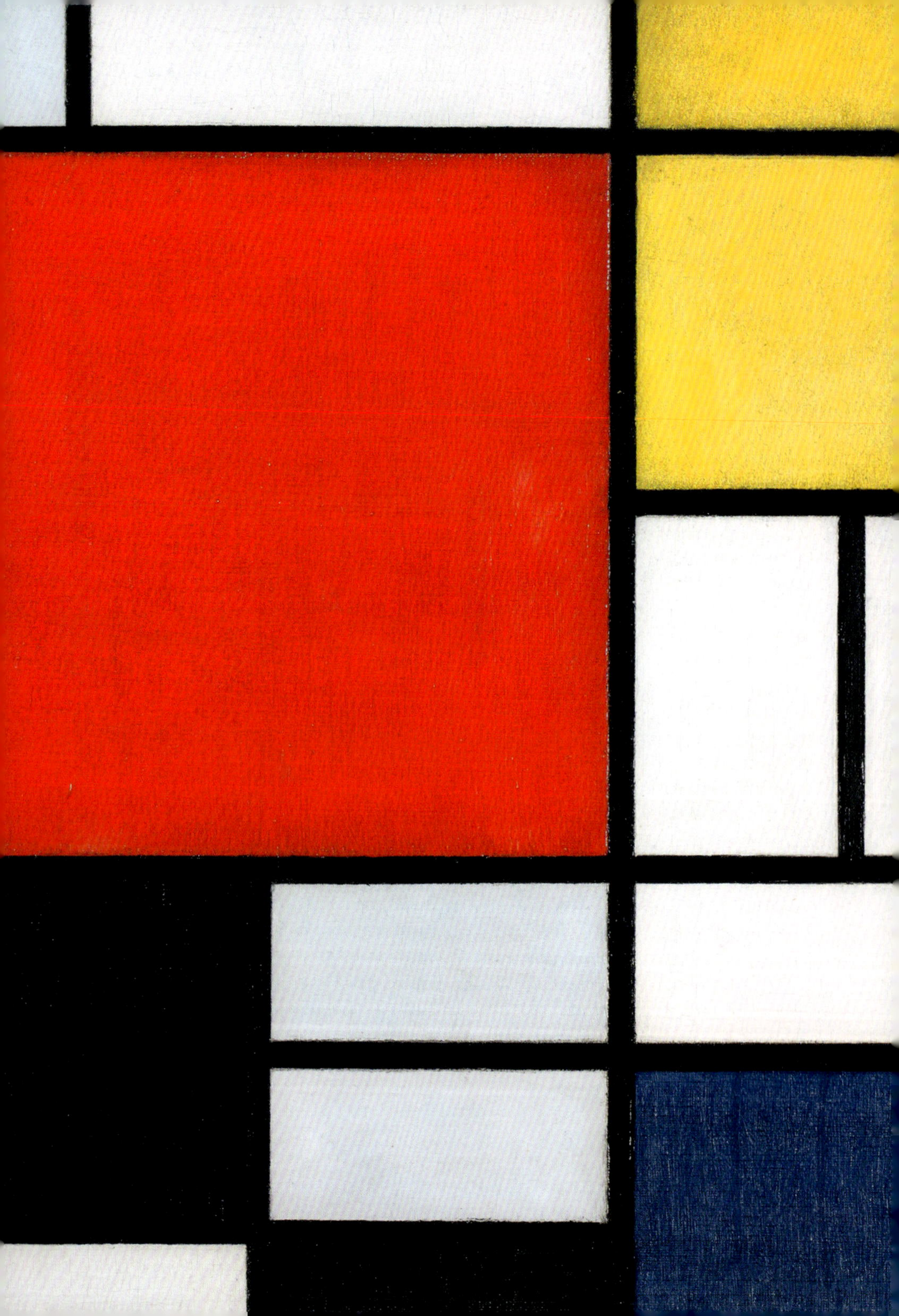

Appendixes

The Meaning of Colors

The symbolism of colors has evolved over time and can differ between cultures, but the following attributes have been associated with specific colors at different times in history.

Black

austerity
darkness
death
despair
emptiness
fear
gravity
grief
impenetrability
malice
masculinity
night
rigor
sin
sobriety
the unknown
turmoil
union

Blue

air
childhood
divine light
  (Christianity)
dream
immortality
  (Ancient Egypt)
indifference
melancholy
pallor
peace
purity
royalty
serenity
sky
the Apostles' robes
the Virgin Mary's robe
truth
vitality (India)

Brown

austerity
brute force
comfort
discovery
earth
filth
humility
mediocrity
nature
poverty
reliability
tradition
trustworthiness
warmth
well-being

Gray

austerity
boredom
calm
elegance
humility
intelligence
melancholy
misfortune
monotony
neutrality
old age
sadness
sobriety
temperance
wisdom

Green

balance
chance
change
ecology
envy
fate
fertility
freshness
hope
nature
plants
progress
prosperity
rebirth
renewal

Orange

abundance
ambition
ambivalence
communication
creativity
enthusiasm
generosity
hypocrisy
malevolence
solace
vibrancy

vitality
warmth
zeal

Pink

beauty
childhood
erotism
femininity
gentleness
gratitude
indulgence
innocence
love
naivety
romanticism
sensuality
sexuality
tenderness

Red

aggressiveness
anger
blood
charity
danger
desire
dignity
excess
fire
Hell
life
love
passion
power

prohibition
revolt
temptation
victory
violence
vivacity
wealth

Violet/Purple

fear
feminism
half-mourning
meditation
melancholy
mystery
peace
penitence
power
reflection
sadness
solitude
spirituality
supernatural
the occult
wealth

White

candor
clarity
cleanliness
emptiness
faith
grief (Asia)
indifference
innocence

light
minerality
peace
precision
purity
rest
simplicity
timelessness
union
virginity
well-being
wisdom

Yellow

betrayal
celebration
cheerfulness
cowardice
energy
enthusiasm
fatigue
friendship
health
illness
joy
light
marriage
  (Republican Rome)
maturity
movement
pride
summer
trust
vibrancy
warmth
youth

Index of Names

Illustrations are indicated in *italics*.
Main entries are indicated in **bold**.

Where to See the Artworks

The artworks in this book can be viewed at the following museums and locations.

AUSTRIA
Kunsthistorisches Museum, Vienna
Mumok, Vienna

DENMARK
Ordrupgaard Museum, Copenhagen

FRANCE
Basilica of Saint-Denis, Saint Denis
Bibliothèque Nationale de France, Paris
Centre Pompidou, Paris
Chapel of the Rosary, Vence
Chauvet Cave, Vallon-Pont-d'Arc
Musée Carnavalet, Paris
Musée d'Archéologie Nationale,
 Saint-Germain-en-Laye
Musée d'Art Moderne de Paris, Paris
Musée d'Orsay, Paris
Musée du Louvre, Paris
Musée du Quai Branly-Jacques Chirac, Paris
Musée Marmottan-Monet, Paris
Musée Soulages, Rodez
Notre-Dame Cathedral, Paris

GERMANY
Nationalgalerie, Berlin

GREECE
The tomb of Agios Athanasios, near Thessaloniki

ITALY
Museo Nazionale Romano, Rome
Uffizi Gallery, Florence
Vatican Museum, the Vatican

NETHERLANDS
Gemeentemuseum, The Hague
Rijksmuseum, Amsterdam
Van Gogh Museum, Amsterdam

SPAIN
Museo del Prado, Madrid

SWEDEN
The Hilma af Klint Foundation, Stockholm

SWITZERLAND
Kunsthaus Zürich, Zurich

UNITED KINGDOM
Barbara Hepworth Museum and Sculpture Garden,
 St Ives
British Museum, London
National Galleries of Scotland, Edinburgh
National Trust Waddesdon Manor, Buckinghamshire
Tate Britain, London
Tate Modern, London
Victoria and Albert Museum, London

UNITED STATES
The Art Institute of Chicago, Chicago, IL
Brooklyn Museum, New York, NY
Cleveland Museum of Art, Cleveland, OH
Dallas Museum of Art, Dallas, TX
The Frick Collection, New York, NY
The Josef and Anni Albers Foundation, Bethany, CT
The Metropolitan Museum of Art, New York, NY
Museum of Modern Art (MoMA), New York, NY
National Gallery of Art, Washington, DC
National Museum of Asian Art, Washington, DC
The Nelson-Atkins Museum of Art, Kansas City, MO
Neue Galerie, New York, NY
Philadelphia Museum of Art, Philadelphia, NY
San Francisco Museum of Modern Art (SFMOMA),
 San Francisco, CA
Solomon R. Guggenheim Museum, New York, NY
Whitney Museum of American Art, New York, NY
Yale University Art Gallery, New Haven, CT

Photographic Credits

Artists' Credits